MW00443107

Custom Shawls

for the Curious and Creative Knitter

Kate Atherley & Kim McBrien Evans

Abrams, New York

Introduction

Look in various dictionaries, and you'll find diverse definitions of the word *shawl*. Some define it by shape. Others, by material. Still others by age or gender or geography. Yet say "shawl" to a contemporary knitter and we all generally agree: A shawl is a piece of fabric of any shape you wish that you wrap yourself up in for warmth, for comfort, to make yourself feel elegant and sophisticated on a special occasion, or to simply revel in the "I made this!" joy that comes from completing a project you're proud of. Shawls are for all ages, genders, and walks of life.

So who are we, and why did we write this book? We are two lifelong knitters, teachers, and designers who come to knitting from very different perspectives:

Kate is analytical and enjoys symmetry. Her favorite color is black. She loves formulas and spreadsheets. Her approach is orderly and technical. She will build your shawl vocabulary of basic shapes, techniques, and stitches so that you can tell the best stories through your hands. She believes that we all have in us the ability to create whatever we put our minds to. And she's created the tools we need to do just that.

Kim has never fully followed a pattern in her life and believes Kate's favorite color is . . . not a color. She likes breaking traditional structures, changing the rules, and taking chances with color and shape. She likes her world a little asymmetrical and off-balance and doesn't see limits in anything she tries. She believes that we all have creative muscles, primed to flex in our knitting.

Our methods are rarely the same, but combined they give all sides of the puzzle, giving confidence to knitters and allowing them to create the shawls of their dreams. We share deep respect for our craft, for each other, and for you: the knitters.

If you are a beginning shawl knitter, we will take you through the basics. You'll learn everything from shapes and techniques to color theory and stitch selection.

If you've knit several shawls, we will strengthen your shawl knitting by expanding your vocabulary of techniques and ideas. You'll learn how to make better fabric, how to mix and match shapes with stitch patterns, and how to combine color like a boss.

And if you are an expert, we will show you how to leap off the cliff to create your own beautiful shawl. To take chances and experiment. To improve your technique, to improve your knowledge of yarn management, and to express yourself in shawl form.

How to Use the Book

We've provided recipes for a broad range of standard shawl shapes, symmetrical and not. They work with any yarn, and you can follow them as written to create fantastic straightforward, everyday sorts of shawls. You can go further and customize them with the addition of pattern stitches from the "Stitch Dictionary" chapter and/or color changes and patterns from the "Color" chapter.

The "Techniques" chapter provides information and tutorials on the key shawl-knitting skills: casting on (including the often-tricky and misunderstood Garter tab), increases, bind-offs, blocking, and much more. There are tools here to help you better knit existing shawl patterns, or to allow you to customize and create your own. Want invisible rather than yarnover increases? We can help you with that. Want a different edging effect? There are suggestions and ideas. Unsure about blocking? We've demystified it.

The "Yarn and Fabric" and "Color" chapters help you become a better shawl knitter by teaching you how to make choices that suit the pattern, your needs, and your tastes.

And the "Breaking the Rules" chapter is all about letting your creativity fly. Take Kate's recipes and follow Kim's path to inspiration.

If you just want to get knitting, we've got thirteen patterns for you. In each case, there are notes to guide you with yarn substitution and alteration. After all, it's all about creating exactly the shawl you want. In this section, we've provided some guidance on how to wrap and wear shawls—because even if the shawl is perfect, it's no good unless you wear it!

The Shapes and Recipes

This chapter provides recipes for all the key shawl shapes. For those that have shaping—that is, all of them but the simple squares and rectangles—the recipes are all written to be worked from the inside out, from the smallest stitch count to the largest. We've done it this way to give knitters the most flexibility with size and yarn usage: You can work until it hits a specific size, or until you've used up a specific quantity of yarn.

Many of these shapes can be worked from the outside edge to the inside, from the largest stitch count to the smallest; indeed, some of them, including the Faroese shawl, are traditionally done this way. This direction avoids a hard bind-off edge, which can impede the stretch of blocking, but working this way is more complicated since you need to determine the desired finished dimensions in advance and make sure you have plenty of yarn. We've chosen to make all our recipes for the smallest-to-largest direction to avoid these challenges. And of course, we've got tips so you can make sure your bind-off isn't too tight.

Notes on the Recipes

For shawls that are worked flat in rows, the recipes use Garter stitch for the body of the shawls. Unless otherwise noted, you can work in Stockinette stitch without significant change to the shape. For shawls worked flat that have increases at the edges, we've used a standard three-stitch Garter stitch border. This can be modified—two stitches work well, or see the "Techniques" chapter (page 27) for other ideas.

For shawls that are worked in the round, the recipes use Stockinette stitch. Unless otherwise noted, you can work in Garter stitch without significant change to the shape.

For shawls that use only increases for shaping, the recipes use yarnovers to create visible increases. If you prefer invisible increases, substitute your favorite Make One increase. See the "Techniques" chapter (page 27) for more information about increases.

For shawls that use both increases and decreases for shaping, the recipes use invisible increases. This keeps the look of the piece balanced—that is, you don't have half with yarnover holes and half without. You can, of course, change the increases to yarnovers for open increases or substitute an increase like kyok for kfbf. If you do this, you'll likely want to make yarnover holes in the decrease section, to match the decrease shaping to the increase shaping. You can do this by working a yarnover accompanied by a double decrease, in place of a single decrease. This is discussed in detail in the "Techniques" chapter (page 27).

See the "Techniques" chapter for information on the various stitches and techniques used.

+

Note on Needles and Yarn

See "Yarn and Fabric" (page 42) for information on needles to use. Unless otherwise noted, a shawl is worked flat and you can use your preferred needles for that.

See page 55 for information on yardage required.

Which Shape Should I Choose?

If you have lots of yarn and time

Rectangle or square

Circle or semicircle

If you have a limited amount of yarn or time

Asymmetrical triangle, narrow

Top-down wide triangle

Vortex

Shallow crescent

If you have a very specific size in mind

Rectangle

Square, straight or on the diagonal

If you like symmetry

Rectangles

Squares

Tip-up, top-down, side-to-side symmetrical triangles

Crescents

Circles and semicircles

If you prefer asymmetry

Side-to-side asymmetrical triangles

Vortex

Kite

If you don't like Garter stitch and you aren't keen on purling

Square from center

Rectangle from center

Circles

If your pattern stitch easily accommodates increases

Square from center or point

Triangles

Circles and semicircles with the rays method

If your pattern stitch doesn't easily accommodate increases

Rectangles and squares worked straight

Circles and semicircles with the pi method

Crescents—particularly the wider, shallow version

Measuring Your Stitch Gauge

To measure your stitch gauge, look at the needles suggested on the ball band, and look for the number of stitches expected in 4 inches (10 cm). (Most list it that way; some brands list it over 1 or 2 inches [2.5 or 5 cm]. In that case, multiply appropriately.)

Using the needles suggested or those appropriate to you (if you know you're a tight knitter, you'll probably want a size larger; if you know you're a loose knitter, you'll probably want a size smaller), cast on about one and a half times the 4-inch (10 cm) stitch count.

Work about 4 inches (10 cm) in the pattern stitch you want to use. Bind off and wash the piece as you intend to wash the finished item, stretching and pinning if appropriate (page 38).

Once it's dry, measure the swatch, counting the stitches over 4 inches (10 cm) of width. Measure in a couple of places to allow for variances in yarn, fabric, and stitch pattern. The average of them is your stitch gauge over 4 inches (10 cm). Divide that by four to get the number of stitches in 1 inch (2.5 cm), or by 10 to get the number of stitches in a cm. Don't round the result; fractions are important.

Yes, yes, we know that the calculations below use the stitches in 1 inch (2.5 cm), but you need to measure over 4 inches (10 cm) so you can get a more accurate result. It's very hard to assess and count fractions of stitches, and if you only measure over a tiny area, you're not taking yarn, fabric, and pattern variance into account.

+

For information about swatching in stitch patterns, see page 52.

Rectangles

The simplest shape to create, this one is excellent if you've got a lot of yarn. A scarf or stole for adults needs to be at least 60 inches (152 cm) long. The width is flexible, but anything narrower than about 6 inches (15 cm) is less practical for warmth and wrapability. A dramatic stole or wrap can be up to 24 inches (61 cm) wide, or even wider.

These are the simplest designs in which to work pattern stitches, as the stitch count doesn't change. The rows are straight.

You will need to know your stitch gauge to be able to calculate the stitch count required to achieve a specific size.

From the Short Side

WORKED IN ONE PIECE

CALCULATE THE CAST-ON NUMBER: Multiply the number of stitches per inch (cm) by the desired width. Adjust for your stitch pattern as required, then cast on.

Work until it's the length you want, then bind off.

For matching edges, use the crochet cast-on with a standard bind-off.

To create a cowl, join the starting and ending edges. The simplest way to do this is to sew up the two ends. To create a seamless/invisible join, start with a provisional cast-on; when the scarf reaches the desired length, undo the cast-on, returning the resulting stitches to a spare needle. Join the ends with three-needle bind-off or Kitchener stitch (page 40).

THE SEAMAN'S SCARF

If you are working a pattern stitch with a visible directionality, then working in two pieces allows you to keep the pattern aligned so that when the scarf is draped around your neck, both sides lie in the same direction.

You can work from the center out, or from the ends in.

CENTER OUT: Cast on with a provisional method and work half the desired length. Undo the cast-on, returning the resulting stitches to your needles. Working on these stitches, make the second side as you did the first.

EDGES IN: Work two identical pieces by casting on normally and working half the desired length. Join the two with three-needle bind-off or Kitchener stitch (grafting).

From the Long Side

CALCULATE THE CAST-ON NUMBER: Multiply the number of stitches per inch (cm) by the desired length. Adjust for your stitch pattern as required.

Work until it's the width you want, and then bind off.

For matching edges, use the crochet cast-on (page 24) with a standard bind-off.

To create a cowl, cast on onto a circular needle of appropriate length (it's easiest to work with one slightly smaller than the target circumference of the cowl; don't use a longer one), place a marker, and join the cast-on stitches for working in the round. Work in the round until it's the depth required and bind off.

TO CALCULATE THE CAST-ON NUMBER FOR THIS SHAPE: Multiply the number of stitches per inch (cm) by the desired width. Adjust for your stitch pattern as required.

Work until it's the length you want, and then bind off.

For matching edges, use the crochet cast-on (page 24) with a standard bind-off.

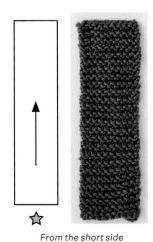

From the short side

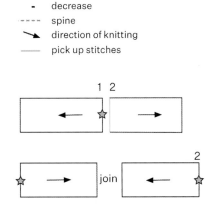

☆ cast on
+ increase
- decrease
---- spine
↘ direction of knitting
— pick up stitches

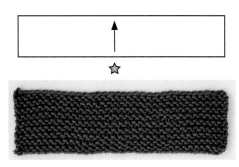

From the long side

Squares

A square is a good shape for a baby blanket. Although it can make for a dramatic shawl, a piece of significant size requires both a lot of knitting and a lot of yarn.

For a square baby blanket, 36 inches (91 cm) square is a good size; an adult shawl needs to be a minimum of 55 inches (140 cm) square.

Straight

Work as for a Rectangle from the short side, stopping when it's as long as it is wide.

The rows are straight, and the stitch count doesn't change, making this an ideal place to work large-repeat or complicated stitch patterns.

On the Diagonal—Straight

The shawl starts at the tip with a small number of stitches, and increases are worked at each end of RS rows until the desired diagonal width is achieved; decreases are then worked in the same place at the same rate, down to the opposite end, ending when you have the same number of stitches as for your cast-on.

This design only results in a perfect square if you work in Garter stitch; working in Stockinette stitch gives you a piece that's longer than it is wide. See page 50 for more on this.

Track and manage yarn usage: Don't use more than half the available yarn in the increase section.

Rows are straight, on the diagonal axis. Invisible increases are used here, since the second half of the shaping is based on decreases.

CO 1 st with a slipknot.

SETUP ROW 1 (RS): Kfbf into the first st. 3 sts.

SETUP ROW 2: Knit.

SETUP ROW 3: K1, kfbf, k1. 5 sts.

Increase section:

RS ROWS: K1, M1, k to last st, M1, k1. 2 sts increased.

WS ROWS: Knit.

Work to desired diagonal width, ending with a WS row.

Decrease section:

RS ROWS: K1, ssk, k to last 3 sts, k2tog, k1. 2 sts decreased.

WS ROWS: Knit.

Work until 5 sts remain, ending with a WS row.

NEXT ROW: K1, CDD, k1. 3 sts.

NEXT ROW: Knit.

NEXT ROW: CDD. 1 st. Cut yarn and pull through final st to secure.

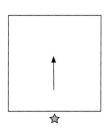

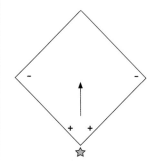

On the Diagonal—Mitered

The shawl starts at the tip with a small number of stitches, and increases are worked on either side of the center stitch until it reaches the desired size.

This design only results in a perfect square if you work in Garter stitch; working in Stockinette stitch gives you a piece that's longer than it is wide. See page 50 for more on this.

Rows are mitered, folded at a 90-degree angle at the center.

CO 1 st with a slipknot.

SETUP ROW: Kfbf into the first st. 3 sts. Place st markers either side of the center st.

RS ROWS: K to center st, yo, sm, k1, sm, yo, k to end. 2 sts increased.

WS ROWS: Knit.

Work to desired size. BO.

To work in Stockinette stitch, purl all WS rows.

From the Center Out

The shawl starts in the center and is worked in the round, so the default fabric is Stockinette stitch. This construction is excellent if you don't want Garter stitch and prefer not to purl.

Cast on a small number of stitches and join in the round. Divide the stitches into four quarters, and increase at each end of each quarter every other round until piece is the size you want.

Another way of dividing it up is to establish four corner spines; the increases are worked on either side of the spines. In the pattern below, the first stitch of the quarter is the spine.

Note: You will need to start with your preferred small-circumference needles and proceed to working on circular needles as the circumference grows.

Rounds are straight within each section, set at 90 degrees from each other, aligned with the sides of the square.

CO 8 sts. Join in the round.

ROUND 1: [K1, yo] around. 16 sts. Divide sts into 4 quarters with 4 sts each.

ROUND 2: Knit.

ROUND 3: (K1, yo, k to end of quarter, yo) 4 times. 8 sts increased.

Repeat Rounds 2 and 3 to desired size. BO.

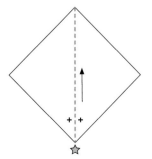

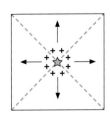

Triangles

Triangles are the classic shawl shape, the most traditional, and the most often seen even in modern projects. There are a number of different constructions, which provide a lot of possibilities: alternate geometries and different alignment of fabric and patterns.

Tip Up

Rows are straight.

You can work as per the first half of Squares, On the Diagonal—Straight (page 12).

A more classic version uses the yarnover increase:

CO 1 st with a slipknot.

SETUP ROW 1 (RS): Kfbf into the first st. 3 sts.

SETUP ROW 2: Knit.

SETUP ROW 3: Kfb twice, k1. 5 sts.

SETUP ROW 4: Kfb, k to last 2 sts, kfb. 7 sts.

RS ROWS: K3, yo, k to last 3 sts, yo, k3. 2 sts increased.

WS ROWS: Knit.

Work to desired size. BO.

The geometry is slightly different, depending on the fabric worked. Worked with the same yarn, at the same gauge, a Garter-based shawl will be a little shorter and wider; a Stockinette-based shawl will be a little narrower and longer. See page 50 for more on this.

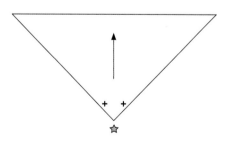

Top Down—Standard

In contrast to the Tip-Up Triangle, the rows on this construction are mitered, folded at a 90-degree angle at the center. The shawl is also wider, as it's actually two of the Tip-Up Triangles put together.

This shawl is best started with a Garter tab. Four increases are worked every RS row—one increase at each end and one on either side of the center—until the desired size is achieved.

Work a 3-st, 4-ridge Garter tab for 9 sts (page 26).

Place st markers either side of the center st.

WS ROWS: Knit.

RS ROWS: K3, yo, k to marker, yo, sm, k1, sm, yo, k to last 3 sts, yo, k3. 4 sts increased.

Work to desired size. BO.

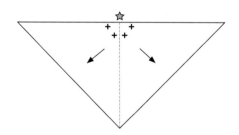

Top Down—Wide

Even wider than the standard top-down shape, this adds two more increases, worked at the ends of the WS rows. Rows are mitered.

Work a 3-st, 4-ridge Garter tab for 9 sts (page 26).

Place st markers either side of the center st.

WS ROWS: K3, yo, k to last 3 sts, yo, k3. 2 sts increased.

RS ROWS: K3, yo, k to marker, yo, sm, k1, sm, yo, k to last 3 sts, yo, k3. 4 sts increased.

Work to desired size. BO.

Note: The yarnovers at the start and ends of the rows aren't visible here. The angle of the wings tends to compress them, but it's still important to use the yarnover rather than a closed and tighter increase, so that the edge can stretch this way.

Faroese-Style

A traditional Faroese shawl is worked from the lower edge up towards the top, but this recipe creates a shawl with the same shape worked from the top down for flexibility. This shape is the same as a Top-Down Triangle (page 14), but instead of a single-stitch spine, a patterned section is worked in the center. Increase the Garter tab stitch count accordingly. For example, if you want a ten-stitch center section, you need to ensure that your Garter tab has ten more ridges, to allow you to pick up ten more stitches.

Work appropriate size Garter tab (page 26).

For the Standard Version

Place st markers either side of the center section.

WS ROWS: Knit.

RS ROWS: K3, yo, k to marker, yo, sm, work center section, sm, yo, k to last 3 sts, yo, k3. 4 sts increased.

You can also use this construction with both the Standard and Wide versions of the Top-Down Triangle.

For the Wide Version

WS ROWS: K3, yo, k to marker, sm, work center section, sm, k to last 3 sts, yo, k3. 2 sts increased.

RS ROWS: K3, yo, k to marker, yo, sm, work center section, sm, yo, k to last 3 sts, yo, k3. 4 sts increased.

The rows are straight in three sections, which follow the line of the bottom edge. The center section is straight across; the side section rows are at 45-degree angles.

This shape is, effectively, a squared-off crescent. Pushing the increases away from the center changes the lower edge—it's angled between the increase points and flat in the center section.

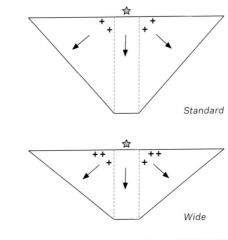

Standard

Wide

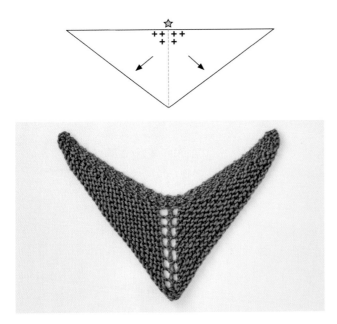

Side-to-Side Symmetrical

This shawl starts at the tip with a small number of stitches, and increases are worked at the end of RS rows—every two, four, or six rows, depending on the yarn available and the depth desired—until it reaches the desired depth; decreases are worked in the same place at the same rate, to the opposite tip.

The more even (non-increase) rows that are worked between the shaping, the shallower the shawl will be.

Track and manage yarn usage: Don't use more than half the available yarn in the increase section.

This recipe has increases/decreases every four rows; to change that, simply adjust the number of rows worked even between the shaping rows.

CO 1 st with a slipknot.

SETUP ROW (RS): Kfbf into the first st. 3 sts.

Knit 3 rows.

Increase section:

ROW 1 (RS): K to last st, M1, k1. 1 st increased.

Knit 3 rows.

Repeat the last 4 rows to desired depth, ending after 3 even rows.

Decrease section:

ROW 1 (RS): K to last 3 sts, k2tog, k1. 1 st decreased.

Knit 3 rows.

Repeat the last 4 rows until 3 sts remain, ending after 3 even rows.

Final row: CDD. Cut yarn and pull through final st to secure.

Rows are straight and vertical when worn.

Side-to-Side Asymmetrical

This shape is ideal if you don't have a lot of yarn. Rows are straight as worked, but when the shawl is worn, they are on the diagonal.

You can work it as for the Increase section of the Side-to-Side Symmetrical version (left), binding off when you reach the desired length and depth. No need to decrease! If you're working it this way, the shawl is worn with the increased edge at the top—that is, with the increase rows facing in, and the WS rows facing out.

Alternately, if it's easier for your pattern, you can work increases at the start of the row, as follows:

RS increase rows, invisible version: K1, M1, k to end. 1 st increased.

RS increase rows, visible version, K3, yo, k to end. 1 st increased.

This version is worn with the increase rows—the RS rows—facing out.

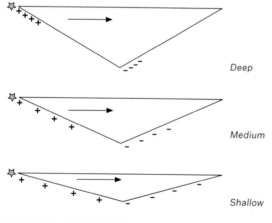

Deep

Medium

Shallow

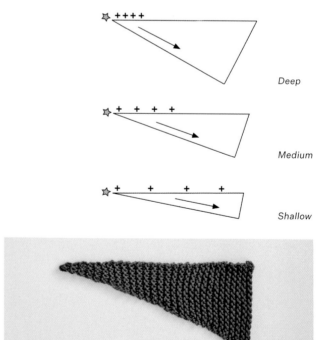

Deep

Medium

Shallow

Vortex

This is closely related to the Side-to-Side Asymmetrical shape, but an additional increase/decrease pair causes the fabric to tilt farther, making for a more extreme diagonal fabric.

As with the Side-to-Side Asymmetrical shape, this one is ideal if you don't have a lot of yarn. Rows are straight as worked, but when the shawl is worn, they are on the diagonal.

The shawl starts at the tip with a small number of stitches. Increases are worked at the start of RS rows, while WS rows start with a decrease and end with an increase.

CO 1 st with a slipknot.

SETUP ROW (WS): Kfbf into the first st. 3 sts.

RS ROWS: K1, M1, k to end. 1 st increased.

WS ROWS: K2tog, k to last st, M1, k1.

Work to desired size. BO.

See "Breaking the Rules" (page 110) for more information about making this shawl even more of a vortex.

Kite

This shawl starts with a mitered increase section created by working an increase at each end of every row, and a CDD in the center of RS rows to establish the miter spine, resulting in two stitches increased every two rows.

In the Straight Section, continue CDD over the same spine stitch, working only one increase per row at the end of RS rows and the start of WS rows. The spine moves over towards the far side edge of the piece. Once the spine hits the end of the row, bind off.

Rows are mitered, folded at a 90-degree angle. In the increase section the miter is at the center; in the straight section, the miter position moves towards the lower edge.

CO 1 st with a slipknot.

SETUP ROW 1 (RS): Kfbf into the first st. 3 sts.

SETUP ROW 2: K1, kfbf, k1. 5 sts.

Place a removable st marker on the center st to mark the spine—this is where the decrease will be worked.

Increase section:

WS ROWS: K1, M1, k to last st, M1, k1. 2 sts increased.

RS ROWS: K1, M1, k to 1 st before marked spine st, CDD, k to last st, M1, k1.

Work until piece is the desired depth, moving marker up as you go so you can keep track of the spine st.

Straight section:

WS ROWS: K to last st, M1, k1. 1 st increased.

RS ROWS: K1, M1, k to 1 st before marked spine st, CDD, k to end. 1 st decreased.

Work until 1 st remains after the spine st.

FINAL ROW (RS): K1, M1, k to 1 st before marked spine st, CDD. 1 st decreased.

BO.

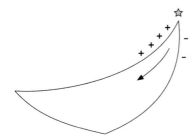

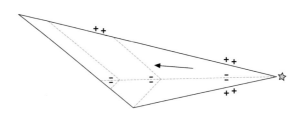

Crescents

These are similar to Top-Down Triangles (page 14). The key difference is that increases are only worked at the ends of the rows.

Because of this, it's easier to add stitch patterns for crescents than for triangles—you've got one larger area in which to place the patterns, rather than two or more smaller wedges. The faster increase rate of the shallow shawl means that the fabric widens quickly, making it easier to incorporate patterns (page 125).

A number of popular crescent shawls use short rows to create clever striping patterns (page 121).

The rows are straight as worked, but when worn they are slightly curved. The deeper version has a more curved edge.

Shallow

This shawl is best started with a Garter tab. Cast on a small number of stitches. Work two increases at each end of RS rows, and one at each end of WS rows, until piece is the desired size.

Work a 3-st, 4-ridge Garter tab for 9 sts (page 26).

WS ROWS: K3, yo, k to last 2 sts, yo, k3. 2 sts increased.

RS ROWS: K3, yo, k1, yo, k to last 4 sts, yo, k1, yo, k3. 4 sts increased.

Work to desired size. BO.

Deep

This shawl is best started with a Garter tab. Cast on a small number of stitches. Work an increase at each end of every row until the piece is the desired size. This version is deeper than the Shallow version, since you need to work more rows to get a specific width.

Work a 3-st, 4-ridge Garter tab for 9 sts (page 26).

ALL ROWS: K3, yo, k to last 2 sts, yo, k3. 2 sts increased.

Work to desired size. BO.

This shape requires a loose bind-off edge and firm blocking to ensure that the top edge is straight.

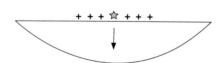

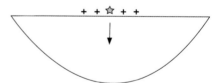

Circles and Semicircles

A circular shawl is a beautiful piece, but a significant commitment of both yarn and time. For an adult shawl, you need a piece at least 55 inches (140 cm) in diameter. Some consider a circular shawl challenging to wear, too.

A semicircle is perhaps a bit more practical—certainly, there's less knitting!

Circular, Rays

This construction is closely related to the Square—From the Center Out (page 13).

This shawl starts in the center and is worked in the round, so the default fabric is Stockinette stitch. This construction is excellent if you don't want Garter stitch and prefer not to purl.

Cast on a small number of stitches and join in the round. Divide the stitches into eight segments. You can either increase at each end of each segment every fourth round, or one stitch in each segment every other round, until the piece is the size you want.

As with the Square—From the Center Out, another way of thinking of this is that you're establishing spines—eight, in this case—and every fourth round you're increasing one stitch on either side of the spine. In the pattern below, the first stitch of each segment is the spine stitch.

Note: You will need to start with your preferred small-circumference needles and proceed to working on circular needles as the circumference grows.

VERSION 1—INCREASE EVERY FOURTH ROUND, VISIBLE INCREASES

CO 8 sts. Join in the round.

ROUND 1: [K1, yo] around. 16 sts. Divide sts into 8 segments with 2 sts each.

ROUNDS 2–4: Knit.

ROUND 5: (K1, yo, k to end of segment, yo) 8 times. 16 sts increased.

Repeat Rounds 2–5 to desired size. BO.

VERSION 2—INCREASE EVERY OTHER ROUND, VISIBLE INCREASES

CO 8 sts. Join in the round.

ROUND 1: [K1, yo] around. 16 sts. Divide sts into 8 segments with 2 sts each.

ROUND 2: Knit.

ROUND 3: (K1, yo, k to end of segment) 8 times. 8 sts increased.

Repeat Rounds 2 and 3 to desired size. BO.

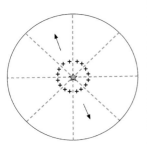
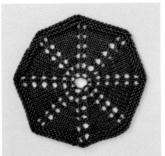

Version 1

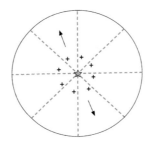

Version 2

Semicircle, Rays

This construction is related to the Top-Down Triangle (page 14).

This shawl is best started with a Garter tab (page 26). Cast on a small number of stitches. Divide the stitches into four segments. You can either increase at each end of each segment every fourth row, or one stitch in each segment every RS row, until the piece is the size you want.

Put another way, you've got three spines, evenly distributed. On each increase row, you're adding eight stitches—one st at each end, and one on each side of the three spines.

In the recipe below, the patterning may seem slightly asymmetrical, but it's just a quirk of where the increases are placed. It works out perfectly even.

VERSION 1—INCREASE EVERY FOURTH ROW, VISIBLE INCREASES

Work a 3-st, 8-ridge Garter tab for 13 sts (page 26).

ROW 1 (RS): K3, [yo, k1] to last 3 sts, yo, k3. 21 sts. Place markers after the first 3 sts, then (after every 4 sts) 4 times; the last marker will be 2 sts from the end.

ROWS 2–4: Work even in Stockinette stitch or Garter stitch (your choice).

ROW 5: K3, (yo, k to last st of segment, yo, k1) 4 times, k2.

Repeat Rows 2–5 to desired size. BO.

VERSION 2—INCREASE EVERY OTHER ROW, VISIBLE INCREASES

Work a 3-st, 8-ridge Garter tab for 13 sts (page 26).

ROW 1 (RS): K4, (pm, yo, k2) 4 times, k1. 17 sts. The markers are placed to indicate the increase positions; increases are worked on one side of the marker or the other, alternating rows.

ROW 2: Knit or purl (your choice).

ROW 3: (K to marker, yo, sm) 4 times, k to end. 4 sts increased.

ROW 4: Knit or purl (your choice).

ROW 5: (K to marker, sm, yo) 4 times, k to end. 4 sts increased.

Repeat Rows 2–5 to desired size. BO.

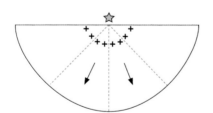

Version 1

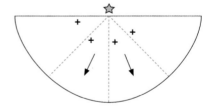

Version 2

Circular, Pi

This shawl starts in the center and is worked in the round, so the default fabric is Stockinette stitch. This construction is excellent if you don't want Garter stitch and prefer not to purl.

Cast on a small number of stitches and join in the round. Knit one round, then double the stitch count on the following round. Continue to double the stitch count with each increase round, while at the same time doubling the number of even rounds between the increase rounds each time. Minor variations to stitch and round counts don't matter.

What's notable—and rather wonderful—about this construction is that the stitch count remains fixed in a given section, between increases. This makes it very easy to incorporate and manage stitch patterns.

Note: You will need to start with your preferred small-circumference needles and proceed to working on circular needles as the circumference grows.

CO 9 sts. Join in the round.

Knit 1 round.

INCREASE ROUND: [K1, yo] around. 18 sts.

Knit 3 rounds.

INCREASE ROUND: [K1, yo] around. 36 sts.

Knit 6 rounds.

INCREASE ROUND: [K1, yo] around. 72 sts.

Knit 12 rounds.

INCREASE ROUND: [K1, yo] around. 144 sts.

Knit 24 rounds.

INCREASE ROUND: [K1, yo] around. 288 sts.

Knit 48 rounds.

INCREASE ROUND: [K1, yo] around. 576 sts.

Knit up to 96 rounds.

Work a border or a stretchy BO.

You can, of course, continue the pattern—after 96 rounds double the stitch count again to 1152, and then work up to 192 rounds. But even if you're working with lace weight and making a bedspread, the shawl is probably big enough before you hit that point.

Semicircle, Pi

Requiring less knitting, and similar to the Circular Pi construction (left), this shawl has the wonderful advantage of tiers of fixed stitch counts for ease of patterning.

This shawl is best started with a Garter tab. Cast on a small number of stitches. Place markers to divide the edging on each side. Work one row even, then double the stitch count between the markers (that is, not including the edging stitches) on the following. Continue to double the stitch count on every increase row while at the same time increasing the number of even rows between increase rows each time.

Minor variations to stitch and row counts don't matter. If working in Stockinette stitch, use the row counts below; if you wish to work in Garter stitch, add a few rows in each of the even sections once you get past 25 stitches.

Work a 3-st, 5-ridge Garter tab for 10 sts (page 26).

Knit or purl 1 row (your choice).

INCREASE ROW (RS): K3, [yo, k1] to last 3 sts, yo, k3. 15 sts.

Work 3 rows even.

Repeat Increase row. 25 sts.

Work 5 rows even for Stockinette st, 7 rows for Garter st.

Repeat Increase row. 45 sts.

Work 11 rows even for Stockinette st, 13 rows for Garter st.

Repeat Increase row. 85 sts.

Work 23 rows even for Stockinette st, 29 rows for Garter st.

Repeat Increase row. 165 sts.

Work 47 rows even for Stockinette st, 57 rows for Garter st.

Repeat Increase row. 325 sts.

Work up to 95 rows even for Stockinette st, 119 rows for Garter st.

BO.

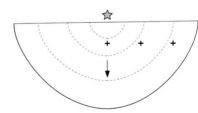

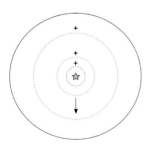

Tech-niques

Casting On

For a Large Stitch Count

If you're working a rectangle or square from a straight edge, you need a flexible cast-on. Two methods are well-suited to the task: the long-tail and the crochet cast-on.

LONG-TAIL CAST-ON

This method creates an attractive and flexible lower edge. To make it stretchy, ensure that you leave room between the stitches when you snug them up to the needle—at least a stitch's width or two. Don't use a larger needle, as that makes the stitches of the first row too big, and they will look sloppy.

You need a long tail—unless you're working with very bulky yarn, 1 inch (2.5 cm) per stitch will be sufficient. If you are using very bulky yarn, double that.

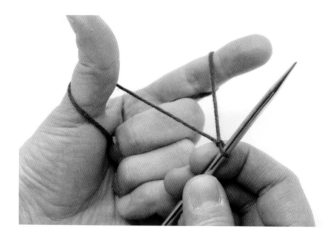

Make a slip knot, leaving the required long tail, and place it on the working needle. Hold the needle in your right hand.

With your left hand, grab both strands of the yarn and make a fist around them, pulling them a little to create some tension. Use your thumb and forefinger to separate the two strands, as if you're opening curtains—your finger and thumb should be pointed in the same direction, coming in from the same side. Turn your left hand so that your palm is upward. Swoop over with the needle, and, coming over it, pick up the strand on the outside of your thumb, to make a loop. Swing the needle tip back, and coming over it, pick up the strand on the inside of your finger. Bring it through the loop around your thumb, and remove your thumb from the loop. Tug both yarns slightly to snug the stitch up to the needle.

CROCHET CAST-ON

This method produces an edge that looks exactly like the standard bind-off, and it is well-suited to any piece where the cast-on and bind-off edges will be close together and easily compared.

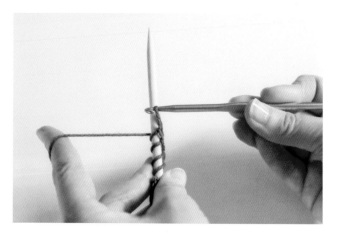

Using a crochet hook close in size to the working needle, make a slipknot and place it on the hook.

Hold the yarn in your left hand and the crochet hook in the right. Hold the knitting needle in your left hand, positioned above the yarn.

*With the hook, come over the needle, grab the working yarn, and draw it through the loop on the hook. 1 stitch made.

Swing the yarn so that it's under the needle again; repeat from *. Work until you're one stitch short of the required number of stitches. For the last stitch, slip the loop from the hook onto the needle.

E-Wrap/Backwards Loop Cast-On

This is a low-profile edge. It's a good choice for a Garter tab (page 26), or for when you have a very lacy pattern stitch and you don't want a ridge or firm edge at the start.

Leaving about a 4-inch (10-cm) tail, make a slipknot but keep it loose; make sure it's not tight around the needle. Use the e-wrap/backwards loop method to cast on the rest of the stitches you need: simply make a backwards loop and place it on the right-hand needle for each stitch. It doesn't matter which way you twist it.

Note that you can also use this method to cast on a single stitch between stitches, or at the beginning or end of a row (see E-wrap/Backwards Loop [M1Z], page 28).

See the Garter tab instructions for details on how to pick up the stitches in this cast-on edge.

Center

For circular or square shawls worked from the center out, there are two good choices.

The traditional one is a technique known as Emily Ocker's Circular Beginning; it's closely related to the crochet magic ring.

If you're a crocheter, work the magic ring as you normally do, but leave each of the loops live on the hook, slipping them to knitting needles once you have all the required stitches.

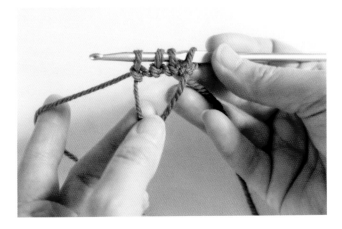

If you've not made a magic ring before: Make a slipknot, but do not pull it tight; leave the loop at the base of the slipknot slightly open so that you can work through the loop. Place the stitch of the slipknot onto your crochet hook. Use the hook to grab the working yarn and pull it through the stitch on the hook. One stitch made. *Going through the center of the loop below the slipknot, grab the yarn to make a loop on the hook, then grab the working yarn and pull it though the loop on the hook. One stitch made. Repeat from * until you have all the required stitches. Slip them to your needles. Once you've worked a few rounds, you can pull on the yarn tail to close up the hole.

You can get almost as good a result with a slight cheat using a standard cast-on. Kate finds it easiest to work this with DPNs, but you'll only need three. Use the long-tail method to cast on the required number of stitches, ensuring you've got at least a 4-inch (10-cm) tail for weaving in. Split the stitches between two DPNs—only two. Use the third DPN to join and work the first round or two. Once you have more stitches, you can then change to your preferred small-circumference method, distributing the stitches as usual. There will be a hole in the center, but you can easily close it up when you weave in the cast-on tail.

Provisional

You need scrap yarn for this: Choose something smooth, in a similar thickness to your project yarn, and in a contrasting color.

With the scrap yarn, work the crochet cast-on method, continuing until you have all the stitches you need—don't place the slipknot on the needle. Once you have the stitches you need, crochet a few chains, then cut the yarn, pulling it through the final chain to finish it up.

Begin working with the project yarn. When it's time to undo the provisional cast-on, use a smaller needle to pick up the lower loops of the first worked row, making sure to pick up the little half-loop at the far end. Count the stitches to make sure you have the correct number. Undo the knot or just cut near the end of those few chains you made, and then carefully unravel the scrap yarn. Change to the working needle and work as instructed.

The Garter Tab

The top-down triangle, crescent, and semicircular shapes are best started with a tab—a narrow strip of stitches typically worked in Garter stitch. This technique ensures a smooth and continuous top edge by establishing the center portion of the border.

The basic method is worked as follows:

Starting with a slipknot, cast on a small number of stitches—the number that will be used for the shawl border, usually two or three stitches. As noted on page 24, the backwards loop method is great for this.

Work a set number of rows in Garter stitch. Work a pick-up row as follows: Knit across the stitches on the needle (these form the first side of the border); pick up and knit stitches along the side edge of the piece (usually one less stitch than the number of Garter ridges) for the shawl body; pick up and knit one stitch for each stitch in the cast-on edge for the other side of the border.

Some instructions have you work a provisional cast-on and then undo it for the second set of border stitches, but it's fairly fiddly. You can get almost as good a result by using a low-profile cast-on method like backwards loop; the difference on so few stitches is barely visible.

There are some tricks to making this easier:

- Make your cast-on looser by working it on a larger needle, and then do the knitting with the appropriate-size needle, ideally one with a good pointy tip.

- To work the pick-up-and-knit along the edge, grab one leg of the edge stitch in the valley, between Garter ridges. You'll be able to get one stitch less than the number of ridges.

- When working the pick-up-and-knit along the cast-on edge, you will be able to get one stitch in the slipknot, and the rest by going between the stitches.

In the recipes, we've specified the number of stitches and rows for the tab, and the number of stitches that will result. For example, a three-stitch, five-ridge tab is worked on three stitches, and you are to knit until you have five Garter ridges visible on the RS of the work. This will result in ten stitches: three at each end, and four in the center for the body of the shawl picked up between the five ridges.

Stockinette Tabs

A tab doesn't always need to be Garter; the Stoclet shawl uses a Stockinette tab. Other than the obvious difference that the strip is worked in Stockinette stitch, the only adjustment in working is the pick-up rate: Rather than one stitch for every ridge, you should expect to pick up three stitches for every four rows. Do, of course, make sure that you pick up the stitches with the RS of the strip facing.

A small strip of Stockinette stitch rolls tidily inward, creating what looks like a rounded edge. See the discussion of borders in the next section for more on this.

Picking up stitches in the edge of a garter tab

Borders and Edges

Shawls worked flat often have a distinct border or edging pattern, at the start and end of the rows. It's particularly common for a shape that has increases worked close to the edges, or where the body of the shawl is worked in a lacy or Stockinette-based pattern stitch.

Garter stitch is used most often in these situations, usually worked over two to five stitches. It helps with blocking (page 38), and for a piece that has a Stockinette-based pattern or fabric, it can reduce the roll of the fabric. Note, however, that the simple presence of the Garter edge doesn't actually stop the roll—the fabric needs to be blocked. An unblocked Stockinette-based fabric with a Garter edge often folds at the edges.

A small border of Stockinette or reverse Stockinette can actually be very effective—you can see an example of a Stockinette border in the Stoclet design (page 165). The roll creates a small and attractive edge, a little bit more refined than Garter stitch. A Stockinette border will curl towards the WS of the shawl; a reverse Stockinette border will curl towards the RS of the shawl.

Although i-cord is often used to create a rolled edge, you have to be careful because the row gauge can be significantly different than the fabric used for the body of the shawl. The risk is that the edging may be much tighter than the fabric and may cause the shawl edges to roll or pucker. If you want to use i-cord, it's worth making a small swatch of your stitch pattern with the i-cord edge, and do a preliminary block to see how it looks. If it is too tight, loosen up with yarnovers: Every RS row, add a yarnover before you work the i-cord stitches; on the WS rows, drop them. This extra yarn gets taken up into the edging stitches, providing more give.

Increases

Open

The classic increase used in shawls, particularly lacy ones, is the yarnover. It's open or visible, in that it leaves a decorative hole.

It's slightly trickier than it might seem, because there are actually four different versions (depending on which stitch is worked immediately before and after) and then two variations (depending on whether you carry yarn in your right or left hand). A lot of information follows, but simply look for the version that applies to your current project and how you carry yarn.

YARNOVER BETWEEN KNITS:
If you work with the yarn in your right hand, just bring the yarn to the front between the tips of the needles. When you work the next stitch, the yarn drapes over the needle to create the yarnover.

If you work with the yarn in your left hand, bring it to the front between the tips of the needles and let it drape over the right-hand needle, in position to work the next stitch.

YARNOVER BETWEEN PURLS:
For either right- or left-hand carry, starting with the yarn in front, take the yarn over top of the right-hand needle, and then bring it around to the front again, into purl position.

YARNOVER AFTER KNIT, BEFORE PURL:
For either right- or left-hand carry, bring the yarn to the front between the tips of the needles, then wrap it all the way around again into purl position.

YARNOVER AFTER PURL, BEFORE KNIT:
If you work with the yarn in your right hand, just leave the yarn where it was after the purl (at the front), and let it drape over the right-hand needle when you knit the next stitch.

If you work with the yarn in your left hand, just drape it over the needle as you do for the between-knits version.

In all cases, the yarnover should be seated on the needle with the right leg forward, so that when it's worked in the following row/round, it stays open.

If your project has a lot of yarnovers created in different situations, you might see some inconsistencies: Because of the path of the yarn, a yarnover worked after a knit and before a purl is a little larger; a yarnover worked after a purl and before a knit is a little smaller. In most cases, you can even them out by just paying attention to those stitches: Shorten the after-knit-before-purl yarnover by wrapping it around the tip of the needle, pulling it tight; lengthen the after-purl-before-knit yarnover by making sure you're wrapping it all the way around the full circumference of the needle and leaving it a little slack.

Closed

There are two types of increases: making a stitch where there wasn't one before, and working multiple times into the same stitch.

MAKING A NEW STITCH

There's a whole set of increases that fit into this category, commonly called the Make One increases.

Aside from a few small considerations as noted below, they're entirely interchangeable.

M1L—LEFT-LEANING MAKE ONE: Insert left-hand needle, from front to back, under the horizontal strand of yarn which runs between the stitch just knit and the following stitch; knit into the back of this loop.

M1R—RIGHT-LEANING MAKE ONE: Insert left-hand needle, from back to front, under the horizontal strand of yarn which runs between the stitch just knit and the following stitch; knit into the front of this loop.

These are the most obvious paired increases— they look good when worked close together. You can also purl rather than knit the loops; these are usually referred to as M1PL and M1PR.

E-WRAP/BACKWARDS LOOP (M1Z): Simply make a backwards loop and place it on the right-hand needle, as in the E-wrap/backwards loop cast-on (page 24). (The *Z* is for Elizabeth Zimmermann, in whose work Kate first found reference to this as an increase. It's not a standard abbreviation, but we use it in these patterns to be specific when it's the best method.)

If you need to work paired increases, two of them close together, you can work the first increase twisted one way and the second increase twisted the other way if you wish, but it's not crucial.

RLI (RIGHT LIFTED INCREASE): Insert the right-hand needle into the right leg of the stitch below the next stitch on the left-hand needle; pick up this loop and place it on the left-hand needle with the right leg at the front, then knit into it.

LLI (LEFT LIFTED INCREASE): Insert the left-hand needle from the front into the left leg of the stitch two rows below the last stitch on the right-hand needle. Knit into this loop.

Choosing a Make One

If a pattern just says "M1" without further detail, it's your choice which one to use. If you're working two increases close together, they look nice if you pair them— make the first one right-leaning and the second one left-leaning.

The e-wrap/backwards loop version is a good neutral increase—it doesn't really have much of a left or right lean—and has the advantage that if you're working into a stitch pattern, you can delay the decision about what the stitch needs to be until the following row/round. (If you've ever tried to increase into Seed stitch, you'll understand why this might be helpful.)

If you need to work a lot of increases close together on a single row/round, the e-wrap/backwards loop or RLI/LLI are better choices. The M1R/M1L increases pull up the yarn from the row below, and you can get a pucker if you're pulling it up too much.

If you need to work a lot of increases close together in a single column, with no or few rows/rounds between them, the e-wrap or M1R/M1L are better choices.

+

On Remembering How to Do M1R & M1L

If you find it hard to remember which is which, this phrase might help: "I'll be Right Back!" Meaning that the first step of the M1R instructions starts with the back, as in picking up the strand from back to front.

WORKING MULTIPLE TIMES INTO THE SAME STITCH

Kfb (knit into the front and back of the stitch) and pfb (purl into the front and back of the stitch) are the most common. They are quick and relatively easy, but can be problematic.

These increases aren't symmetrical, as they both create the new stitch on the left side of the existing one. Kfb in particular is pretty visible, in that the new stitch is a little bump rather like a slightly-too-small purl stitch. They disappear well enough into Garter or other textured stitch patterns, but can be easily seen in Stockinette. They can provide a nice subtle border effect, but they do interrupt a plain fabric.

This asymmetry means that they're not a straightforward substitute for the Make One group of increases.

If working increases close to the edge, you usually want to position the visible part of the increase in the same place, the same number of stitches from the edge. With a Make One increase, this is simple:

K3, M1, work to last 3 sts, M1, k3.

For the equivalent increase placement with kfb, you'd need to do the following:

K2, kfb, work to last 4 sts, kfb, k3. This will make the little purl bump the fourth stitch in from each edge.

If you want to substitute a kfb for an M1 increase, you have to be careful with the counting. If you've got 10 stitches, and your instructions tell you to k5, M1, k5, you can work the instructions without any problems. But if you try to replace the M1 with a kfb and work k5, kfb, k5, you won't have enough stitches to work it. The M1 is worked between stitches, whereas the kfb is worked on an existing stitch (stitch number 6 in this case), so you only have 4 stitches left at the end of the row, not 5. To work this row correctly, you would have to work the kfb on stitch number 5, as follows: K4, kfb, k5.

Neither of these issues make the kfb increase unusable; they just require that you plan ahead.

Multiple Increases

MULTIPLE YARNOVERS

The simplest and most visible method is to add extra wraps to the yarnover and then work into it multiple times on the following row/round. If working multiple times into yarnovers, you need to alternate between knits and purls because it's impossible to knit twice into yarnover wraps. It doesn't matter if you're on a knit or a purl row, just alternate k1 and p1 as many times as you need to for the number of wraps you worked.

Note that the number of wraps doesn't need to correspond to the number of times you work into the yarnover. For example, you can create a really dramatic hole by making two or more wraps and only working into it once. Multiple wraps start to get a little difficult to handle, and the hole gets large quickly. Even if she needs to make three new stitches, Kate will most often only work a double wrap, and then work into it three times. (See the Ancoats shawl on page 141 for an example of where she's used this.)

WORKING MORE THAN ONCE INTO THE SAME STITCH

The tidiest method is what's commonly referred to as a KYOK: working (k1, yo, k1) into the same stitch. You can take this further, too: (k1, yo, k1, yo, k1) is fairly common in Estonian lace patterns to create nupps.

This method is tidy and symmetrical; the yarnover in the increase doesn't really make much of a hole, since the new stitches all gather together.

And of course, just as there's kfb, there's also kfbf. You can take it even further, working four (kfbfb) or even five times (kfbfbf). As with kfb, this isn't symmetrical, but that may or may not matter.

With either method, the more times you work into the stitch, the more stretched out that stitch will be. The result is not exactly invisible, but it's not a big yarnover hole, either.

Decreases

Single Decreases

A quick note about the direction of increases and decreases: When we say an increase or decrease is right-leaning or left-leaning, that is the direction in which it leans on either side of the piece on which it is worked.

RIGHT-LEANING

K2tog and p2tog (knit or purl two stitches together) both result in a stitch that has a visible right lean.

LEFT-LEANING—KNIT DECREASES

Skp: Slip the next stitch knitwise, knit the following stitch, then lift the slipped stitch up and over the just-knit stitch, as if binding off.

Ssk: Slip the next two stitches, individually, knitwise to the right-hand needle. Return them to the left-hand needle without twisting them and knit them together through the back loops.

K2tog-tbl also leans to the left, but it's imperfect, because the stitch that lies on the top is twisted. This makes it look different from other stitches and decreases, and tends to tighten up the stitch. Whether this matters is your choice; if you're not going to be able to see it, if you're working in a darker yarn, or if there aren't a lot of them, then it's perfectly fine to use it.

LEFT-LEANING—PURL DECREASES

Ssp is a perfect analog to ssk:

Slip the next two stitches, individually, knitwise to the right-hand needle. Return them to the left-hand needle without twisting them and purl them together through the back loops. It's a little tricky to work, requiring good pointy needles, but it looks great.

In most situations, p2tog-tbl works just fine. Although it's not a perfect equivalent, since the stitch that lies on top is twisted, it's usually not all that visible hidden under the bump of the purl stitch.

On Substituting and How They Look

Skp and ssk do look slightly different but are otherwise utterly interchangeable. Use the one you prefer. The choice is often driven by whether the left-leaning decrease will be positioned close to a right-leaning decrease. Many feel that the ssk is a better match for k2tog, but it often depends on your own knitting tension. Experiment and see which you prefer.

If you find that the ssk looks a little loose or untidy, you can try one of these three tricks: Slip the second stitch purlwise, slip the second stitch purlwise through the back loop, or work the stitch that sits above the ssk in the following row/round through the back loop.

There are occasions when you might want an open decrease (i.e., one with a hole)—for example if you want to continue a line of yarnovers from a section of increases into a section of decreases. To do this, either work a yarnover next to a double decrease [e.g., (yo, k3tog)], or work decreases on either side of the yarnover [e.g., (k2tog, yo, k2tog)].

Double Decreases

You can create right- and left-leaning double decreases by just expanding the existing ones: K3tog and p3tog lean to the right; sssk and sssp lean to the left. They can be challenging to work—you'll need pointy needles—and they do affect the fabric somewhat, causing it to pull in strongly from one side or the other.

More often, you want a centered decrease. There are two, and they're not really interchangeable:

SK2P: Slip the next stitch knitwise, k2tog, then lift the slipped stitch up and over the just-knit stitch, as if binding off.

CDD (CENTERED DOUBLE DECREASE): Slip two stitches knitwise as if working a k2tog, knit one, then lift the two slipped stitches up and over the just-knit stitch, as if binding off. This is also known as s2kp2 and s2kpo.

Both of the above decreases are centered, in that they pull the fabric in equally from left and right; however the first version leaves a stitch with a very pronounced leftward lean lying on top while the second version creates a central vertical line. In most cases, you likely want the CDD version.

There is also an analog to the sk2p that leaves a pronounced right-leaning stitch on top: Work an ssk, return it to the left-hand needle without twisting it, lift the second stitch on the left-hand needle up and over the first stitch (as if for binding off), and then return the slipped stitch to the right-hand needle.

You may find using these two preferable to struggling with k3tog and sssk.

Lifelines

A lifeline is an excellent tool when working a large or complex project. It gives you the ability to safely undo a section of your work without the risk of losing everything.

You need smooth, contrasting-color yarn, finer than the yarn you're working with. Crochet cotton is great, or a smooth sock yarn; some knitters use unwaxed dental floss and even fishing line for this. And of course, you'll need a reasonably small tapestry needle.

Without taking the stitches off the knitting needle, thread a length of your lifeline yarn through the live stitches—but not the markers—following the path of the needle. Using a circular needle makes this easy: slip the stitches down onto the cord so there's more room to run the threaded tapestry needle through them.

After running your lifeline, keep working. If you make a mistake above the lifeline, you can remove the needle and safely undo your work back to where the lifeline was threaded. The stitches caught on the lifeline are safe; return them to the needle, following the path of the lifeline yarn. Using a smaller needle can make this step easier; just remember to resume working with the appropriate size needle for the project.

How often do you need to do this? It's entirely up to you. How much work are you willing to risk? And don't make the mistake Kate did the first time she used one—don't thread a lifeline above a section with a mistake in it!

Short Rows

Short rows can be used to alter shapes of shawls, or even the shape of color or stitch pattern sections within a shawl (page 121).

A short row is worked simply by turning before you reach the end of a row and leaving stitches unworked. You can do this with no special techniques or adjustments, but when you work across the full row the next time, passing over the turning point, a gap will result. The various methods listed below are used to close up that gap, to make the turning point less visible.

There are several short-row methods. Although they achieve similar things, we recommend these two for different situations:

Wrap & Turn (abbreviated as *w&t*) is the most well-known. It's straightforward but is only suited to a few situations: in a Stockinette-based fabric that is not intended to be reversible; in Garter stitch; or when multiple turns are worked in the same place, stacked on top of each other, as in Radialactive (page 174).

The German (aka Double Stitch) method suits reversible fabrics very well and works seamlessly in mixed fabrics with right-side purls and wrong-side knits. Which you use is a case of personal preference—it's worth experimenting with both methods. You might find one slightly better than the other for your own personal tension and fabric.

Wrap & Turn

In this method, you create a wrap around the stitch after the turn point, and then when working back over the wrapped stitch, you work the wrap and the stitch together to hide the wrap and tidy it up.

Work to the turn point indicated in the pattern. Wrap the next stitch as follows:

Slip the next stitch purlwise, move the working yarn between the tips of the needles to the other side (if it's in knit position, bring it to the front; if it's in purl position, take it to the back), and then return the slipped stitch to the left-hand needle. Turn, ready to work the following row. Bring the yarn to where you need it for the following row, ready to continue in pattern.

RESOLVING THE SHORT ROW GAPS

If you're working in Garter stitch, don't bother; the wraps look like tidy little purl ridges and fill in the gap on their own.

If you are working in Stockinette stitch, and the piece is not intended to be reversible, you will want to hide the wrap, working the wrapped stitch and the wrap together so that it falls to the WS of the work.

If the wrapped stitch is to be knit: Insert the tip of the right-hand needle into the wrap from underneath, and then insert the needle into the stitch as normal; knit the wrap and the stitch together, making sure that you come out through the wrap. This pushes the wrap to the back of the work.

If the wrapped stitch is to be purled: Going over to the RS of the work, use the tip of the right-hand needle to come from underneath, scoop the wrap up, and place it on the left-hand needle; purl the stitch and the wrap together. This pulls the wrap to the WS of the work.

German or Double Stitch Short Rows, the DS

Work to the turn point in the pattern, work the following stitch—knit or purl as required—and turn the work. Bring the working yarn to the front and slip the first stitch on the left-hand needle purlwise to the right-hand needle. Tug on the working yarn, bringing it up and over the needle, around to the back, so that the slipped stitch is pulled up tight, and two strands (the two legs of the stitch) are sitting on the needle. If you're to knit the next stitch, leave the yarn at the back, keeping the tension, and work back in pattern. If you're to purl the next stitch, bring it around the needle to the front as if for a yarnover, keeping the tension.

Wrap & Turn

This creates what looks like a doubled stitch, a stitch with two legs up on the needle. To resolve these gaps when you encounter one of these on a subsequent row, just work into it as normal, catching the two strands.

In the patterns, this is abbreviated as DS. Note that if you're working from a pattern written for German short rows, the row immediately before will include instructions to work the turning point stitch, and then turn the work. The DS is the slipping-and-pulling-on-the-yarn move only, and will always be worked at the start of the row after the turn. If you wish to make a substitution, remember that the turn for a German short row happens a stitch later than for a wrap & turn. The final stitch worked before the turn—the one that gets slipped on the following row—is the stitch that gets wrapped in the wrap & turn.

German Short Rows

At least one knitter reports that the following small variation produces a tidier result: If the stitch immediately before the turn is purled, then after working the turn, slip that stitch knitwise rather than purlwise. Try it both ways (slipped purlwise as is the traditional way, or slipped knitwise) to see which you prefer.

Joining Yarn

For a project that uses more than one color, or more than one skein, at some point you're going to need to join new yarn.

    If the edges of the piece are going to be exposed—most likely in a shawl project—then join in the middle of a row. If you're working in the round, of course, you'll have to do this anyway. Only join at the start of a row if you're going to be seaming that edge or picking up stitches there. This may seem counterintuitive, but it's very hard to neatly weave in an end at the edge.

Quick and Easy

Quick and Easy

This method is very straightforward and broadly applicable. When about 6 inches (15 cm) of the old yarn remains, grab the new yarn, and leaving a tail of about 4 inches (10 cm), work three stitches with both ends of the yarn held together.

    This is very secure, because the ends are already partially woven in, and there's no risk of loose or sloppy stitches. Three stitches will be doubled, of course, but in the larger project you'll find that they're really not very visible at all. It's as if the yarn just got a bit thicker in that area. If you're working a very lacy pattern stitch, it's less visible if you change yarns in a more solid area, with few or no yarnovers.

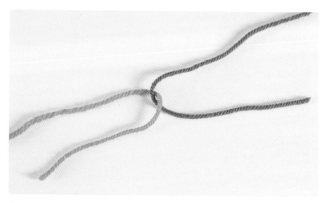

Russian Join

Splicing

If the fiber felts—specifically, if it's a sheep's wool that has not been treated to be machine washable—you can do a spit-splice. If you're at all unsure whether your yarn is suitable, try this on two short lengths of the yarn. Once it's dry, soak it in water and try to pull the two pieces apart; if you can, then the join won't be permanent and you shouldn't use this method.

    When there are about 3 inches (7.5 cm) left, gently tease apart any plies of the yarn, on both the old and the new yarns. If it's a single ply, gently rub the yarn a little between your fingers to open it up a bit. Lay the two ends together, end to end, overlapping and intermingling the plies.

    Spit on your palm (yes, spit! Saliva has enzymes which make this work better) and rub the two ends together, felting them.

Do make sure your saliva is clear—tea, coffee, soft drinks, and wine can all stain your tongue, which can color your saliva and transfer to the yarn.

    Tug on the join to make sure it's strong before you proceed. There's no need to wait for it to dry to continue working, although you might find it more pleasant that way.

Russian Join and Variants

An extra secure join is the Russian method. The basic method is to fold the two ends over, about 3–4 inches (7.5–10 cm) from the end, looping one over the other.

    Depending on the stickiness of the yarn, you can secure this a number of ways. The simplest is to just work with the yarns doubled for a couple of stitches either side of the change-over, letting the extra tails hang to be woven in later. If it's a feltable yarn, you can felt the overlaps as if splicing; again, consider thinning the plies if you feel the resulting join is too thick.

Binding Off & Finishing Edges

A too-tight bind-off can damage the look and use of a shawl by impeding the drape or blockability of the fabric. You need to make sure that there's give in the bound-off edge to match the give in the fabric.

How much give is determined by the fabric and how it will be blocked—see below for more information on that.

If it's not going to be stretched, you need a medium-stretchy bind-off method; if it's going to be stretched, you need a very stretchy bind-off.

In general, if you're not sure how loose an edge you'll need, feed a lifeline in the final row before you bind off. Work the method you've chosen, and when you cut the yarn, leave yourself a very long tail—two or three times the length of the final row. Tie that up into a little butterfly knot, and block as desired. If the edge isn't right, it's easy enough to undo it back to the lifeline and rework it.

Medium-Stretchy Bind-Offs

SLIGHTLY LARGER NEEDLES

Sometimes you can get what you need by using a larger needle to work the stitches of the bind-off row.

A FEW CHEEKY YARNOVERS

To soften the edge a bit more without too much flaring out, create a yarnover on the right-hand needle every third or fourth stitch as you're working across, and immediately bind off that new stitch.

Very Stretchy Bind-Offs

RUSSIAN LACE

This method has many names: Russian Lace, Estonian Lace, or just plain lace bind-off. Kate finds it's very stretchy, plenty for all but the most open of lace patterns. It creates a chain edge that looks just like the standard bind-off. It does tend to flare out, so it's appropriate for pieces that are going to be stretched or need lots of drape.

K1, *k1, return the 2 stitches to the left-hand needle and k2tog-tbl; repeat from * until all stitches have been worked. Cut the yarn and pull through the final stitch to secure.

General Bind-Off Rules

If you're working in a knit/purl pattern and the edge is going to be exposed as is—the end of a scarf, for instance—it's better to bind off in pattern, knitting the knits and purling the purls. This gives an edge that sits on top of the work, which lies and moves nicely with the fabric. Working the bind-off edge as all knits or all purls makes the edge curl to one side and flare out.

If, however, you're going to be seaming the bind-off edge—making a scarf into a cowl, for example—then it's better to bind off all stitches knitwise. When you cut the yarn, leave a tail about four to five times the width of the row, to use for the join. See instructions for Joining on page 40.

Russian Lace BO edge

You can make this even stretchier by working purlwise: Purl all the stitches, and work a p2tog. Don't use a larger needle, as that makes the top edge untidy.

THE YARNOVER METHOD/JENY'S SURPRISINGLY STRETCHY BIND-OFF

This is a different use of yarnovers than the one mentioned above. The basic technique is that you're creating a yarnover before every stitch and dropping the yarnover over the stitch when you lift the previous stitch over. This lets the bind-off stretch, because each stitch has extra yarn in it. That extra yarn sits around the base of each stitch like a collar—when you tug on the bound-off edge, the stitches have enough yarn in them to expand.

K1, *yarnover on right-hand needle, k1; lift both yarnover and right-most knit stitch over the stitch just worked; repeat from * until all stitches have been worked. Cut the yarn and pull through the final stitch to secure.

The yarnover method is a knitwise bind-off. The popular Jeny's Surprisingly Stretchy method is a variant of this specifically for ribbing—one adjustment makes it slightly easier to work. You can work the standard knitwise version with ribbing and other knit/purl pattern stitches, and there's not really much difference in the end result.

The No-Bind-Off Bind-Offs:

CROCHET BIND-OFF

You need a crochet hook of a size close to your knitting needles.

Slip the first 5 stitches to your hook, grab the yarn. and pull it through those stitches. *Chain 5. Slip the next 5 shawl stitches to your hook, grab the yarn, and pull it through the shawl stitches and the loop of the chain. Repeat from * until all the stitches have been worked. To finish, cut the yarn and pull it up and out so it knots.

Stoclet shawl edge, using the crochet bind-off.

This edging was used in the Stoclet shawl (page 165) to create a crochet chain between the columns of dropped stitches.

You can vary this edge somewhat by shortening or lengthening the crochet chain loops. You can also work fewer stitches together, slipping three or four stitches rather than five. A longer crochet chain makes for larger and more dramatic loops; slipping fewer stitches means that you'll have more loops along the edge—these are more design than technical decisions.

ATTACHED EDGINGS

Attached edgings are stitch patterns that are worked perpendicularly to the direction of the shawl. New stitches are cast on, and then a pattern is worked across only the new stitches. The last of the new stitches is attached to the shawl body with a decrease. That decrease, effectively, decreases one stitch of the shawl body.

These types of edgings provide two—sometimes three—excellent benefits over a standard bind-off edge: They're more attractive, they're much stretchier, and if you choose one with points or scallops, they make pinning for blocking that much easier.

An attachment decrease is worked every other row, and so you decrease 1 shawl stitch for every 2 rows of the edging pattern. When choosing a stitch pattern, consider the number of rows in the repeat and the number of stitches in the shawl—for example, a 12-row edging repeat would decrease 6 stitches, so you want the shawl's final row to have a multiple of 6 stitches. If it doesn't line up, work increases or decreases in the final shawl row to get the right stitch count. Typically, the final row of the edging is worked as a RS row, binding off all but the last of the edging stitches, and working the final attachment decrease on the last of the edging stitches and the last of the shawl stitches. The yarn is then cut and pulled through the final stitch to secure it.

If you're working a square or circular shawl, where the edging goes all the way around, it's traditional to start with a provisional cast-on method. Once you've worked all the way around, you can close the edging gap by grafting the remaining stitches to the cast-on.

If working these types of edgings on a triangle, when you reach the point, you should work twice in the same place: The first time, skip the decrease, just knit the last stitch of the edging, then turn and work back; work the decrease as normal on the following row. This provides enough fabric and a bit of give to allow the edging to bend around the point.

If working on a square or rectangle, when you hit the corner, work three times in the corner: Work a pair of rows, skipping the decrease; work the decrease and its following row, then work another pair of rows skipping the decrease again.

See the "Stitch Dictionary" (page 86) for a selection of edging patterns. The simplest version is a plain Garter edging, worked on any number of stitches. The downside to the Garter edging is that the side edge is straight and therefore requires either wires or an awful lot of pins if you plan to stretch it.

Plain Garter Edging

CO any number of sts at the start of a RS row. The number of sts you cast on sets the width of the edging.

ROW 1 (RS): K until 1 CO st remains, ssk (last st of edging tog with 1 st of shawl), turn.

ROW 2: Sl 1 wyif, k to end.

Rolled Edge/Stockinette Edging/Faux I-Cord

CO 3 sts at the start of a RS row.

ROW 1 (RS): K2, ssk (last st of edging tog with 1 st of shawl), turn.

ROW 2: Sl 1 wyif, k2.

This looks much like an i-cord bind-off, giving a small rolled edge. It's better suited to most shawls in that it's looser than i-cord, and it has sufficient give to accommodate a stretch blocking.

Top: Plain garter edging. Bottom: I-cord bind-off

I-Cord Bind-Off

This method creates a very tidy and attractive edge, but it doesn't have much stretch.

CO 3 sts at the start of a RS row.

ALL ROWS (RS): K2, ssk (last st of edging tog with 1 st of shawl); slip 3 sts back to left-hand needle.

Repeat this row until all sts have been bound off and only 3 i-cord sts remain. Bind those off or join to starting sts.

Each decrease decreases one stitch of the shawl body.

This edge can be fairly tight, and you need to make sure that you're not causing the edge to pucker. Work a few rows and do a rough blocking—get that section of the shawl wet and see how it looks. If it's too tight, try working the i-cord on a larger needle. Or consider working one row periodically without joining to the body of the shawl.

Blocking

There's a fairly common misunderstanding about the term *blocking*: that it is synonymous with *stretching*. It's absolutely not.

How you block depends on the fibers in the yarn and the fabric of the project.

If the fabric is lacy, then absolutely, you want to open up the yarnovers to make the fabric look its best. Typically, this is done by stretching the fabric. (But even in this case, stretching isn't always required—it depends on the fibers used.)

Other fabrics, non-lacy ones, just don't need to be stretched out—indeed, stretching them out can have a negative effect. Stretching can flatten fabrics like Garter stitch, or take the bounce and texture out of a pattern stitch. For most fabrics and yarns, washing is sufficient.

If there's any seaming or grafting to do, you should wash the piece beforehand. The fabric should be settled, for more even and tidy joins. If you're going to be working a graft, and there are live stitches remaining, slip them to scrap yarn. Cut the working yarn, leaving about five or six times the width of the final row, and tie it in a loose butterfly so it doesn't tangle in the wash. If it's going in the machine for wash or spin, use a mesh washbag.

Step One: Wash

No matter the yarn or fabric, whether you plan to stretch or not, always start with a wash. Wash the piece according to the care instructions on the ball band. You need to wash the piece to even the stitches out, let the fibers bloom, and rinse out anything that might have settled on the project as you were working: pet hair, cookie crumbs, dust; even hand cream can transfer to yarn as you're working with it.

If the yarn is hand-wash only, soak in lukewarm water and a wool-safe washing product. Rinse if required—not all of the products require rinsing—and then squeeze as much moisture out as possible. Roll the piece in a towel and squeeze hard, or even step on it. If you have a front-loading washing machine, you can use the spin cycle; higher-speed spinning is

A Wool-Wash Is Important

A proper washing product—a soap, a no-rinse wool-wash, etc.—is crucial for moth prevention. Moths aren't really after your wool; they're after all the good stuff that settles on your wool: the oils off your hair and skin, skin cells, food crumbs. A moth thinks about wool the way many of us feel about the plate of veggies that often accompanies a dip; it's just a way to more easily eat the good stuff. Plain water doesn't get all the good stuff off the yarn.

an excellent way to get moisture out. If you intend to stretch the fabric out, put it in the machine loose; if you don't want to stretch the fabric, put it in a mesh washbag. Even with the most delicate fabrics, a high-speed spin in a front-loading washing machine is very gentle—the centrifugal force keeps the piece motionless against the side of the washing machine tub. Don't be afraid! And if you're really not sure, buy a hand-wash-only sweater from a secondhand or vintage clothes shop, and try it out.

Step Two: Dry

The key question: Do you need to stretch it out for drying?

If it's a lacy fabric, and you've used silk, wool, other animal fibers, or some blend of these, then you should stretch. Otherwise not.

IF NOT STRETCHING

Once the piece is damp rather than dripping, lay it flat to dry.

It's best to put it on towels on a laundry rack or similar. (I use the dog's crate when he's not in it.) Better a surface that allows air to circulate underneath for faster drying. We don't recommend laying a piece on towels on a bed or carpet, as that can slow the drying significantly, and if the piece is too wet, you risk smelly fabric and even mildew. Even if the ball band recommends a clothes dryer, we would avoid it: Using a dryer can hasten pilling and fading, making a fabric look worn more quickly.

If your piece is lacy and you've used acrylic or acrylic-blend yarns, then once it's dry you can open up the yarnovers and smooth the fabric with a gentle application of steam. A purpose-made garment steamer works great, but in a pinch use a clothes iron with a steam setting—just don't let it touch the fabric.

If your piece is lacy and you've used cotton or linen, steaming can create a nice effect but isn't necessary: The yarnovers will open up on their own.

IF STRETCHING

If you do want to stretch it, you will need a bit more equipment: pins, mats, wires, etc.

When it's damp, lay it out on mats, stretch it out, and pin to secure.

If the piece has straight edges, wires or blocking combs help enormously. If you're using wires, run them along the edge of the piece—this is why Garter edges

are so common, as you can easily catch each Garter bump with the wire. Place pins every 4–6 inches (10–15 cm) to anchor the wire. If you don't have wires, you can create a decent straight edge by placing pins every inch (2.5 cm) or so. Blocking combs are clever— they're little plastic handles with a few pins placed side by side, so that the process is quicker—and you can be guaranteed the pins are lined up and evenly spaced.

The best blocking wires are fairly stiff, so that they don't bend under pressure.

If the edge has points or scallops, use pins to catch them.

You want to be reasonably aggressive with the stretch: Pull until there's no give in the fabric. And then just let it dry.

Wool, silk, and other animal fibers have elasticity— the ability to stretch—and a memory so that you can stretch them out when they're wet, and they remember that stretched-out position when they're dry. You're actually stretching out the yarn, not just the fabric. The bad news, however, is that these fibers also have bounce-back; the next time the piece gets wet, it will forget that stretched-out position, requiring you to pin it out again. The degree to which it bounces back does depend on the fiber; sheep's wool bounces back very well indeed to its original size, while alpaca and silk will retain some of the stretched position permanently.

The reason that cotton, linen, and acrylic (or yarns that have significant percentages of these in a blend) don't require this treatment is that they don't have a memory. You can absolutely stretch them out to dry, but they'll just return to their original shape and size when you remove the pins. It doesn't mean that these yarns are bad choices for lacy stitch patterns; just know that the results will be different.

Cotton and linen loosen up naturally over time— linen fairly significantly—and so the yarnovers will naturally be pretty open. And acrylic needs to be steamed to open up the yarnovers, but once it's done, that's permanent. (You're actually slightly melting and reshaping the yarn.)

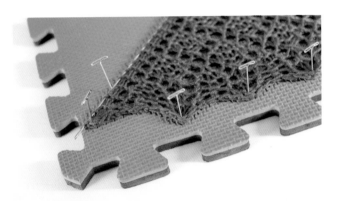

Weaving In Ends

Once the piece has been blocked as required, the ends should be woven in. In general, you should plan to weave in about 4 inches (10 cm) of yarn—more if the yarn is particularly smooth or slippery. If you're using a highly-textured animal fiber, particularly one that will felt, you don't need to work quite as hard. Work in two different directions, roughly half and half.

For a Reversible or Very Lacy Fabric
Duplicate stitch is the best answer here. It's very secure and disappears most easily into the fabric. As the name suggests, you are duplicating the stitches in the fabric by tracing the path of the stitches with the yarn. Work from the WS if the fabric has one.

It's more precise work than other methods but absolutely worth it.

For a Mostly Solid Fabric with Defined Right and Wrong Sides
If you're weaving into a Garter stitch fabric, catch every other leg of the stitches just tucked under a ridge, first in one direction, then back again.

If you're weaving into ribbing, run the end up through one side of a column of WS knit/RS purl stitches, and then back down again in another stitch column.

For a Stockinette-based fabric, weave up and down, following the paths of the stitches on the WS of the work. This is a sort of casual duplicate stitch, and it's very secure.

Before you cut, wiggle the fabric around to make sure it's lying naturally. And don't cut right down to the surface of the fabric; leave a short little tail sticking out on the WS—1/8 inch (3 mm) or so. It's less likely to start coming out that way.

Joining

If working a cowl flat, you'll need to join the two ends. Make sure you've washed and blocked the piece first, and use either the cast-on or bind-off tail for working the join.

Seaming
This method is straightforward but does create a ridge on the WS of the cowl. This is less suitable for a cowl with a twist.

To join a cast-on to a bound-off edge, use the invisible horizontal seaming method as follows:

Align the two edges with RSs facing. With the tail threaded onto the tapestry needle, weave the end under the points of the stitches closest to the edges. Pull it tight as you go, so that the joining yarn is invisible.

Three-Needle Bind-Off
Quicker and simpler than seaming, it does still leave a ridge. Use a provisional cast-on, and leave the stitches of the last row live. Return the cast-on stitches to a needle, making sure you have the same number of stitches on both needles.

Hold the two needles parallel, with the RSs of the work held together. Using a third needle, knit together one stitch from the front needle and one stitch from the back needle; *knit together one stitch from the front needle and one stitch from the back needle; lift the first stitch on the right-hand needle over the second, as for a standard bind-off. Repeat from * until all stitches have been worked and one stitch remains on the right-hand needle. Cut the yarn and pull through the final stitch to secure.

Grafting (Kitchener Stitch)

A grafted join is a little fussy to work, but the result is utterly invisible.

Use a provisional cast-on, and leave the stitches of the last row live. Return the cast-on stitches to a needle, making sure you have the same number of stitches on both needles.

Hold the needles parallel, with the work hanging down—as if for three-needle bind-off. If you're working in Stockinette, reverse Stockinette, or a knit/purl pattern, hold them so that you're looking at the RS of the front piece and the WS of the back piece.

If the pieces are in Garter stitch, hold them so that there's a Garter ridge right up against the needles on the RS of the front piece and the WS of the back piece.

With the yarn tail threaded onto a tapestry needle, work as follows:

+ Controversial Advice

Always wash before you weave in the ends. The fabric should have settled first. If you weave in the ends, and then the fabric stretches or changes shape, you risk creating a pucker in the fabric. If you're using a sticky, feltable wool yarn, the traditional advice is to block after you've woven in the ends. This can absolutely help the ends stay in place, but if you're weaving into an unblocked fabric, there is a significant risk of a visible end because the fabric has shifted.

A well-woven end shouldn't be escaping anyway, but if Kate were using a yarn that felts and wanted a bit of extra security, she might apply a little steam or some water to the area where she had woven in the end.

Fabric	Stockinette Stitch	Reverse Stockinette Stitch	Garter Stitch
Setup	Front needle: Through first stitch purlwise, pull yarn through. Back needle: Through first stitch knitwise, pull yarn through.	Front needle: Through first stitch knitwise, pull yarn through. Back needle: Through first stitch purlwise, pull yarn through.	Front needle: Through first stitch purlwise, pull yarn through. Back needle: Through first stitch purlwise, pull yarn through.
Repeat	Front needle: Through first stitch knitwise, slip st off, pull yarn through. Through next stitch purlwise, pull yarn through. Back needle: Through first stitch purlwise, slip st off, pull yarn through. Through next stitch knitwise, pull yarn through.	Front needle: Through first stitch purlwise, slip st off, pull yarn through. Through next stitch knitwise, pull yarn through. Back needle: Through first stitch knitwise, slip st off, pull yarn through. Through next stitch purlwise, pull yarn through.	Front needle: Through first stitch knitwise, slip st off, pull yarn through. Through next stitch purlwise, pull yarn through. Back needle: Through first stitch knitwise, slip st off, pull yarn through. Through next stitch purlwise, pull yarn through.
Finish	Front needle: Through last stitch knitwise, slip st off, pull yarn through. Back needle: Through last stitch purlwise, slip st off, pull yarn through.	Front needle: Through last stitch purlwise, slip st off, pull yarn through. Back needle: Through last stitch knitwise, slip st off, pull yarn through.	Front needle: Through last stitch knitwise, slip st off, pull yarn through. Back needle: Through last stitch knitwise, slip st off, pull yarn through.

Yarn and Fabric

Keeping you warm outside on a snowy day, or cozy inside as a storm rages. Adding elegance and sophistication to an evening out. Celebrating a special occasion like a wedding, an anniversary, or a significant birthday. Giving comfort to someone ill or in pain, reminding them they are loved and cared for. Adding a touch of color and whimsy to your everyday life.

There are many reasons for knitting shawls. The choice of yarn and the fabric you knit with it are essential to how your shawl will make the wearer feel, the appearance of the shawl, and its suitability for the intended purpose.

In this chapter, you will find the tools to help you become a yarn and fabric expert. Fiber content, yarn structure, and needle sizes all work together in building your fabric. In the patterns, Kate and Kim will tell you about the yarns we chose and why, to give you a better sense of how all of this works in real-world situations. We will also offer yarn substitution tips to make it easier to knit the shawls you love with the yarns that make you happy.

Choosing Yarn

Fiber content, yarn construction, and how yarn is dyed (or not dyed) combine to influence how yarn behaves and what kind of fabric it will produce. All three factors determine the right yarn for a project. Start with yarn you love. Choose the very best yarn you can afford, remembering that best does not always equal the most expensive. The best yarn for you is about quality of fiber, the quality of color, and how suitable it is for your project. You should love everything about the yarn, for the purpose intended, whether it's a wedding shawl or something to go hiking in. Love the color. Love how the yarn feels in your hands. Choose yarn that you will love working with from start to finish.

Fiber Content

Different fiber types have different qualities. Once you know what the primary purpose of your shawl is, you can start to narrow down the kinds of fibers you want your yarn to contain. Natural fiber-based yarns make quality fabrics that last for years. They breathe and carry warming and/or cooling properties. They offer a wide range of options and variations that will contribute to your project's success. Man-made fibers offer durability and washability and come at a price point that's accessible to knitters at all incomes. We have so many options, and room to try them all.

ANIMAL FIBERS/PROTEIN FIBERS

Sheep: Wool yarn is spun with fleece sheared from sheep. There are hundreds of breeds of sheep used for textiles worldwide, each producing fleece with different qualities. Staple length is the average length of the fibers in the fleece. Short staple length makes softer yarns, while longer staple length makes more durable yarns. Micron count—the diameter of the fibers—determines how soft yarn feels against your skin. The smaller the micron count, the softer the yarn. Crimp is all about the texture of the fibers. Wools with finer crimp and more texture create yarns with lots of elasticity, bounce, and memory, all things that add to the "squoosh" factor we love in our knitted fabric. Elasticity is the ability of the fibers to spring back after being stretched. When plied together, that characteristic translates into "bounce." Take a strand of yarn made from fine wool fibers, and you'll notice a spring to it. Between your fingers, the strand will compress and then bounce back into shape when you release it. A strand held between your hands will spring when you pull your hands away from each other and then bounce right back in shape when you're done. Long wools—from sheep with large, curly locks—tend to be smoother and shinier, resulting in less elasticity and less bounce in the yarn, but more drape.

Good elasticity in shawl yarns means that the shawl always returns to its original size and shape. Memory is important for lace, in particular. If you stretch wool when it's wet and let it dry in that stretched-out position, it will remember the stretch. That's how we make lace beautiful, how we open up the holes of yarnovers and smooth the fabrics. By the same token, when you have a wool shawl knit with a textured fabric, like Radialactive (page 174), laying it flat to dry in a relaxed state—laid out flat and patted into shape, with no stretching—the wool will remember that shape as well, and return to it after washing.

Wool is insulating, wicks moisture away from the skin, and dries quickly when it gets wet. Difficult to believe when you're standing over your just-washed shawl whispering "dry . . . DRY!," but when you're out on a cold, snowy day wrapped in wool, even when the wool is wet, you feel warm. Wool also breathes, offering a cooling effect on the skin. This makes lightweight wool yarns an excellent choice for even the warmer seasons.

Cashmere: Oh, cashmere—soft, luxurious cloud of a fiber! Cashmere fiber, combed from cashmere goats, is warm, light, and delicate and adds a light halo to yarn. Cashmere has a short staple length, giving your yarn a matte, downy surface. The result is a very soft feel, but also a high likelihood of pilling. If your budget doesn't stretch to 100% cashmere, look for blends. Even in tiny amounts, cashmere makes a yarn feel luscious and luxurious—and adds warmth.

Camelids: Alpaca, llama, and camel are the most commonly found camelids in our yarn. Camelid fibers drape well, provide a soft halo, and add a significant amount of warmth to yarns they're in. These fibers tend to be heavy, and they lack the elasticity that sheep's wool has. Look for these fibers combined with more stable ones like wool in a yarn blend. Their softness makes for cozy, warm shawls that don't need to retain size.

Qiviut: Qiviut is fiber obtained from the softest undercoat of the musk ox. The fibers are short and retain a lot of elasticity. Curiously, it's the only animal fiber that resists felting in its natural state, making it a surprising easy-care choice. Because of the level of difficulty in gathering this fiber, qiviut is extremely expensive. You can get 100% qiviut yarn for the most special of projects, but qiviut blends with other fibers provide many of the benefits while keeping the cost down. Either way, qiviut yarn is a delight—a very special yarn perfect for shawls for the most knit-worthy in your life.

Mohair: Mohair is light and airy with a wide halo. We most often see it spun with a central binder thread made from a strong fiber like silk or nylon, however it can often be found carded and spun with other fibers like wool. Its smooth surface and long staple length add shine but also contribute to lack of memory and elasticity. Blended with wool or other fibers, mohair adds pockets of air, allowing you to knit at a much looser gauge while still maintaining fabric with stability. Carrying a strand of a mohair yarn, blended with a silk or nylon binder or center, along with another yarn gives you the ability to play with blending colors and textures for multi-layered fabric. The halo (page 49) obscures fine stitchwork, so mohair is best used for plainer fabrics or larger-scale pattern stitches.

Yak and Bison: Yak and bison are becoming increasingly popular in yarn fiber blends. As with cashmere and qiviut, these fibers are harvested by combing from the softest undercoat of the animals. The fibers are short, and as these fibers are much warmer than wool and costly to gather, these are most often found in blends. This also helps mitigate the pilling you can expect with any soft fiber. A tiny bit of yak or bison can make your yarn warmer and give it more drape. Keep the pattern stitches simple to let this depth of color be the star, but otherwise these fibers are a good choice for all types of pattern stitches.

SILK

While silk is technically a protein fiber, it is a unique fiber with special characteristics that make it a category of its own.

Silk is luxury. It adds sheen to a yarn and has excellent drape, making it ideal for special-occasion shawls. It possesses both warming and cooling qualities which make it a popular choice for a variety of climates. It has limited elasticity and memory, which means it will stretch out over time. When washed, silk shawls will come back to their original shape and size but with limitations. Eventually all remaining memory in the fibers will be gone, and the shawl will settle at a larger size.

PLANT FIBERS

Plant fibers are favored by those who are sensitive to animal fibers and for the cooling effect they give in warmer climates. These fibers are strong and hard wearing and machine washable and indeed often benefit from a trip to the dryer. They make excellent shawls for warm-weather wear, like adding a layer to a summer outfit without adding considerable warmth.

Cotton: Cotton yarns have no elasticity, meaning that they don't stretch out when wet. They can shrink when washed in hot water and dried in a dryer, only to stretch out again when worn. Cotton yarns make for beautiful, relaxed fabrics that are excellent for warm weather shawls. It's an excellent choice for textured pattern stitches, but be more careful with lace and openwork. Because cotton lacks elasticity, you can't open up the fabric with stretching or blocking. It doesn't mean lace is a bad idea in cotton, but know that you're going to harness the power of gravity to open up a lace pattern. This means that the larger the shawl is, the better a lace pattern looks.

Linen: Linen is produced from the flax plant, a fiber that can take a beating. The stalks of the flax plant are harvested, soaked to remove unwanted pieces, dried, pounded, and combed to produce fibers that are still fairly coarse. In the skein, linen yarns can be hard and rough to the touch. Yet the resulting fabric is soft and drapes beautifully, only improving over time—indeed, linen benefits from both a machine wash and dry. Linen fabrics are extremely durable, lasting for years and years of regular wear. Linen is also its own cooling system, wicking moisture away from the skin and evaporating it.

Nettle: Nettle is a durable fiber that adds texture, visual interest, and strength when blended with other fibers in your yarn. The fiber comes from the stem, after the bark is removed. The fibers are long and strong, and can often be mistaken for linen.

We've used two very different yarns in this book that both contain nettle. Hespero (page 161) uses Erika Knight's Wild Wool, a wool and nettle blend. At first glance the yarn has a rustic look, but when you touch it, it's soft and slightly textured. Soundscape (page 157) makes the most of Middle Brook Fiberworks Vintage No. 6, a yarn designed by shepherdess Anne Choi. Vintage No. 6 combines fibers from Anne's Shetland flock, local fine wools, and nettle to create a yarn with a crisp and textured hand.

Bamboo and Rayon: Bamboo and rayon are typically processed in a way that imitates the qualities of other fibers like silk and cotton. They both provide drape and sheen in yarns but have drawbacks. Rayon is fragile when wet. Bamboo stretches with time and gravity—and has no bounce-back at all, meaning your shawl will keep getting bigger. To mitigate this, work on smaller needles than you might expect to help the fabric retain stability, and keep it for smaller shawl projects.

Although the source plants are fast renewing and the yarns are often touted as eco-conscious choices, the process to create them is water-intensive and problematic.

MAN-MADE FIBERS

Nylon, polyamide, and acrylic are some common names for various synthetic fibers developed for use in clothing. They are inexpensive, widely available, and easy to care for. Developed to mimic the texture of wool and silk, polymer-based yarns add strength, durability, and elasticity to fiber blends. They're stable; they never stretch or change shape. This means that fabrics knit with them can't be stretched or blocked—how it comes off your needles is how it's going to stay. Choose your projects and pattern stitches with this stability in mind: A synthetic blended with wool would be an excellent choice for a deliberately oversized shawl, as it would retain its shape. It's common advice to tell you to avoid lace patterns or openwork in synthetics, as you can't stretch the fabric to smooth and open it up. This isn't strictly true: You can't do it with a wash, but a gentle application of steam can work wonders.

Yarn Construction

The general guidance when matching yarn to pattern stitch and vice versa is that the smoother the yarn, the more complex the patterning can be; the more textured the yarn, the simpler the patterning should be. A highly textured yarn obscures fine details of pattern stitches. There are, of course, exceptions—smooth yarns that fight pattern stitches, or highly textured yarns that work with textured stitches—so understanding yarn construction helps you make informed choices about which yarn to choose.

WORSTED VS. WOOLEN SPUN

How yarns are spun greatly affects how they behave when knit, how gauge affects the final fabric, and how much stitch definition they have. When fibers are neatly combed, with all fibers going in the same direction, the resulting yarn is said to be worsted spun. Worsted-spun yarns are smooth and sleek, giving wonderful stitch definition. Woolen-spun yarns are created when fibers are carded and allowed to mix in different directions. You'll notice woolen-spun yarns are lighter as the process allows more air to be trapped between the fibers. These yarns are cozy and more textured than worsted-spun yarns.

Worsted-spun (left) vs. woolen-spun (right)

TWIST AND PLY

Twist is what makes our yarn. It's twist that holds the fibers together and determines how fluffy or smooth our yarn is. It determines durability and strength, softness and bounce. The tighter the twist, the stronger the yarn. The looser the twist, the softer the yarn. Twist gives our yarn its personality at the very core of its being: the ply.

What is a *ply*? It's the very beginning of what yarn is. It's the strand at the start of the yarn building process. The moment fibers are twisted, they form a ply. Add plies together, and you build the strands and layers that form the final construction.

SINGLE PLY

A single-ply yarn is a single twist of fiber—easy! The looser the twist, the more pilly the yarn is likely to be.

Fabrics made from these yarns tend to *bias*: The fabric can develop a twist in the same direction as the yarn's twist. With these yarns, you might notice that one leg of each stitch stands perfectly vertical, while the other tilts to one side. As you work further, you will notice that the fabric starts to bias: tilt on an angle. The tighter the twist, the greater chance of the fabric biasing. This is a quality that can usually be resolved with a good soak and block once the shawl is complete.

TWO-PLY YARNS

Two-ply yarns are balanced: Each ply is twisted in one direction, and those two plies are twisted together in the other direction, equalizing the force the twist places on each ply. As a result, the fabric doesn't bias. Two-ply yarns are not quite round. A slight texture in the skein means it will create a slight texture in your fabric.

As the number of plies increases, the likelihood of pilling reduces. Consider whether the piece is going to experience wear and rubbing, and let that guide your choice. Kate has a sad tale of a shawl that she ruined: It was loosely knitted with a loosely plied single. She used to wear it cape-style over the shoulders of her coat, and the strap of her messenger bag created a very unattractive stretch of pilling along one side.

THREE-PLY AND FOUR-PLY YARNS

Three or four plies create a round, balanced yarn, similar in shape to spaghetti. Fabrics knit with three- and four-ply yarns generally have very good stitch definition. Lace patterns and cable patterns especially benefit from this kind of construction.

CABLED

Cabled yarns are created by taking two, four, or six two-ply yarns and plying them together in the opposite direction. This creates a textured, abrasion-resistant yarn that creates an interesting textured fabric. These types of yarns work fantastically well with textured pattern stitches, further enhancing the difference between the knits and the purls—finer lace patterns can sometimes be overwhelmed.

BOUCLÉ

Bouclé yarn looks like a series of loops on a string. The loops are created by plying two strands together: one held taut and the other looser. Loops can be small or large. Fabric knit with bouclé yarns has deep texture. Simple Stockinette or Garter stitch works best with this yarn, as the loops tend to obscure stitch definition.

TWEED

Tweed yarns are woolen-spun yarns. Fibers are carded and allowed to go in many different directions. Small bits of contrasting fibers are added to the batts in the carding process to add pops of color to the yarn. Tweed has a reputation for being a rough and coarse yarn, however in recent years mills have started creating tweed yarns that are made using softer fibers. Even hand dyers can access yarns with *neps* spun into them, allowing them to created hand-dyed versions of tweed yarns.

SLUB YARNS

Slub yarns, often called *thick-and-thin yarns*, are characterized by their uneven and irregular appearance. They produce blatantly uneven fabrics that can appear to be thick and dense in some areas and almost see-through in others. Most of these yarns are bulky or chunky yarns, which emphasizes the difference in changes in fabric. Simple stitch patterns like Garter, Stockinette, and Seed stitch are the best use of these: Anything else gets lost in the yarn texture.

HALO

When soft, light fibers like mohair and alpaca are spun loosely around a central binder made from nylon, silk, or an equally strong fiber, you get halo yarns. When knitting with these yarns, you're really knitting with the binder and allowing the fluffy and fuzzy outer fiber to fill in space between stitches. You can use a larger needle than usually recommended with these yarns for this reason.

The fuzzier the yarn, the harder it is to see pattern stitches, so keep it simple. A large-scale lace pattern can work well in a yarn with halo, but know that you won't be able to see the details of the decreases and other stitches as well—it's really about letting the yarnovers star.

CHAINETTE

Chainette yarns consist of one or more strands of yarn machine knitted into a chain. They are essentially yarns made into a very long i-cord. This tube construction traps air, creating lighter yarns—more yardage per ball than a more traditional type of yarn construction. These can also create yarns that bring elasticity to fibers that don't normally have it, like linen and cotton. They vary in texture, but the same general rules apply: highly textured yarns lend themselves better to simpler fabrics; less textured yarns look great with all sorts of pattern stitches.

What Does Good Shawl Fabric Look Like?

Socks, mittens, and sweaters require sturdier fabric with little room to move. We want our socks and mittens to wear like iron. We want our sweaters to keep their shape so that they always fit us well.

Shawls are different. The fabric we want to create for shawls needs to drape well and show off our hard-working stitches. The fabric needs to have enough drape to wrap around us and follow the shape of the person wearing it.

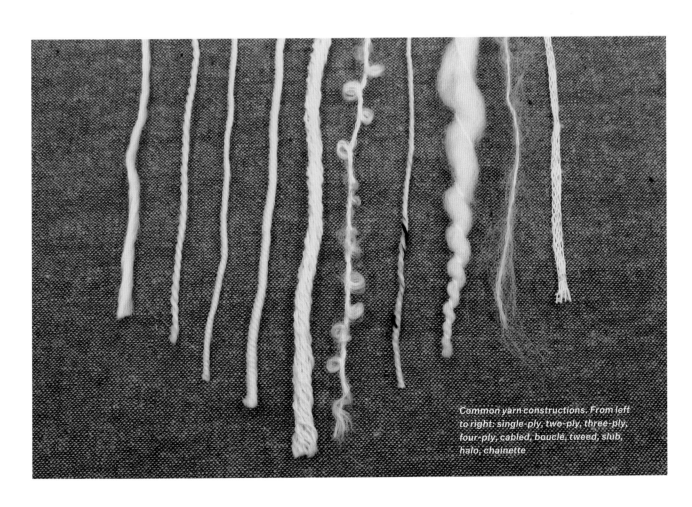

Common yarn constructions. From left to right: single-ply, two-ply, three-ply, four-ply, cabled, bouclé, tweed, slub, halo, chainette

How Stitch Patterns Affect Fabric

Stockinette Stitch

Stockinette stitch occurs when you knit every second row and purl on alternate rows. Knit stitches and purl stitches create force in different directions, so when stacked on top of each other, they hold each other up, stretching their little "yarny" arms vertically. Stockinette stitch is the standard we compare all other stitch patterns with, as it's the most commonly used. We can also use Stockinette stitch gauge as a tool for yarn substitution. Find a yarn that has the same construction, fiber content, and recommended gauge as the yarn used in a pattern, and you'll have a close match to the original yarn.

Stockinette stitch will show off the qualities and texture of your yarn like no other stitch pattern. Tight twist, loose twist, slubs, tweed, and changes in texture will all be evident in Stockinette stitch.

If you love the feel of Stockinette stitch fabric but want another stitch pattern, look for one that contains large portions of Stockinette stitch. If a stitch pattern predominantly contains large portions of Stockinette, then that pattern is more likely to behave like Stockinette stitch fabric in the same gauge. The Seaweed stitch pattern (page 94) is an example of this. While it contains both knit and purl stitches on each side, the overall fabric behaves like Stockinette stitch fabric.

Garter Stitch

Farrow Rib

Garter stitch occurs when you knit every row. Knit stitches stacked on top of knit stitches fold over each other, compressing stitches horizontally down toward the cast-on. Garter stitch stitches are square, making this an excellent stitch for square shawls, because the geometry of the shawl matches the geometry of the stitch.

If you love the feel of Garter stitch fabric but want to use another stitch pattern, look for stitch patterns that contain large portions of Garter stitch. If a stitch pattern predominantly contains large portions of Garter stitch, then that stitch pattern is more likely to behave like Garter stitch fabric in the same gauge. Farrow Rib (page 91), for example, has the depth and layered feel of Garter stitch, which contributes to how it behaves in a shawl fabric.

Garter stitch will emphasize the qualities of the yarn you've chosen, evening out textures in slub yarns, showing off clear purl bumps with smooth and sleek yarns and adding a bouncy underpinning to fabric made from haloed yarns.

Lace

Stoclet Crescent shawl (page 165)

Lace stitches purposely put holes in your knitting. Because holes create space, they stretch the fabric out in all directions. Even putting a single hole in your knitting will change the quality and shape of your fabric.

If a stitch pattern predominantly contains large portions of lace stitch, you can expect lots of changes to the shape and size of the fabric compared to a Stockinette swatch of the same stitch count. More yarnovers in a lace pattern will create greater length and width in places where those yarnovers occur. In the image below, diagonal lines of yarnovers evenly spaced in the fabric make the fabric larger than the other three fabrics that use the same number of stitches. Stitch patterns like Zigzag Version 1 (page 105) that use fewer yarnovers create a denser lace fabric.

Lace stitches benefit from smooth, sleek-surfaced yarns with high twist. Like using a fine-tipped fountain pen, these yarns outline each stitch composition cleanly.

Cables

Cable stitches cross over each other, folding the fabric in from the side edges, compressing it on a vertical plane. For this reason, when working with cables in a shawl pattern, you usually need to make your shawl wider than you would a similar shawl in Stockinette stitch. Every time one stitch crosses another, they cancel each other out, folding two stitches into the space that one took up previously.

On the next row (rest row), that space comes back, widening the fabric again. Every cable crossing causes a compression; every rest releases some of that compression. The overall effect of a cable stitch pattern is vertically compressed fabric in comparison to Stockinette stitch fabric.

Cables knit in round yarns (for example, three- or four-ply yarns) have beautiful, clear stitch definition. They don't need high-twist yarns. In fact, plumper yarns with looser (but not too loose!) twist fill in the spaces naturally created in cable constructs.

Geometry and Stitches

While both simple stitch patterns, Garter stitch and Stockinette stitch create vastly different geometries when applied to shawl shapes. Garter stitches are square, which means that shawl shapes made entirely of Garter stitch will be squatter in height than those made entirely of Stockinette stitch. Stockinette stitches are taller than they are wide. Back in the "Shapes and Recipes" chapter (page 6), there are some shapes that benefit from the square qualities of Garter. The Mitered Square, for example, can only truly be a square when worked in Garter stitch. The angle of the point of increase runs diagonally across the square, requiring stitches to be the same height and width. If worked in Stockinette stitch, the "square" becomes a squat rectangle instead.

In the images on this page, each of these swatches has the same number of stitches and the same number of rows, and they were worked using the same needles. It's an excellent snapshot of what happens to the geometry of a shawl with different kinds of stitch patterns. The Garter swatch is shorter; you need more rows to get the same height fabric as Stockinette.

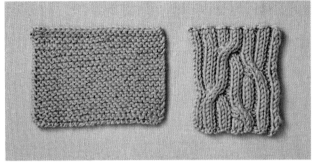

Top: Stockinette stitch, lace. Bottom: Garter stitch, cables

The cabled swatch pulls in at the sides, making a narrower shape. And lace stitches open up fabric in all directions, taking up more space. All of this will affect your yardage usage. Swatching in both the yarn and stitch pattern(s) you'll be using in your shawl is an essential step in not only what it will look like, but how to manage your yarn throughout (see page 55 for more on yardage).

Stitch Definition

Good stitch definition means that the stitch pattern is visible, the individual elements are discernible, and the overall pattern is easy to see. This includes uniformity of stitches. You should be able to see the shape of each stitch, and each stitch of the same kind should look like the others. When looking at lace patterns, stitch definition is also about negative space. Openwork should be open, with no closed holes or eyelets.

Make Fabric You Love

To make fabric you love, the process is simple: Take yarn you love, work with needles that feel good in your hands, and begin to knit. Repeat until you have fabric you love.

That's it.

In all the projects in this book, we have done just that. We start with beautiful yarns we are in love with and needles that feel good in our hands, and we knit. If we don't like the fabric—how it feels in our hands, how it drapes, and how it shows off the stitch patterns we've chosen—we rip out and start again with a different size needle or a different stitch pattern.

All of this comes from developing our knowledge about knitted fabric through experimentation, experience, and getting it wrong as much as we get it right. Over time, we've developed instincts that tell us what needle size to try first and how to recognize when the fabric is just right for our project. What follows is how to get yourself there.

Needles: Where to Start?

Every skein or ball of yarn should come with guidelines to help you determine the best needle size. The tag or ball band should have recommendations for what needle size to use with the yarn, and in rare cases where it doesn't, Ravelry becomes a good resource for crowdsourcing what sizes other knitters have tried for similar projects. The yarn label will also tell you what the recommended gauge for each yarn is: a range that can represent fabrics from the densely packed stitches needed to make durable socks to looser fabrics used in shawls and scarves.

How to Sample Yarn and Needle Combinations

In an ideal world, every yarn company would have swatches available in every yarn, every colorway, every possible stitch pattern, and every single knitter's gauge. We do not live in that world. And so, we swatch samples to learn about the yarn and how it interacts with our hands, and sometimes we even try different needle materials to create fabric we cannot wait to wrap ourselves up in. Swatching became a joy when Kim stopped looking at it as a race to meet another knitter's gauge and started looking at it

as an opportunity to play with yarn and stitches to make beautiful fabric. When she has to meet another other knitter's gauge, it irritates her and annoys her impatient, project-hungry knitter-self; when she plays to create fabric she loves, everything changes.

1. Gather your needles: the recommended size (or for shawls, the largest of the recommended sizes) plus needles both larger and smaller by a size or two.

2. Cast on a "good number" of stitches. In order to fully understand how fabric behaves on a larger level, you need to create a good-sized piece of fabric that will mimic the fabric in your finished shawl. My go-to cast-on numbers for shawl fabric:

- Fingering weight: 30–35 stitches
- Sport or DK weight: 25–30 stitches
- Worsted or Aran weight: 25 stitches
- Bulky or chunky weight: 15–20 stitches

(Kim has a very nerdy knitting friend who *always* casts on 42 stitches, because according to Douglas Adams's *The Hitchhiker's Guide to the Galaxy,* 42 is the ultimate answer to Life, the Universe, and Everything.)

3. Work about 4–6 inches (10–15 cm) in the stitch pattern you've chosen for your shawl. Some knitters like to build in a Garter stitch border when sampling a new yarn—a few rows of Garter stitch, then start and end each row with 2–3 stitches in Garter, and finally a few rows of Garter to finish before binding off. Kim doesn't do this. She likes to see what the stitch pattern does to the edges of the fabric. Are they straight or wavy? What is the shape of the finished sample? These things are important for her to know. These could be qualities that she's thrilled to play with in her final shawl design, or they could be detrimental to the final shape. It's only through swatching and sampling that she gets this information.

3. Measure your gauge (page 10), and write it down. Kim keeps a handful of tags in her knitting bag that she uses to label her swatches. She puts information about her gauge(s) down on a tag, along with yarn name and needle size(s) used. This gives her important information to compare with washed and blocked swatch measurements.

4. Wash and block your sample as you will wash and block the finished shawl (page 38). We cannot stress this enough. Are you are the kind of person who will wash your shawl, squeeze out (never wring!) excess water, and throw your shawl over a railing to dry? That is how you should treat your sample. You want to preemptively figure out how your finished shawl fabric will behave in your life.

5. Once your swatch is dry, measure the gauge(s) again. Write them down and compare them to your prewashed numbers. How do they compare? If your gauge has not changed at all, your fabric is stable and won't change much in the finished shawl. If your gauge numbers have grown by a few stitches over 4 inches (10 cm), it might be worth taking the extra step of hanging your swatch up for a day with binder clips attached, to see how gravity will affect the fabric after a full day of wearing.

6. Evaluate the fabric.

DRAPE: Does it drape well? Hanging the swatch over a finger or two, or even poking your index finger into the center of the swatch and letting it hang over, can tell you a lot about your fabric. If the fabric is stiff and barely bends, your shawl will not drape well. The fabric should fold softly over your hand and feel good to touch, while not feeling like your fingers will poke through.

STITCH DEFINITION: Are your stitches clear and easy to read? If you used a stitch pattern, can you see the texture, lines, and designs it's supposed to make? Do you like how this stitch pattern looks in this yarn?

DURABILITY: Will the fabric stand up to being worn? If knitting something that will be worn often and needs to survive everyday use, treat the swatch in the same way. Putting a swatch in your bra, a pocket, or the bottom of a tote bag will mimic what the fabric will go through on a daily basis. If the fabric pulls, pills, and shows signs of wear, it may not be the best choice for everyday wear. If the fabric shows signs of being delicate, reserving it for special-occasion wear is a better choice.

Shawl Fabric and Pasta

Compare shawl fabric to pasta. The two extremes of this are raw pasta and the pasty, shapeless goop that results from cooking pasta too long. The ideal pasta is somewhere in between: cooked through, but still holding its shape. The same goes for shawl fabric. At a tight gauge, the fabric will stand up on its own. Perfect for making a house of wool (and let's face it, we've all thought about that at least once!), but do you want to wrap it around yourself? Unlikely. Some of us like our pasta al dente with a little firmness—not crunch, mind you, but firm. Others like their pasta on the soft side. Whichever is your preference is fine, but keeping fabric somewhere in that middle range is important.

How to Avoid Swatching
Call it knitting.

You like to knit. You like to knit beautiful things. Swatching is the first step toward that. Whether you knit a gauge swatch before you start your project or dive in with both feet into the full-sized shawl, what you are knitting is a swatch: sampling yarn, pattern, and fabric. When you knit a swatch to fall in love with the pattern, the yarn, and the fabric—making sure all three are perfect—your knitting life changes and swatching is no longer the chore you have to do before the real knitting. Knitting a swatch is real knitting.

Trust your hands and experience. Even if you've knit one shawl in your life, you already have experience. If you loved everything about that shawl—the yarn, the stitch pattern, the shape, and wearing it—then you already know one set of parameters that will help inform future shawls. If there are any one of those factors you wish were different, then you have ideas for what to avoid in the future.

THE G WORD

When you knit someone else's pattern, getting the same gauge as the designer is important to replicate the designer's vision and for a number of structural reasons. If your gauge is looser than the designer's, you'll end up with a larger shawl, but you may run out of yarn before finishing it. If your gauge is tighter, your shawl will be smaller and may drape differently. But what happens when that perfect gauge match is elusive? As a knitter with free will to be the boss of your knitting, you also have a choice.

If you're set on matching gauge as closely as possible, there are a few strategies you can try:

1. Try a different needle size. Going up a needle size when your gauge is smaller, or down a needle size if your gauge is larger, can be just enough difference to balance your gauge and match the designer's.

2. Try a different needle material. Sometimes the material your needles are made of can make a really big difference in the quality of your fabric, and by extension, your gauge. Metal needles are slippery and can be immobile, which makes it difficult to work with sleek yarns like silks, but can be the answer to the drag that some wools have on your needles. Wood or bamboo both create a slight drag with their texture, which helps when working with sleeker and more slippery yarns like silk. Carbon brings smoothness and strength to the table—a lightweight alternative to metal; plastic needles provide flexibility, which makes them easy on your hands.

+
Teaching Your Hands

Gather up a small bag or bowl of leftover yarns from different projects. When you're not sure what to knit, or just feel experimental, pick up a ball, choose a shape from the "Shapes and Recipes" chapter or a pattern from the "Stitch Dictionary" chapter, and make a sample. Learn how the same stitch pattern looks in different colors, in different yarn constructions, in different yarn weights. Kim keeps these swatches, labeled with all the information she needs to repeat this combination on a larger scale. They become inspiration for future projects.

If that's not your thing, then you have a series of coasters, or squares to make a blanket, or even contrasting patch pockets for your next sweater.

When Gauge Is Elusive

If you don't win the gauge lottery, but you do like the fabric you've created, there is nothing wrong with continuing as you were with caution and an understanding of what to expect.

CHECKLIST FOR THE RENEGADE SHAWL KNITTER:

- Does the fabric have enough structure to hold its shape? Your initial swatch should tell you (page 52).

- Does the stitch pattern have enough definition at this stage? Do you like how it looks?

- If your gauge is different than the pattern calls for, do you have enough yarn to finish the project (page 55)? Will you be comfortable with any changes in finished size that may occur?

On Yardage

Predicting required yardage for a shawl pattern is more complicated than for other types of projects; the type of fabric and stitch pattern used significantly affect how much yarn is used.

For things like socks and sweaters, yardage tables are fairly easy to figure out, and there are listings and apps to help you shop. It works because we know we're comparing apples to apples: The fabric is the same. All of these apps and tables assume that the pieces are worked in Stockinette stitch with small ribbed edgings.

But when you're talking about shawls, it all changes.

You don't use the same amount of yarn if you're working a very open lace pattern, compared with a densely cabled pattern or Stockinette stitch. Cables use much more yarn than Stockinette; lace uses less. Even the difference between Stockinette and Garter is remarkable. Garter stitch compresses vertically, so that you need to work a lot more rows per inch, and therefore you need significantly more yarn per inch than Stockinette stitch—on average, about 50 percent more. (See the photos on page 51.)

One Key Truth

There is one fact we can guarantee to be true: If you work exactly the same pattern in two yarns, to create two pieces of the same size you need less of the thicker yarn and more of the finer yarn. Consider the Hollerith shawl: To create a piece of the same size in fingering-weight yarn (worked to a fingering-weight gauge/fabric), you'd need to do a lot more knitting, and you'd therefore need a lot more yarn.

And interesting things happen when you push the gauge of a yarn. If you work two very different yarns at the same gauge—e.g., a fingering weight and a worsted weight at 5 stitches per inch (2.5 cm)—the yardage used to knit a piece of the same size is not the same. The diameter of the yarn takes up some of the curve of the stitch, and so you tend to use more of thicker yarns.

All of which is to say that we can't offer a tidy "finished size vs. gauge" table. But it's not a hopeless cause or an entirely unanswerable question.

Working from the Patterns and Recipes

All of the recipes and patterns in this book are easily adjusted to accommodate different yardages: They're all *work until it's the length you want, or until you run out of time and/or yarn.* Shaped shawls all start with the smaller stitch count, working up to the largest, so that you never run out before the shaping is complete. And the thirteen designs were all specifically created so that you can substitute for gauge and yardage with impunity: When there are pattern transitions or borders to be worked, the transition point is flexible, allowing you to use different amounts of yarn.

And then there are tools below that can help out, too.

First, there are guides to help you when you're buying yarn or assessing your stash.

There are also solutions to help you determine how big a shawl will get once you're working the project. There's some geometry, which may or may not be your thing; if you're not into that, a spreadsheet is an excellent tool.

Finally, at the end of this section, there are tips for yarn management and how to plan for and deal with possible shortages. This is useful whether you enjoy geometry, spreadsheets, or neither.

Before You Start the Project: Shopping or Stash-Diving

Minimum Requirements

Don't plan to start a project of the listed type or size unless you have approximately the indicated amount of yarn.

The lower number is for a fabric that's mostly Stockinette- and/or lace-based; the larger number is for a Garter-based or heavily cabled fabric.

Gauge	Scarf, Medium Cowl	Shawlette	Medium Shawl	Full Circular Shawl, Personal Blanket
Lace 9 sts per inch	490–735 yards (445–670 m)	550–825 yards (500–750 m)	920–1,380 yards (835–1,255 m)	2,295–3,445 yards (2,090–3,135 m)
Fingering/sock 8 sts per inch	440–660 yards (400–600 m)	495–745 yards (450–675 m)	830–1,245 yards (755–1135 m)	2,070–3,105 yards (1,885–2,830 m)
Heavy fingering 7 sts per inch	400–600 yards (365–550 m)	450–675 yards (410–615 m)	745–1,120 yards (680–1,020 m)	1,870–2,805 yards (1,700–2,650 m)
Sport 6.5 sts per inch	385–580 yards (350–530m)	430–645 yards (390–585 m)	720–1,080 yards (655–985 m)	1,800–2,700 yards (1,645–2,460 m)
DK 6 sts per inch	350–525 yards (320–480 m)	395–595 yards (360–540 m)	655–985 yards (595–900 m)	1,645–2,470 yards (1,505–2,2460 m)
Worsted 5 sts per inch	320–480 yards (290–435 m)	360–540 yards (330–495 m)	605–910 yards (550–830 m)	1,510–2,265 yards (1,380–2,070 m)
Aran 4.5 sts per inch	295–445 yards (270–405 m)	330–495 yards (300–450 m)	550–825 yards (500–750 m)	1,375–2,065 yards (1,255–1,890 m)
Chunky 4 sts per inch	265–400 yards (240–365 m)	295–445 yards (270–405 m)	495–745 yards (450–681 m)	1,240–1,860 yards (1,130–1,700 m)
Bulky 3 sts per inch	180–270 yards (165–250 m)	200–300 yards (180–270 m)	335–505 yards (305–460 m)	835–1,255 yards (760–1,144 m)
Super bulky 2 sts per inch	120–180 yards (110–165 m)	295–445 yards (270–405 m)	225–340 yards (205–310 m)	565–850 yards (515–775 m)

+

Big Disclaimer

Any numbers we give here, any calculations you make—these are estimates. If you're managing a very small quantity of yarn, or are trying to fit in specific pattern repeats, it's good to make sure you have a little extra yarn on hand, have a plan for what you might do if you run short, and monitor the usage as you work through the project. Remember that yardage requirements can change radically between different types of pattern stitches, and so calculations and estimates you made based on a plain Garter or Stockinette section will not be applicable for sections worked in other stitches.

A Bit More Detail: Predicting Yardage Requirements by Shawl Size

Always weigh each skein or ball in grams before you start working with it. You'll need this information for the calculations outlined below.

STEP 1: Calculate the Surface Area of the Shawl You're Aiming to Make

Shape	Measurements	Calculate the Surface Area
Square	Side = length of one side	Side × Side
Rectangle	Short Side = length of short side Long Side = length of long side	Short Side × Long Side
Triangles – including Kite and Vortex	Top Edge = length of top (longest) edge Depth = measured straight from top edge down to tip	(Top Edge × Depth) ÷ 2
Faroese	Width = width of the center panel Depth = measured from center of top edge to bottom of center panel Top Edge = length of top edge of one side triangle, measured from one edge of center panel to tip	Width × Depth + Depth × Top Edge
Crescent	Top Edge = length of top (longest) edge Depth = measured straight from top edge down to tip	(3.14 × Top Edge × Depth) ÷ 2
Circle	Radius = measurement from center to outside edge	3.14 × Radius × Radius
Semicircle	Radius = depth or half of top width	(3.14 × Radius × Radius) ÷ 2

Divide the surface area by 100 and multiply it by the appropriate number from this table: presto, a yardage estimate!

For example, a triangular shawl 60 inches (152 cm) along the top edge and 25 inches (63.5 cm) deep has a surface area of (60 × 25) ÷ 2 = 750 square inches.

And 750 square inches (surface area) ÷ 100 = 7.5.

Working a Stockinette-based piece at worsted-weight gauge, 5 stitches per inch, you'll need about 7.5 × 65 yards = 487.5 yards.

Estimated yardage required to work 100 square inches (254 square cm)

Fabric Gauge	Fabric: Stockinette Stitch, Lace, Openwork	Fabric: Garter Stitch, Cables
Lace 9 sts per inch	100 yards (91 m)	150 yards (137 m)
Fingering/sock 8 sts per inch	90 yards (82 m)	135 yards (123 m)
Heavy fingering 7 sts per inch	85 yards (77 m)	130 yards (118 m)
Sport 6 sts per inch	80 yards (73 m)	120 yards (109 m)
DK 5.5 sts per inch	75 yards (68 m)	115 yards (105 m)
Worsted 5 sts per inch	65 yards (59 m)	100 yards (91 m)
Aran 4.5 sts per inch	60 yards (55 m)	90 yards (82 m)
Chunky 4 sts per inch	55 yards (50 m)	85 yards (77 m)
Bulky 3 sts per inch	35 yards (32 m)	55 yards (50 m)
Super bulky 2 sts per inch	25 yards (23 m)	40 yards (36 m)

Once Your Project Is Under Way: Estimating How Far You Can Go

A digital scale and a spreadsheet program are fantastic tools for shawl knitters, as they allow you to make calculations to predict how much of a shawl you can make with the yarn you have available.

Weigh each ball/skein (in grams) before you start working with it. Yarn is rarely exactly the same weight as listed on the ball band, and even 3 or 4 grams can make a difference in yardage, particularly for finer yarns.

Once you've worked about a quarter of your first skein of yarn, you will have enough to get an accurate measurement. It's important to measure in grams, rather than ounces, as it's much more accurate.

Weigh the yarn you have left over in your skein, and subtract that from the starting weight of the skein to see how much you've used. For example, if you started with a 115 g skein, and there's 80 g left, you've used 115 – 80 = 35 g so far.

Then count your stitches in the current row.

This solution is all about being able to calculate based on how many stitches or how much fabric you've worked, and how much yarn you've used. You can do it for any shape by stitch count, and some of the simpler shapes also have a shortcut straight from geometry class.

Either way, don't be afraid of the calculations: Your computer is there to help.

Method One: For Pieces Worked Without Shaping

This is easy, and you may have already done this type of estimation.

Measure the length of the piece you've worked. Divide the number of grams used by the length worked. This tells you how many grams you need to work 1 inch (or 1 cm if you're using metric). Then divide the total number of grams of yarn by that number.

For example, if you've got 200 grams of yarn, and you've worked 8 inches of a scarf using 30 grams, the calculation goes as follows:

30 (grams used) ÷ 8 (inches worked so far) = 3.75

This is how many grams of yarn you need to work 1 inch.

200 (grams of yarn available in total) ÷ 3.75 (number of grams required to work an inch) = 53.3

This means you can expect to get a scarf about 53 inches (135 cm) long.

Method Two: By Surface Area

This works for the following shapes: squares (those worked with shaping), top-down triangles with the standard shaping (not the wide version), and rays and wedge shaping for circles and semicircles. (That is, this only works for shapes where there is one variable measurement.)

To do it this way, you need to measure your piece. Slip the stitches to scrap yarn and measure the key dimensions as listed below, twice—once before blocking and once after blocking. Block, of course, the way you intend to block the finished piece. (See page 38 for more information.) Both measurements are important: Pre-blocked measurements will help you keep track as you're working, and post-blocked measurements will give you a true sense of how big the finished item will be.

STEP 1: Calculate How Much You've Worked So Far

Consult the table below to determine what to measure, and calculate the surface area. It doesn't matter if you're working in inches or cm; just stay consistent with all your measurements.

Make a note of the measurements pre- and post-blocking, but use only the post-blocking measurement for this calculation.

The result of this calculation is the *Surface Area*—how many square inches or centimeters—of the knitting you've worked so far.

Shape	Measure	Calculate the Surface Area
Square	Side = length of one side	Side × Side
Top-Down Triangle, Standard	Depth = measured from center of top edge to tip	Depth × Depth
Circle	Radius = measurement from center to outside edge	3.14 × Radius × Radius
Semicircle	Radius = depth (or half of top width)	1.57 × Radius × Radius

STEP 2: **Calculate How Much Knitting You Can Do per Gram of Yarn**

You'll need to weigh your work for this. For the most accurate measurement, slip the stitches to scrap yarn—so the weight of the needle isn't affecting the result—and use a digital scale set to grams (much more accurate than ounces).

Take the result from the previous calculation (Surface Area) and divide it by the number of grams of yarn you've worked. This tells you how much knitting—how many square inches or cm—you get per gram of yarn. We'll call it *Knitting Per Gram*.

STEP 3: **How Much Knitting Can You Make with All Your Yarn?**

Multiply Knitting Per Gram by the number of grams of yarn you have available. This tells you how much knitting—how many square inches or cm—you can do with the full quantity of yarn you have.

Let's call that number *Total Knitting Area*.

STEP 4: **How Far Will That Take You?**

Once you know the surface area you've worked so far, the formulas for surface area can tell you how far you'll get. (This only works for mathematically regular shapes, those with only one variable measurement.) The result of this calculation gives you a very good sense of how big your piece will get with the yarn you have available.

Shape You're Making	Calculate	What The Result Means
Square	The square root of Total Knitting Area	The maximum length of the Side
Top-Down Triangle, Standard	The square root of Total Knitting Area	The maximum Depth
Circle	The square root of (Total Knitting Area ÷ 3.14)	The maximum Radius
Semicircle	The square root of (Total Knitting Area ÷ 1.57)	The maximum Radius/Depth

Difference Between Blocked and Unblocked Fabric

As you're working, remember that this measurement is relative to the blocked fabric. If your fabric changed significantly with blocking, one more quick calculation will help.

Divide the post-blocked dimension by the pre-blocked one. This gives you the growth factor. Then divide your target dimension calculated above by the growth factor to give you a sense of how big it will be as you're working.

For example, if the shawl measured 24 inches before blocking and 28 inches after, your growth factor is 28 ÷ 24 = 1.167. And if your predicted target measurement from the calculation above is 32 inches, your pre-blocked estimate is 32 ÷ 1.167 = 27.4 inches.

after blocking ÷ before blocking = Growth Factor

If you're struggling to get a good measurement on your needles, you might want to slip the stitches to scrap yarn or a lifeline, take the needle out, and lay the stitches flat.

Method Three: By Stitch Count

This method words for all shapes. What you're doing is calculating the number of stitches and rows you've worked with the yarn you have, and then you work out how many stitches you can work total.

STEP 1: Count the Stitches You've Worked So Far

You'll need a spreadsheet program to do some arithmetic. Microsoft Excel, Numbers, Google Sheets—any of these tools will work.

Look at the pattern: How many stitches did you start with? That's the first number in your calculation. (Note: If you worked a Garter tab, count the stitches and rows in that, and add it to your total.)

Then look at the increase pattern. For example, are you increasing 2 stitches every other row? If so, it means that you work 2 rows with your initial stitch count (which gives you 2 × the number of stitches initially cast on), and then add 2 to the stitch count; work 2 rows with that stitch count, and add 2 to that count; and work 2 rows with that stitch count, and so forth.

Put another way, you are adding up:

2 × cast-on number

2 × (cast-on number + 2)

2 × (cast-on number + 4)

And so forth, until you get all the way to your current stitch count. If you've worked both RS and WS rows, include 2 × that number, too!

If you're increasing on both RS and WS rows, you need one line for each row. For example, if you're increasing 4 stitches on the RS rows and 2 on the WS rows, you are adding up:

Cast-on number

Cast-on number + 4

Cast-on number + 6

Cast-on number + 10

Cast-on number + 12

And so forth, until you get all the way to your current stitch count. (Note that Kate doesn't actually type all these numbers in; she just sets up formulas in her spreadsheet.)

For the first example above, Kate starts with 2 × the cast-on number, and then all cells below that are just 2 × (value from cell above + 2). She copies the formula down the column until she sees the number of stitches from her current row.

For the second example, Kate starts with the cast-on number, and then she has two alternating formulas below that: The first one is (value from cell above + 4), corresponding to the RS row; the second one is (value from cell above + 2), corresponding to the WS row. She then copies these two formulas down the column until she sees the number of stitches from her current row.

It would be something like this:

	A	B	C
1	Starting stitch count	8	8
2	RS row increases	4	= C1 + B2
3	WS row increases	2	= C2 + B3
4	RS row increases	4	= C3 + B4
5	WS row increases	2	= C4 + B5

When you copy and paste a formula, the references are automatically updated, so if the formula refers to the previous cell, that gets sorted out.

Once she has reached the current stitch count, Kate uses the addition tool/ sum formula to add up this long column. This value is Total Stitches, representing the total number of stitches you have worked up to now. (Kate actually finds this calculation both amusing and illuminating. She thinks it's nice to be aware of how many stitches you've actually worked.)

	A	B	C	D
1	Starting stitch count	8	8	
2	RS row increases	4	= C1 + B2	
3	WS row increases	2	= C2 + B3	
4	RS row increases	4	= C3 + B4	
5	WS row increases	2	= C4 + B5	
6	RS row increases	4	= C5 + B6	
7	WS row increases	2	= C6 + B7	
8	RS row increases	4	= C7 + B8	
9	WS row increases	2	= C8 + B9	
10	RS row increases	4	= C9 + B10	
11	WS row increases	2	= C10 + B11	
12	RS row increases	4	= C11 + B12	
13	WS row increases	2	= C12 + B13	
	. . .			
80	RS row increases	4	= C79 + B80	
81	WS row increases	2	= C80 + B81	= sum (C1:C81)

This column is long, but it allows you to easily check to make sure the formulas are correct—just as your mathematics teachers used to ask you to show your work to make sure they understand how you got to an answer, you're asking your spreadsheet to show you its calculations. For example, if you see that you have 96 stitches in one row, and 200 stitches in the next row, you know that you've goofed somewhere. (If Kate were doing this calculation by hand, she wouldn't do it this way—but she's not! You actually should do it electronically, so you can keep track of the calculations.)

There are other ways to this, of course. If you're more comfortable with spreadsheets, do this in whatever way makes sense to you. Either way, though, save your spreadsheet; you'll use it for the last step, and you can use it for future shawls that are worked the same way.

STEP 2: How Many Stitches Are You Getting per Gram?
Take Total Stitches and divide it by the number of grams worked so far. That gives you the *Number of Stitches Per Gram*.

STEP 3: How Many Stitches Can You Work with the Rest of Your Yarn?
Take the total number of grams of yarn you have (all that you've worked and the rest that you haven't) and multiply that by Number of Stitches Per Gram. This should be a gratifyingly big number: the total number of stitches you can work with the yarn available. Let's call that *Full Stitch Count*.

STEP 4: How Far Will That Take You?
Go back to your spreadsheet. You need to create a new entry, and then you're going to start adding more lines.

In the cell to the right of the current row's stitch count, enter the Total Stitches total. In the example below, Kate used Excel's SUM function to add up the values of all the rows 1 to 81.

In the next row(s), in the left column, copy the formula(s) for the stitch counts as before. In the right column—Column D in the example here—below the Total Stitches entry, create a new formula that takes the entry above and adds the stitch count from the Column C to it. In the example below, the D column contains the new entry—the total number of stitches worked up to this point. After each row, Kate takes the previous total and adds the new row's stitches to it.

Keep copying both your Stitch Count Per Row and the Total Stitches worked formulas down, and predicting future rows worked, and watch the total number of stitches worked grow.

When the total number of stitches worked (the value in the D column) gets close to—but absolutely not over—the Full Stitch Count, then stop. Kate usually stops when she's about 10–15% from the Full Stitch Count. From this, you can get a sense of how far you can increase: the stitch count you can expect to hit as you approach the end of your yarn. Note that you need to allow yourself more than one row's worth of yarn for binding off, so Kate will usually start to weigh her yarn as she approaches that stitch count, to make sure she doesn't run out on the bind-off. See the "Yardage Management" section below for more details.

Again, there are other ways to do this. Kate likes this method because it allows her to track it precisely, row by row, and check for mistakes in the formulas or calculations.

	A	B	C	D
1	Starting stitch count	8	8	
2	RS row increases	4	= C1 + B2	
3	WS row increases	2	= C2 + B3	
4	RS row increases	4	= C3 + B4	
5	WS row increases	2	= C4 + B5	
6	RS row increases	4	= C5 + B6	
7	WS row increases	2	= C6 + B7	
8	RS row increases	4	= C7 + B8	
9	WS row increases	2	= C8 + B9	
10	RS row increases	4	= C9 + B10	
11	WS row increases	2	= C10 + B11	
12	RS row increases	4	= C11 + B12	
13	WS row increases	2	= C12 + B13	
	. . .			
80	RS row increases	4	= C79 + B80	
81	WS row increases	2	= C80 + B81	= sum (C1:C81)
82	RS row increases	4	= C81 + B82	= D81 + C82
83	WS row increases	2	= C82 + B83	= D82 + C83
84	RS row increases	4	= C83 + B84	= D83 + C84
85	WS row increases	2	= C84 + B85	= D84 + C85
86	RS row increases	4	= C85 + B86	= D85 + C86
87	WS row increases	2	= C86 + B87	= D86 + C87

Yardage Management

Avoiding Yarn-Shortage Disasters

If you're managing a limited amount of yarn, or trying to work to the very end of it, it's a very good idea to have an escape plan—that is, a plan for how to manage if you find your yarn isn't going to get you as far as you predicted.

There's nothing worse than running out in row 21 of a 24-row pattern repeat. And if you're working a shawl with an attached edging, you're in serious trouble if you run out of yarn before the edging is complete.

Ideas

Whether it's an attached edging, or just the final rows of the main body of the piece, you can always work the edging in a contrast color or different texture of yarn. Kate made a shawl for a friend's wedding many years ago, with a specifically purchased yarn: a gorgeous, smooth silk-and-wool blend. The body was mostly plain, with a deep lace edging. She realized she didn't have enough for the full shawl in the existing yarn, so she chose to work the plain section with that, and she found a very fine, fluffy mohair and silk blend in the same color for the edging. It looked fantastic and entirely intentional.

- If you're going to add a second color only for the last section, it needs to either be a fairly substantial area or a very narrow section. Working the last inch (couple of cm) of the shawl in another color makes it fairly obvious that you ran out, but 4 inches (10 cm) or so looks like a significant, attractive, and planned color change. Or, if required, work only the bind-off in the contrast color, to create an effect of decorative piping. Consult the section on Color Blocking (page 82) for ideas for using color in this way.

- Stripes are an excellent solution, of course. It looks very effective if you work the stripes somewhere in the middle of the shawl, rather than at the end. Save yourself some of your main project yarn for working the last few inches and the bind-off. Consult the "Color" chapter (page 66) for ideas for striping patterns and color placement.

- Use a pattern stitch with a small number of rows/rounds in the repeat, so that the row count doesn't matter as much. Kate did this with Hollerith (page 153), working the last third of the yarn in a simple two-row repeat that allowed her to end when she ran out of yarn.

- Or pick a pattern stitch that looks attractive no matter where you stop in the repeat. For example, the Rib and Welt pattern (page 95) would look great no matter where you ended.

- If the pattern stitch you want to use has a lot of rows, work it earlier. That is, work the patterned section near the middle of the piece, and work a deep edging that matches the section before the pattern. Kate particularly loves a top-down triangle shawl that begins with a substantial section of Garter stitch, has a nice deep lace stripe, and then has another swath of Garter stitch to balance out the first one.

Making Sure You Have Enough to Bind Off

As you approach the end of your yarn, your digital scale can be very helpful to make sure that you don't get caught short in your bind-off. Weigh the yarn before and after working a few rows. If you're working with fairly thick yarn, you should be able to get an accurate measurement from one or two rows' worth of yarn. With something very fine, you might need four or even six rows' worth of yarn to get an accurate measurement. (This is because these fine yarns are very light, they don't weigh much, and you need to use enough yarn so that the scale can get a good measurement.)

Make sure you allow yourself at least two rows' worth of yarn to work your bind-off. A standard bind-off requires more yarn than if you were to just knit the row, and stretchy methods require even more. And if you're working a shawl with increases, you'll need more again to allow for those extra stitches you've acquired in the final few rows.

Color

Color in knitting is universally revered. We marvel at the intricate detail of the colorwork in Fair Isle patterns. We're awestruck when presented with a wall of hand-dyed yarn, feeling inspired just by picking up a skein. Color can change moods and inspire emotion. Who isn't filled with joy at the sight of their favorite color? In a shawl, color has the power to change your whole look from fun and whimsical to sophisticated and elegant or to confident and powerful.

The prospect of choosing and combining colors strikes fear in many knitters. We don't trust ourselves. Somewhere along the way, someone told us that working with color requires a special talent granted to a lucky few creative people. That's simply not true. With a little knowledge and practice, anyone can learn how to work with color.

Color is a technical skill, just like learning a different cast-on or stitch pattern. Like every other skill in our knitting lives, it gets easier to be bold in color decisions when you do it. When you pull random skeins off the yarn store shelves or out of your stash and play with putting different colors together, you're learning color skills. When you start looking at every color as a potential new favorite and stop putting colors back on the shelf—because at that family event in 2009, your second cousin twice removed told you yellow is a terrible color on you—you're taking chances. Push your boundaries. Try new things. Trying is playing; playing is practicing. Practicing is how you develop an instinct for working with color that expands your palette, and prompts that "oh wow!" factor from others.

Color wheel, using yarn

Yes, there are lots of very old rules. But here's what's important about those rules: They are guideposts that help us sort and build color combinations that we fall in love with based on centuries-old ideas from others who also played, practiced, and honed their instincts for color. They teach us patterns. And knowledge of how the patterns are supposed to work allows us—in fact, encourages us—to break them.

Color Language: Speaking in Color and Knowing Their Names

Color theory is the language based in how experts talk about color. There is also common, everyday language used when casually talking about color. We talk about *light* and *dark* colors, *bright* and *deep*, but often in different ways than color theory intends—in fact, often in different ways than others in the same room. Knowing the commonly used words that correctly belong to the technical terms, we can build a vocabulary that assists in categorizing any color, which in turn helps us use color theory skills to combine colors in interesting ways.

Every color we come into contact with consists of three elements: hue, value, and intensity.

1. Color or hue: name of the color

SORTING WORDS

yellow, orange, red, violet, blue, green: alone, or in combination such as yellow orange, red violet, blue green

Note: Black, white, and any gray created by mixing only black and white aren't colors—they are *achromatic*: without color. Grays that fall into this category are called *neutral grays*.

WHAT YOU NEED TO KNOW ABOUT HUE

Pure hues happen when no black, white, or neutral gray is added to a color. They are colors created only by mixing with each other. .

HOW TO PRACTICE IT

Go to a source of yarn, such as your stash or your local yarn shop, and sort by color. Look at the differences among different greens and blues and even oranges. Try to name each color using only the sorting words. All of this will show you how you see color, how you categorize it, and how to recognize patterns in your preferences that we will show you how to leverage later in this chapter.

2. Value: how light or dark a color is

SORTING WORDS

very light, light, medium, dark, very dark, and variations on these

WHAT YOU NEED TO KNOW ABOUT VALUE

Value helps you distinguish whether a color is lighter or darker than another. What matters most is how the values of the colors you've chosen compare to each other. So in this case, it's not about sorting into specific boxes; it's about making sure the colors you've chosen will have the desired effect.

Detail of Flexture. The black-and-white photo illustrates shifts in value between the main gradient and the contrasting stripes (page 70).

Top: Value scale in yarn. Bottom: When you look at our color wheel of yarn in black and white, it shows the range of values.

in the main body, the gradient is striped with an accent color that has very little difference in value. In other places, the value difference is higher in contrast. Why? This draws your eye to different places in the shawl and not just a singular focal point. The blue violet in the gradient with a streak of yellow, and then contrasting the orange with a stripe of dark violet, are examples of using a light and a dark color to create impact.

Value can most easily be seen in a scale from black to white, with various shades of gray in between (left). True grays are made only with black and white. Note that this is very different from the vast range of colors we commonly identify as gray.

HOW TO PRACTICE IT

Here are simple ways to perceive value:

1 Squinting at two side by side skeins of yarn will tell you whether they are the same value or not. When you squint, you change the shape of your eye, making objects out of focus and eliminating most light, leaving you only with the monochromatic leftovers. When you squint, if the colors blend and look like one big blob of the same color, there is no difference in value between these colors. If you see a stark difference, there is a large difference in value.

2 Take a black-and-white photo. Every camera phone becomes a color-choosing tool when you take a photo of a color combination and then put a black and white filter over it. The filter eliminates the hue, leaving you looking only at the values of the colors you've chosen. You will be able to see right away whether your chosen colors are the same value or different values and by extension, how much contrast your finished project will have.

At left is our color wheel of yarn in black and white. Within each group of the same color family (red, yellow, etc.), you can see differences in value. Also look at the wheel as a whole. Different color families have different values in comparison to each other. Yellow will generally be lighter in value than red and blue, for example. Cool colors will generally be darker in value (page 73). This is another trick to keep in the back of your brain for color-choosing purposes: If you're trying to find a contrast to a cool color, look for a warmer color.

Combining colors of very different values creates a dramatic contrast. From a great distance away, you can see a color pattern that has both very dark and very light colors. These combinations are high impact, bold, and exciting. They draw attention. They get noticed. Using colors that have the same value has the opposite effect. In this case, differences between the colors become blurred. From a distance, the color pattern may appear to be a single color. Details are softened and often disappear.

Flexture (page 145) is all about playing with changes in value. The gradient yarn used in the main body has shifts in both color and value. In some places

3. Intensity/saturation

This determines how bright or dull a color is and is the most difficult of the three qualities of color to understand and internalize. There are no easy tricks to assist you, so don't worry if it takes some time to fully understand this. Kim works full-time with color every day, and this is the one aspect of color theory that she's still challenged by.

SORTING WORDS

very bright, bright, medium, dull, very dull, or variations

WHAT YOU NEED TO KNOW ABOUT INTENSITY/SATURATION:

Intensity or saturation tells you how bright or dull a color is. In common usage, many times we interchange *bright* and *light* easily to describe a color that is not dark. In color theory, however, *bright* is distinguished from *light*, and they are considered entirely different qualities, with light belonging to value and bright used to compare to dull. Another way to think about the word *dull* as used in color theory is to think of dull colors as muted versions of a pure hue. *Bright*, *dull*, and varying degrees of these (*very bright*, *medium bright*, etc.) are words used to describe how pure a color is. Pure hues are the brightest. If a color is found in the rainbow of the basic color wheel, then it is considered a pure hue. When you add black, white, or a neutral gray to a hue, the hue becomes duller because the pure hue is diluted. Each of these changes the language we use further.

Red, as a pure hue, is bright. When you add white to red, you get light red, or pink. Pink is a tint. The more white you add, the more dull or muted the red becomes. If you add black to red, you get a dark red. The more black you add, the duller or more muted the red becomes. Finally, when you add a neutral gray to red, it doesn't necessarily make the color darker or lighter; it just slowly takes away the red hue, leaving you with a red-hued gray.

You can also create dull colors by mixing a pure hue with colors from the opposite side of the color wheel (page 68). The more you add, the less intense the color becomes, making it appear dull. This is where the term *muddy* comes in. Muddy colors fit within the medium-to-dull range of the intensity scale. Hues that contain enough gray to barely distinguish them as

Top: Red as pure hue, shade (add black), tone (add gray), and tint (add white). Bottom: A range of dull colors

colors at all are the dullest. Unless the gray is a neutral gray (page 69), what we call gray is really color. When you talk about a *blue gray* or a *green gray*, what you're really describing is a very dull blue or green or red violet, and so on.

As with value, what's most important about intensity is how bright or dull a color is in comparison to others. When considering color combinations, if something appears too bright or intense, a duller color will help tone it down and give the combination something to ground it.

In Travelogue (page 134), that color is the non-neutral gray (actually a very dull violet). The other colors in the shawl range from medium to very bright and have a lot of strong personality. The non-neutral gray pulls them together.

HOW TO PRACTICE IT

Look for extremes. Using a basic color wheel as reference, compare other colors with the wedges of color on it. If a blue looks less bright than the blue wedge of the color wheel, then the color is duller. If a colorway looks muddy to you and it's difficult to find a comparison on the color wheel, then it is dull.

When building your color skills, using limited language to describe color helps you communicate and narrow down what you're looking for. Simplify as much as you can. We all see color, value, and intensity a little differently, so getting a general sense of where each color stands in comparison to the others matters more than agreeing on the exact level of value or intensity. When putting colors together for a project, it's the comparison of hue, value, and intensity that matters most. The photo at right shows yarn samples of different hues, values, and intensities. Try to narrow down the language you use to describe these colors:

1 What is the hue of each of these colors?

2 What is the general value of each of these colors? Is it the lighter end of the scale? The middle? The dark? Remember you can squint or take a photo with a black-and-white camera to help you.

3 What is the general intensity of these colors? Are any of them pure hues?

+

Answers

This is how Kim sees these colors. Do you agree?

TOP ROW: 1. yellow orange, blue, blue green; 2. medium light, medium, light; 3. medium bright, bright, medium

MIDDLE ROW: 1. red violet, yellow orange, yellow green; 2. medium, dark, very light; 3. medium, dull, medium dull

BOTTOM ROW: 1. violet, blue violet, red; 2. very dark, very light, medium dark; 3. dull, dull, pure hue

The Yarn Shelves

A color wheel is a rainbow in circular form. Color wheels show us the relationships between colors and help us predict how they will interact with each other. As knitters, our color wheel is a giant source of yarn. That yarn can be your stash, your friend's stash, your local yarn shop, a fiber festival, or any place you find many different colors of yarn together.

WARM VS. COOL

Colors can also be classified as *warm* or *cool*, a concept that is quite simple and can also give us clues to where they might compare in value to each other. Warm colors are generally the color of warm things like fire and the sun: yellows, oranges, reds. Cool colors are generally the color of things that are cool, like ice, winter, and water: blues and greens.

Warm colors stimulate your brain, project energy, draw attention, and are active. Red is the most active and energetic of the warm colors and therefore the best example of the extreme of what warm colors can do. Red is rumored to make you smarter when you look at it. Now before you go and paint everything you own red, here's the bad news: It only makes you smarter for about thirty seconds. Because it's the most stimulating color, it wears out your brain quickly. If you were to take an IQ test immediately after staring at a red wall for one minute, chances are your score would be lower than if you didn't. Red is proven to raise your heart rate. It is the color of stop signs, flashing ambulance lights, and other things that demand we pay attention immediately. It provokes striking responses. In class, when Kim talks about red as an example of a color that anyone can wear, the response is immediate, passionate, and polarizing. Love it or hate it, the feelings are strong, deeply seated, and unlikely to change quickly.

Cool colors, on the other hand, have a calming effect and are peaceful and serene. They calm the eye and brain, creating color harmony. They make us feel safe, lower heart rates, and soothe anxiety. Blue green is the calmest of the cool colors. It's the color of the ocean, which at first thought promotes calm and serenity. Green rooms—the backstage waiting rooms in theaters or television stations—are traditionally painted blue green to help calm nerves and reduce anxiety. Hospital rooms, linens, and even doctors' scrubs are also often blue green, and that is not by accident. Cool colors have been linked to creativity, likely because when we feel safe and secure, we are more likely to explore.

Left: Warm color palette. Right: Cool color palette

1: *Cool (left) and warm versions of the same hues.* **2:** *The yarn in this shawl mimics the colors in* Finding Nemo. **3:** *Draw a straight line across the color wheel from one color to its complement. (Here we've used blue and orange.)* **4:** *Split-complementary colors are the colors on either side of the complement, forming a narrow V shape from the starting color—in this case, yellow orange and red orange.* **5:** *Analogous colors are next to each other on the color wheel.* **6:** *Triadic colors are equal distances from each other around the color wheel.*

As you move around the color wheel in an orderly progression, you will travel from warm (red) to cool (blue) and back to warm again. Subsequently, you will notice a progression in the temperature of your colors. Red violet is warmer than blue violet. Yellow green is warmer than blue green. However, even within a single color family, you can have warm and cool versions of that hue.

Classic Color Combinations

The best color combinations bring both energy and harmony to the table. When combining colors from different parts of the color wheel, you get varying proportions of active and energizing stimulation and serene, calming harmony. This determines how the colors are perceived. A color wheel is a ready-made tool for showing you the basics. In front of your yarn source, pick out a rainbow of options, put them in a circle to create a "yarny" color wheel, and try the below concepts to create connection points between colors.

TWO-COLOR COMBINATIONS: STRAIGHT LINES FOR COLORS THAT COMPLEMENT

Complementary colors are directly opposite each other on the color wheel.

They intensify each other and bring out each other's best qualities. Yellow green makes red violet richer and more vibrant. In the movie *Finding Nemo*, the bright-orange Nemo springs off the screen against the blue water. He is the star of the show, and the color contrast shows us this immediately.

If you're working with two colors in a shawl, choosing a complementary color combination means both colors will shine and make each other better. I've found that in many cases, a person's least favorite colors are the complements to their favorite colors. Kim is a person who has avoided yellow and orange like the plague her entire life and thought they were

colors she would never wear or even use. Her absolute favorite color is blue violet. When she puts yellow orange next to blue violet, it's magical. Her favorite color appears richer and warmer next to the glow of yellow orange, and her least favorite color becomes one she loves when surrounded by the blue violet.

Never discount any color. It may be the one that makes your favorites shine.

THREE-COLOR COMBINATIONS: V-SHAPES FOR SPLIT-COMPLEMENTARY COLORS

Split-complementary color combinations give similar effects to complementary colors while also toning down the intensity. If you want the impact of a complementary color combination but want to soften it a little, choose this kind of combination. The filmmaker Wes Anderson creates a world that is largely cloaked in a split-complementary color scheme. We're drawn in and pay attention, but the overall impact of the colors on screen is softened.

THREE OR MORE COLOR COMBINATIONS: NEIGHBORS MAKE GOOD ANALOGOUS COLORS

Analogous colors are neighbors. They are found beside each other on the color wheel. These are combinations commonly found in nature: the range of green to yellow green to yellow wild grasses in a field. Each color in the combination has its role. One will stand out, one will support, and one will act as an accent or *pop*.

THREE-COLOR COMBINATIONS: TRIANGLE FOR TRIADIC

Triadic colors are three colors equal distance apart on the color wheel. This gives them a balance of energy (when your eyes and brain are stimulated) and harmony. All three primaries (blue, red, yellow) are an example of a triadic color scheme as are all three secondaries.

Translating Skein into Shawl: Reading Your Yarn

You bought that amazing skein of yarn last year in a haze of yarn fumes. You're in love with how the yarn feels and the colors in it, but you're apprehensive about digging in with your needles, uncertain how the colors and tones will behave in knitted fabric. Your yarn has secrets wrapped up in its skein. Let's delve into how to learn them before we commit to a shawl-length relationship.

Who Made Your Yarn?

Commercially dyed yarns tend to be very uniformly dyed, as the process is mechanical. In some factories, skeins of yarn are dyed in a big vat. Dip dyeing is one method, where skeins are loaded onto a rail or arm that turns the yarn slowly as it's dipped into a large vat of dye. This method is used to make variegated yarn as well as solid-colored yarn. Another method loads large, loose skeins into a specially designed vat, where dye is added and the vat is turned to ensure the yarn and dye mix well together.

Hand-dyed yarns, like most handmade objects, show the mark of the human that made them. Hand dyers use a variety of immersion and direct application methods. Hand-dyed yarn is beautiful and amazing because no two sets of hands will do it exactly the same. For this reason, it should be assumed that every skein of hand-dyed yarn is unique and different, even when from the same dye lot from the same studio.

Undyed yarns are generally even in tone. There are exceptions to this rule, especially when fibers from different animals are used. But for the most part, natural yarns can be considered a solid color.

What Does Your Yarn Look Like?

If the yarn is in a ball, it's difficult to determine exactly what it will do. If it's a solid color, you can count on no variation in color. However, if the ball is variegated, you are dependent on the information the seller can give you about the yarn through photographs and shop samples or by looking at projects on Ravelry.

Try This

What happens when you lay other shapes (square, rectangle) on top of a color wheel?

What do you think about the combinations they make?

Remember that the color wheel is not only a way to organize color but a tool for helping you find patterns in how colors work together.

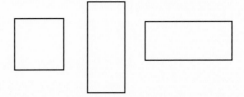

Let Your Camera Choose

Taking a photo of color combinations puts distance between you and the yarn. Looking at a photograph of the yarn, even when the yarn is right in front of you, can help determine whether you love it or not. This method also allows you to compare color combinations side by side.

If the yarn is in a skein or hank form, you can tell a lot by opening it up and laying it in a big ring on a table. Variations in color will be apparent. You can see whether the variations are close in value (page 69) or have strong contrasts. If the yarn is hand dyed, you can get clues about how the yarn was dyed. A skein (aka hank) is a giant, floppy spiral. Because of this, strands can cross each other, float up, or crunch down to the bottom of the pot. The skein may have been handpainted or dipped in dye or had dye speckled on it. The inside of the loop in front of you has a smaller circumference than the outside of the loop, because when skeins are wound, the yarn lies on top of itself in layers. This means that how the colors are spaced is variable. Anyone who has ever knit a pair of socks with variegated yarn has noticed that the color patterning is not quite the same from the first sock to the second. This is why: The color lengths are never quite the same throughout the skein.

So open the skein and look at your yarn. What do you see?

SOLID, SEMI-SOLID, AND TONAL

Here we have an almost-solid skein, a semi-solid skein, and a tonal skein. In the almost solid one (left), there is very little variation in color. The semi-solid (middle) uses the same color dye in different concentration through the strands of yarn. The tonal (right) uses blue, blue green, green and, violet in similar values to create rich depth of color in a quiet, subtle way.

Solid yarns are evenly dyed. There is no shift in color or tone.

Semi-solid yarn is dyed using one dye color. You will often see highlights and lowlights that are simply slightly different values of the same color. These variations in color give more depth to the color and therefore more depth to the resulting fabric, making your eye move across the fabric and pay more attention to the fabric.

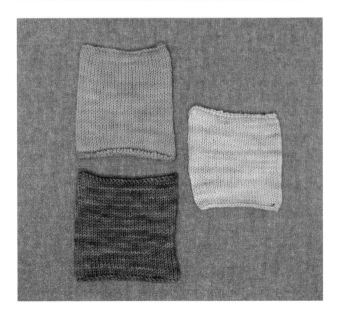

Tonal yarns use different colors of dye that are close in value to each other. Again, these variations add more depth to the overall color of the yarn. Individual colors close in value can also appear to mix together from a distance, fooling your eye into thinking the yarn is a single hue. When you look at it closely, the individual hues become apparent.

VARIEGATED

Variegated yarns have lengths of different colors and often values in one skein. These lengths can be short, long, or a combination of both.

Short-variegated yarn has short lengths of each color (under 3 inches [7.5 cm]). Shorter color lengths mean that only a few stitches at a time will be the same color before shifting to the next color in line. Speckled yarn falls into this category.

Long-variegated yarn has long lengths of each color (3 inches [7.5 cm] or longer), making it prone to *pooling* or *flashing* (page 81).

Changing gauge and stitch count will also change how the colors behave in your knitting. Here we show a short-variegated skein using two different stitch counts. There is a small change in how the colors behave in each swatch. In the example using the long-variegated skein, the differences at 30, 40 and 45 stitches are larger. In the 30-stitch example, the yarn almost stripes. In the 40- and 45-stitch examples, the colors start to pool at the edges of the swatch. When you use these yarns in a shawl shape that doesn't change, like a straight square or rectangle, you can control the way the colors behave by changing the stitch count or gauge. When you use these yarns in a shawl shape that increases or decreases, the colors will shift throughout the fabric and may stripe, pool, and flash, all in one piece of fabric.

Alternating Skeins

Alternating is the method of changing skeins periodically (usually every two rows with two skeins, or every row with three skeins) to minimize differences in working with hand-dyed yarn, working between dye lots of commercially dyed yarn, fading between colors, or working with stripe patterns. When alternating skeins, the strand is not cut at the end of every yarn change. Instead, it's carried up the edge of your knitting (page 85).

Whenever working with more than one skein of hand-dyed yarn in the same colorway, always alternate skeins. Every skein of hand-dyed yarn is different, and many times the skeins that look exactly alike are the ones that cause the biggest problems, show the most difference, and lead to long, mournful cautionary tales told over bourbon or ice cream. Alternating skeins eliminates this issue by breaking up any color lengths, showing them only every second or third row. This also reduces the chances of pooling or flashing (page 81). Differences in a dye lot are spread out through the knitted piece, so that even vastly different skeins can be combined to give an overall even appearance to your fabric.

1: *Skeins of long-variegated, short-variegated, and speckled yarn in the skein.* **2:** *Same skeins laid flat. Note the longer color lengths in the long-variegated skein (top). The shorter color lengths (middle) show a choppier color sequence. Speckles (bottom) have random, unpredictable placement.* **3:** *Note the lengths of color in the skein and how those knit up.* **4:** *Changing the number of stitches also changes how the colors knit up. Top to bottom: 30, 40, and 45 stitches (page 78).*

1

2

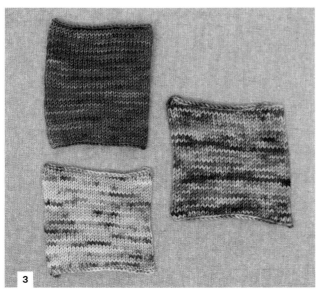

3

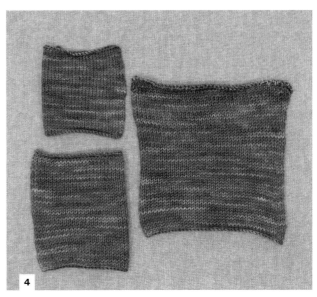

4

SELF PATTERNING

Self-patterning yarn is dyed to create a specific pattern. This can be stripes, a checkerboard, faux isle, an ombré, a gradient that cycles through several different colors, and so on.

Companies who make yarn this way will make it clear on the label and in the pricing of this yarn. It will cost significantly more than other yarns of the same fiber and quality. They will also show you what their yarn will do when it's knit up. It's important to note there is a difference between yarns that create patterned stripes and yarns that create fixed stripes of solid colors. For our purposes here, when we talk about

self-striping yarns, we are talking about yarns that yield fixed stripes when knit as directed.

Self-striping sock yarn results in a regular, fixed stripe pattern that will be easy to predict. This means you can predict the number of stitches in each stripe and apply that idea to other shapes. In Askew (page 184) and Adjacent (page 179), this idea was applied to small, squat rectangles and triangles, allowing each shape to be a different color without having to cut yarn and sew in ends.

Shawl-striping yarns are the same concept but engineered to work with specific shawl shapes and generate a predictable stripe pattern when knit as recommended.

Ombré yarns yield a slow and gradual color change. In Radialactive (page 174), two skeins of the same ombré colorway were alternated from opposing ends of the colorway to create a fading effect.

Gradient yarns gradually cycle through at least two colors, but often more. Flexture (page 145) uses a gradient yarn that cycles through several colors. They can be found in many formats, such as yarn cakes that show the range of colors, a sock blank (yarn that has been loosely knitted into a sheet of fabric and dyed or hand painted), and mini-skein sets. You can also create your own gradient by lining up yarn from your stash and finding colors that blend well into each other.

MIXING IT UP

Yarn can fall into more than one of these categories. Yarn can be tonal and short variegated in the same skein or semi-solid for half the circumference of a skein and speckled for the other half. When this happens, look at suggestions for both categories and try the techniques to find the perfect yarn/pattern match.

What Stitch Pattern with What Yarn?

The more complex the yarn, the simpler the stitch pattern; the more complex the stitch pattern, the simpler the yarn.

Take a wildly variegated yarn with a range of colors and values. If you try to knit a complex lace pattern that depicts vines or leaves, all your beautiful stitches will disappear. The colors and the contrasts in the yarn will outweigh the contrast in the stitches, rendering the design unreadable.

Now try that same stitch pattern in a solid or a semi-solid yarn, and the yarn and pattern balance each other out.

However, the lace pattern used in one of the panels of the Travelogue shawl (page 134) is an allover, simple mesh pattern. Because it was used with the intention of matching the visual texture of the variegated yarn with a stitch pattern that created tactile texture in the fabric, it fulfills its goal.

Yarn is beautiful. Stitch patterns are beautiful. Neither should outshine the other. Stitch patterns should always be in proportion to the patterning in the yarn.

✓✓✓= **Yes!** Go ahead without reservations.

✓✓= **Sometimes.** Worth taking a chance. With caution. This becomes more of a personal preference, combined with the knowledge that the more complex the yarn is—more colors, more contrast between colors, wild speckles—the simpler the stitch pattern should be. By the same token, the simpler the yarn is—semi-solid, tonal, softly toned speckles—the more complex the stitch pattern can be.

✓= **Rarely.** These combinations rarely work. They tend to make the yarn's color patterning look muddy, and the beauty and complexity of the stitch patterns get lost.

This system gives you guidelines around where to start. In all cases, you will need to swatch the stitch pattern with the yarn you want to use it with to determine whether it works or not (page 52).

If your yarn is solid/semi-solid/tonal:

✓✓✓	Stockinette
✓✓✓	Garter stitch
✓✓✓	textured stitches (knit/purl)
✓✓✓	cables
✓✓✓	lace
✓✓✓	colorwork (Fair Isle, intarsia, color blocking)
✓✓✓	stripes

If your yarn is short variegated/speckled:

✓✓✓	Stockinette
✓✓✓	Garter stitch
✓✓	textured stitches (knit/purl)
✓	cables
✓	lace
✓✓	colorwork (Fair Isle, intarsia, color blocking)
✓✓	stripes

If your yarn is long variegated/speckled:

✓✓✓	Stockinette
✓✓✓	Garter stitch
✓✓	textured stitches (knit/purl)
✓	cables
✓	lace
✓✓	colorwork (Fair Isle, intarsia, color blocking)
✓✓	stripes

If your yarn is self patterning:

✓✓✓	Stockinette
✓✓	Garter stitch
✓✓	textured stitches (knit/purl)
✓	cables
✓✓	lace
✓	colorwork (Fair Isle, intarsia, color blocking)
✓	stripes

The How and Why of Pooling and Flashing

Every skein of variegated yarn will pool or flash for every knitter at some point. There is no such thing as a variegated yarn, especially one with long color lengths, that will not pool for anyone.

Variegated yarn is dyed in a skein, which is essentially a giant spiral with one beginning and one end. The circumference of a skein is determined by either the mill or the company and can vary but is usually between 1½–2 yards (1.35–1.8 m). Dye is applied across the skein in blocks of color. Smaller blocks (short variegated) of color are less likely to stack up in your knitting, and when they do, they are likely to last a few stitches and move on to the next color.

When you knit from a hank or skein of yarn, you are knitting with a giant spiral. When knitting, you are cycling through the same color blocks in the same order over and over again. Because larger blocks of color mean longer lengths of color, it is inevitable that these lengths will stack up in your knitting. When this happens in large pools of color, we call it *pooling*. When it happens in zigzag lightning bolts, we call it *flashing*.

Lots can be done to control flashing and pooling in our knitting. We can try different stitch patterns. We can alternate skeins, making it more challenging for the long lengths of color to meet up. We can change needle size, adjust gauge, and even adjust stitch counts to change how the blocks of color line up. All of these things can prevent our yarn from pooling. But it's important to note that all of these techniques can also be used to manipulate your knitting to pool on purpose, creating *planned pooling* patterns in your yarn.

Color Blocking and Stripes: Color in Design

Color blocking and stripes are two simple ways to combine two or more colors in your shawl.

Both techniques are addictive, urging us to keep going so we can start a new color. Every new stripe or color block feels like a fresh start. They are great stashbusters, allowing you to use up those single skeins or leftovers that are languishing in your collection. Both are a great opportunity to use color in daring ways, work with new colors, and introduce those colors into your wardrobe in a less intimidating way.

Size Matters

You can create amazing effects simply by changing the size of your blocks of color. Thin stripes and small blocks visually reduce size. They minimize our attention, giving the impression of finer, more sophisticated fabric. Thick stripes and large blocks visually expand and draw our attention. They make bold statements. When you vary the size of your stripes or blocks in the same shawl, you open up the opportunity to explore color and pattern in visually exciting ways.

Color Blocking Ideas

What happens to your eye when you move a block of color to different places in the construction? In all of these examples I've used the same color combinations, but have moved the lighter value color to different sections of the shawl. This changes where your eye is drawn, where your attention is guided to, and where the focal point of the shawl is.

Here are examples of color blocking. By moving the position of the lighter value color, your eye is drawn to different parts of the shawl. When the color block is

Echoing the shawl shape in a contrasting color adds visual interest by reinforcing the shape. Add a different stitch pattern to the contrasting block and you add textural interest as well.

Add strategically placed blocks of color to help the eye travel across the length of the shawl.

Contrasting floats draw your eye to a specific spot in the shawl— an excellent use for small amounts of leftover yarn!

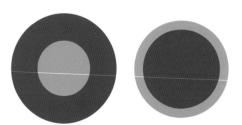

Circular shawls benefit from color contrast in the center to draw the eye in, or on the edge to outline the shape.

at the edge of the shawl, it draws attention to the shawl shape. When it's in the center, your eye is drawn to the body of the shawl. And when you use the spine as a color blocking area, the eye is drawn up and down.

Fading Away

Working stripes in alternating colors to avoid an abrupt line between color blocks is a way to blend from one color into the next. This is called a gradation, but we hear it most often talked about as a *fade* in contemporary knitting. The closer in value your colors are to each other, the more gradual and gentler the fade. When colors contrast greatly with each other, the fade still works but is less subtle.

To fade from one color to the next, work alternating stripes in the two colors. Two-row stripes are the simplest way to do this.

You can also create a long fade with stripes starting with wide stripes of color A and thin stripes of color B, gradually changing until the B stripes are wider and the A stripes are smaller.

 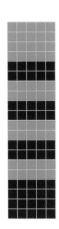 

Why Do White Stripes Look Bigger?

Light colors make things look larger or bring them forward. Dark colors make things look smaller; they appear farther away. All of this happens in relation to other colors. A dark object will only look farther away when placed beside a light object; the light object will only seem closer compared with the dark object. This is because light colors reflect more light and draw our attention to them. They like being in the spotlight. Dark colors absorb light; they suck it in and remain in the shadows. Your eye will always be drawn to light colors first. This can easily be applied to our knitting in color blocking and in stripes. Light valued stripes will draw more attention than dark ones.

Stripe Patterns

Because of the shape of our stitches, one-row stripes—especially in Stockinette stitch—give a slightly wavy appearance. This can add interesting visual texture to your shawl, but if strong, solid stripes are what you're looking for, add more rows. Two rows or more yield well-defined stripes.

To step beyond working stripes that are all the same size, try patterns that are based on mathematical sequences. Each sequence will tell you how many rows to work for each stripe. It's also possible to take a portion of any of these sequences and repeat it for the length of your stripe pattern.

ARITHMETIC SEQUENCE

1, 2, 3, 4 . . .

The difference between each of these numbers is 1.

4, 8, 12, 16 . . .

The difference between each of these numbers is 4.

PRIME NUMBER SEQUENCE

The number of rows in each stripe is a prime number. A prime number is a whole number (no fractions or decimals) that can only be divided by 1 and itself.

2, 3, 5, 7 . . .

5, 7, 11, 13 . . .

FIBONACCI

Each number is the sum of the two previous numbers.

1, 1, 2, 3 . . . 1 + 1 = 2, 1 + 2 = 3 . . .

The next number in the sequence would be 5 (2 + 3).

GEOMETRIC

Each number in the sequence is multiplied by a constant to determine the next number.

1, 2, 4, 8 . . .

The constant here is 2. To find the next number in the sequence, multiply the previous number by 2.

$1 \times 2 = 2, 2 \times 2 = 4, 4 \times 2 = 8$ . . .

The next number in the sequence would be 16.

1, 3, 9, 27 . . .

The constant here is 3. To find the next number in the sequence, multiply the previous number by 3.

$1 \times 3 = 3, 3 \times 3 = 9, 9 \times 3 = 27$

COLLATZ CONJECTURE

The Collatz Conjecture creates a pattern of numbers that rise and fall, giving visual variety to a stripe pattern. This is often called the Hailstone sequence, as the rise and fall of the numbers resembles the behavior of hailstones in a storm.

Choose any positive whole number (larger than zero, no decimals or fractions).

If the number is even, divide it by two to get the next number in the sequence.

If the number is odd, multiply it by 3 and add 1 to get the next number in the sequence.

$3, 10, 5, 16, 8, 4, 2, 1, 4, 2, 1 . . . 3 \times 3 + 1 = 10, 10 \div 2 = 5, 5 \times 3 + 1 = 16$ . . .

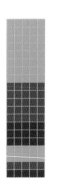

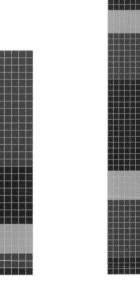

Arithmetic sequence   Prime number sequence   Fibonacci   Geometric   Collatz Conjecture

How to Carry Yarn for Stripes and Other Cases of Alternating Skeins

Working Flat: Even Number of Rows (2, 4, 6 . . .)

In most cases, you will start and end your stripes at the right-hand edge of your knitting. Unless you're excited about weaving in a million ends, you will want to carry the color changes up the edge of your work. There are two effective ways to do this:

Lightly twist your yarn along the right edge. If you drop your working yarn at the end of a row and then pick up the new working yarn at the beginning of the following row, the yarns will twist naturally. Kim finds that if she picks up the new working yarn behind the yarn just dropped, then she doesn't see the twist on the RS of the shawl, and the change is relatively hidden. It also ensures she has a consistent, not-too-tight twist.

Knit the first stitch of every RS row with both colors. Drop the nonworking color after the first stitch. This method is more visible, but not so much that it's unattractive. This method gives a lovely elastic edge that behaves more like knitted fabric than the twist method.

Working Flat: Odd Number of Rows (1, 3, 5 . . .)

Odd-row stripes are worked similarly to even-row stripes, except you change yarns on both the right and the left edge of your work.

If working with three skeins or colors, one row per skein/color:

Using a circular needle, work one RS row with yarn 1.

Drop yarn 1, attach yarn 2, and work one WS row.

Drop yarn 2, attach yarn 3, and work one RS row. At the end of this row, yarn 1 will be waiting to work a WS row.

Continue in this manner until a further change is needed.

Working in the Round: Helical Stripes

There are a variety of methods for alternating skeins in the round, but by far the most seamless and neatest version is the helical stripe method. When knitting in the round, you are knitting a spiral. The helical method stacks one spiral on top of another, ensuring the yarn never starts and stops in the same place. This method works best when working single-row stripes or alternating skeins of a single color. In shawl knitting, we see this most often in any shawl shape that works from the center out.

Work the first round in yarn 1.

Work the second round in yarn 2, stopping 3 stitches before the end of the round.

Slip the last 3 stitches to your right needle.

Pick up yarn 1 where you dropped it off.

Work the third round with yarn 1, stopping 3 stitches before the point where you stopped working with yarn 2.

When to Cut

When knitting a stripe pattern, if you have a long expanse of a single color, it makes less sense to carry yarn. This becomes an individual decision. In cases where Kim has stripes that are longer than six rows of each color, she cuts the yarn at the end of each stripe, leaving a tail of approximately 4 inches (10 cm) and attaching a new strand of yarn in the next color (see page 34). Weave in these tails after the shawl is finished and blocked.

Stitch Dictio- nary

This stitch dictionary contains a selection of stitch patterns that represent the types that work well for shawl projects. They are categorized by type/application:

▲ ▲
▲ ▲ **Background Patterns:** Fairly neutral small-repeat stitch patterns suitable for large sections of fabric, which act as good allover or background patterns

||| **Vertical Insertions:** Narrower stitch patterns that can be used as vertical dividing elements

≣ **Horizontal Insertions:** Stitch patterns that look good worked over a small number of rows and can be used as borders or transitions between other patterns

▼▼▼ **Edgings:** Stitch patterns that create shaped edges, suitable for working on the sides or edges of a piece or as an attached edging in place of a hard bind-off. See "Techniques" (page 22) for more details on how these work.

Some stitch patterns fall into more than one category; many of the background and motif patterns can also be used as vertical insertions if you work only a single repeat or across a small number of stitches.

When a fabric is described as reversible, we mean that it's the same on both sides. Borrowing from Cecelia Campochiaro's masterwork *Sequence Knitting*, we use the term *aesthetically reversible* to mean a fabric that is attractive on both sides, but not the same.

Stitch Key

☐ RS: knit
WS: purl

• RS: purl
WS: knit

ⅴ RS: slip purlwise with yarn in front
WS: slip

○ yo

╱ RS: k2tog
WS: p2tog

╲ ssk

⅄ k3tog

Λ CDD

⟋ RS: p2tog
WS: k2tog

╲ ssp

⌐ bind off

⌣ RS & WS: kfb

⌄³ (k1, p1, k1) in 1 stitch

+

Note about charts

All charts are shown with row/round numbers on the right-hand side, for convenience. If you're working flat, odd-numbered rows are worked on the RS and read from right to left; even-numbered rows are worked on the WS and read from left to right. If you're working in the round, all rounds are read from right to left.

The Classics

Stockinette and Garter stitch fit into this category and are commonly used in shawl patterns. The following stitch patterns might be less common, but are just as effective. These are all good background patterns and can be used as vertical insertions. They look great on their own or combined with a pattern-heavy section.

Double Garter Stitch

Reversible. Lies essentially flat, although if left unblocked, the ridges are inclined to fold up, rather like a ribbing pattern. Great as a background or horizontal insertion, if there are enough rows to see the pattern emerge.

Worked Flat

ROW 1: Knit.

ROWS 2 AND 3: Purl.

ROW 4: Knit.

Worked in the Round

ROUNDS 1 AND 2: Knit.

ROUNDS 3 AND 4: Purl

You can expand these, of course. As written, it's two rows/rounds of Stockinette followed by two rows/rounds of reverse Stockinette. Work more rows/rounds in one pattern before changing to the other, to create a more dramatic horizontal accordion effect, much like a horizontal ribbing.

Ribbing Patterns

Great as background or vertical insertions.

These pattern stitches do lie flat, in that they don't curl up, but they tend to buckle and pull in laterally, making the fabric appear narrower than it actually is. The knit ribs pull forward, while the purl ribs pull to the back; at its most extreme, you can get a fabric that is only the knit ribs showing. If you don't want this effect, work the project using a yarn with a memory, and block it aggressively. As with Stockinette and reverse Stockinette, leaving the fabric unstretched and letting it fold can create good drape and movement.

If the number of stitches in the knit and purl ribs is the same—e.g., (k1, p1)—the fabric is fully reversible. If the knit and purl ribs are different—e.g., (k3, p2)—the fabric is aesthetically reversible.

When working in the round, you should have full multiples of the ribbing pattern so that it looks the same all the way around and it's completely reversible. That is, if you're using a pattern that needs 3 stitches, you should work on a multiple of 3 (e.g., 81, 84, 87, and 90 are good; 82, 86, and 88 wouldn't work).

If you're working in rows, make the fabric symmetrical (but ever-so-slightly break the reversibility) by beginning and ending with the same rib. For example, if you're using (k2, p2), work over a multiple of 4 stitches plus 2 so that you begin and end the rows with either a k2 or a p2. This looks best if you want to use ribbing as a vertical insertion. Beginning and ending with a knit rib makes a clean division between textured patterns; a purl rib makes a clean division between Stockinette stitch-based patterns. If you're using K1, P1 Ribbing as an insertion, make sure you have an odd number of stitches so that it begins and ends with either k1 or p1.

KNIT 1, PURL 1 RIBBING

Over an Even Number of Stitches

ALL ROWS/ROUNDS: [K1, p1] to end.

Worked Flat over an Odd Number of Stitches

ROW 1: [K1, p1] to last st, k1.

ROW 2: [P1, k1] to last st, p1.

KNIT 2, PURL 2 RIBBING

Over a Multiple of 4 Stitches

ALL ROWS/ROUNDS: [K2, p2] to end.

Worked Flat over a Multiple of 4 Stitches + 2

ROW 1 (RS): [K2, p2] to last 2 sts, k2.

ROW 2: [P2, k2] to last 2 sts, p2.

+

Alternate Ribbings

There are a lot of stitch patterns created with combinations of Stockinette or standard ribbing patterns and broken rib elements. The Farrow Rib adds a column of Seed between the knit and purl of a K1, P1 Ribbing. Mistake Stitch and Seeded Ribbings extend this to create a 4-stitch repeat by adding Seed stitch columns after both the knit and the purl ribs. These patterns pull in less than ribbing and make the fabric lie flatter. You can experiment and get creative with all sorts of combinations.

The Seed, Moss, and Broken Rib Stitches

These stitches are reversible, and the fabrics lie flat. They are all excellent as background or vertical insertion patterns. The patterns with smaller numbers of rows/ rounds can also work as horizontal insertions; the key is to make sure you're working enough rows to make the pattern visible.

These are all, effectively, broken rib stitches. That is, each row is a ribbed pattern, but the patterning is deliberately misaligned. Rather than knitting the knits and purling the purls, you will sometimes be purling over knits and knitting over purls. The standard versions as given below are based on K1, P1 Ribbing.

You can create further variations by working with other rib patterns. For example, you can create a Basketweave pattern based on K2, P2 Ribbing by working 2 rows/rounds in pattern before swapping the position of the knits and the purls. Work a 4-stitch Basketweave on a multiple of 8 stitches: Work 4 rows of K4, P4 Ribbing, and then swap the knit and purl positions—put another way: change to P4, K4 Ribbing— and work 4 rows like that, then repeat the 8-row pattern. You can also create broken ribbing patterns by working more rows of one given stitch alignment before changing to the other.

Note: The nomenclature for this family of stitches can be a little confusing, as there are some regional differences in the terms. We're using the US terminology here.

SEED STITCH—BROKEN K1, P1 RIBBING

Over an Even Number of Stitches

ROW/ROUND 1: [K1, p1] to end.

ROW/ROUND 2: [P1, k1] to end.

Tip: If you're working in the round, cast on an odd number of stitches. There's no need to place a start-of-round marker; just work [k1, p1] around.

Worked Flat over an Odd Number of Stitches

ALL ROWS: [K1, p1] to last st, k1.

MOSS STITCH—BROKEN K1, P1 RIBBING WITH REPEATED ROWS

Over an Even Number of Stitches

ROWS/ROUNDS 1 AND 2: [K1, p1] to end.

ROWS/ROUNDS 3 AND 4: [P1, k1] to end.

FARROW RIB

Worked Flat over a Multiple of 3 Stitches

ALL ROWS: [K2, p1] to end.

Worked in the Round over a Multiple of 3 Stitches

ROUND 1: [K2, p1] around.

ROUND 2: [K1, p2] around.

MISTAKE-STITCH RIBBING

Worked Flat over a Multiple of 4 Stitches

ROW 1: [K2, p2] to end.

ROW 2: [P1, k2, p1] to end.

Worked in the Round over a Multiple of 4 Stitches

ROUND 1: [K2, p2] around.

ROUND 2: [K1, p2, k1] around.

SLIP-STITCH RIBBING/CARTRIDGE BELT RIB

This stitch is reversible and lies flat. The brilliance of this pattern is that it looks like a ribbing, but when worked flat, it doesn't have a single purl stitch. It's not quite as easy to work in the round, but it's such an attractive and effective stitch pattern that it's still worth it.

Worked Flat over a Multiple of 4 Stitches

ROW 1 (RS): [K2, sl 1 purlwise wyif, k1] to end.

ROW 2: [K3, sl 1 purlwise wyif] to end.

Worked in the Round over a Multiple of 4 Stitches

ROUND 1: [K2, sl 1 purlwise wyif, k1] around.

ROUND 2: [Sl 1 purlwise wyib, p3] around.

DIAGONAL RIBBING

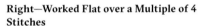

Right—Worked Flat over a Multiple of 4 Stitches

ROWS 1 AND 2: [K2, p2] to end.

ROW 3: [K1, p2, k1] to end.

ROW 4: [P1, k2, p1] to end.

ROWS 5 AND 6: [P2, k2] to end.

ROW 7: [P1, k2, p1] to end.

ROW 8: [K1, p2, k1] to end.

Right—Worked in the Round over a Multiple of 4 Stitches

ROUNDS 1 AND 2: [K2, p2] around.

ROUNDS 3 AND 4: [K1, p2, k1] around.

ROUNDS 5 AND 6: [P2, k2] around.

ROUNDS 7 AND 8: [P1, k2, p1] around.

Left—Worked Flat over a Multiple of 4 Stitches

ROWS 1 AND 2: [K2, p2] to end.

ROW 3: [P1, k2, p1] to end.

ROW 4: [K1, p2, k1] to end.

ROWS 5 AND 6: [P2, k2] to end.

ROW 7: [K1, p2, k1] to end.

ROW 8: [P1, k2, p1] to end.

Left—Worked in the Round over a Multiple of 4 Stitches

ROUNDS 1 AND 2: [K2, p2] around.

ROUNDS 3 AND 4: [P1, k2, p1] around.

ROUNDS 5 AND 6: [P2, k2] to end.

ROUNDS 7 AND 8: [K1, p2, k1] to end.

Brioche & Fisherman's Rib

Sometimes known as tuck stitches, these patterns create deep and textured ribbings. There are two ways of working them, but the end results are rather unexpectedly the same. There can be a slight difference in tension, but that's it. The instructions here use the k1b method—known as Fisherman's Rib—rather than the sl1yo method, which is known as *Brioche*. See Hespero (page 161) for instructions that use the Brioche method.

They make excellent background patterns and bold vertical insertions. As with other ribbings, make them symmetrical: Begin and end with the same stitch.

They don't roll but do tend to accordion in, like any ribbing pattern. The standard patterns are all reversible.

Fisherman's Rib/Single-Color Brioche Rib

If you're working from a cast-on edge, work a setup row/round of K1, P1 Ribbing before you begin the pattern.

Worked Flat over a Multiple of 2 Stitches + 3

ROW 1: P1, [k1b, p1] to end.

ROW 2: K1, p1, [k1b, p1] to last st, k1.

If you're working this as an insertion, you can eliminate the two Stockinette selvage stitches (the first and last stitches of the pattern).

Worked in the Round over an Even Number of Stitches

ROUND 1: [K1b, p1] around.

ROUND 2: [K1, p1b] around.

VARIATIONS

Brioche patterns are actually just K1, P1 Ribbing, so you can do everything you can with K1, P1 Ribbing patterns. You can create really interesting fabrics by mixing things up—work some normal ribs with some brioche ribs interspersed.

When the ribbings are uneven, the fabrics are aesthetically rather than perfectly reversible.

Partial-Brioche Fabrics

A half-brioche fabric is created by working Brioche Rib on the first row/round, and standard ribbing on the alternate rows/rounds. The fabric isn't exactly the same on both sides, but it's an interesting textural effect: You get one more prominent column, one less prominent.

Taking this to an extreme, a single column of Brioche Knit adds an excellent texture to a larger section of reverse Stockinette. And starting and stopping a Brioche Rib partway through another fabric opens up all sorts of possibilities too . . .

TWO-COLOR BRIOCHE RIB

▲▲ ||| ▼▼
▲▲

If you're working from a cast-on edge, work a setup row/round of K1, P1 Ribbing before you begin the pattern.

Worked Flat over an Odd Number of Stitches

ROW 1A (RS): With MC, p1, [k1b, p1] to end. Do not turn; slide sts to other end of needle.

ROW 1B (RS): With CC, p1, [k1, p1b] to last 2 sts, k1, p1. Turn.

ROW 2A (WS): With MC, k1, [p1b, k1] to end. Do not turn; slide sts to other end of needle.

ROW 2B (WS): With CC, k1, [p1, k1b] to last 2 sts, p1, k1. Turn.

If you're working this as an insertion, you can eliminate the 2 selvage stitches (the first and last stitches of the pattern).

Worked in the Round over an Even Number of Stitches

ROUND 1: With MC, [k1b, p1] around.

ROUND 2: With CC, [k1, p1b] around.

Other Texture Stitches

These make great background stitches; they're less suited for use as insertions because either the repeats are fairly large, or you need to work a fairly large area to see the effect of the pattern.

Unless otherwise noted, these patterns are all perfectly reversible. Even the ones that aren't have an interesting and attractive WS. All lie flat.

Seaweed

A clever variation on a diagonal rib; aesthetically reversible.

▲▲
▲▲

Chart rows (right to left, columns 6 5 4 3 2 1):

```
· · ·       ·   12
· · ·       ·   11
· ·         ·   10
· ·         ·    9
·           ·    8
·           ·    7
        · ·      6
        · ·      5
      · ·        4
      · ·        3
    · · · ·      2
    · · · ·      1
6 5 4 3 2 1
```

Worked Flat over a Multiple of 6 Stitches

ROW 1 (RS): [P4, k2] to end.

ROW 2: [P2, k4] to end.

ROWS 3 AND 4: [P3, k3] to end

ROW 5: [P2, k4] to end.

ROW 6: [P4, k2] to end.

ROW 7: [P1, k4, p1] to end.

ROW 8: [K1, p4, k1] to end.

ROW 9: [P1, k3, p2] to end.

ROW 10: [K2, p3, p1] to end.

ROW 11: [P1, k2, p3] to end.

ROW 12: [K3, p2, k1] to end

Worked in the Round over a Multiple of 6 Stitches

ROUNDS 1 AND 2: [P4, k2] around.

ROUNDS 3 AND 4: [P3, k3] around.

ROUNDS 5 AND 6: [P2, k4] around.

ROUNDS 7 AND 8: [P1, k4, p1] around.

ROUNDS 9 AND 10: [P1, k3, p2] around.

ROUNDS 11 AND 12: [P1, k2, p3] around.

Thick and Thin Basketweave

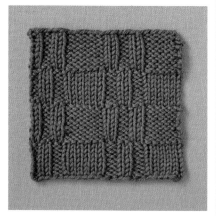

▲ ▲
▲ ▲

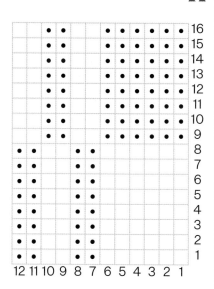

12 11 10 9 8 7 6 5 4 3 2 1

Worked Flat over a Multiple of 12 Stitches

ROW 1 (RS): [K6, p2, k2, p2] to end.

ROW 2: [K2, p2, k2, p6] to end.

ROWS 3–8: Repeat Rows 1 and 2 three more times.

ROW 9: [P6, k2, p2, k2] to end.

ROW 10: [P2, k2, p2, k6] to end.

ROWS 11–16: Repeat Rows 9 and 10 three more times.

Worked in the Round over a Multiple of 12 Stitches

ROUNDS 1–8: [K6, p2, k2, p2] around.

ROUNDS 9–16: [P6, k2, p2, k2] around.

Rib and Welt

▲ ▲
▲ ▲

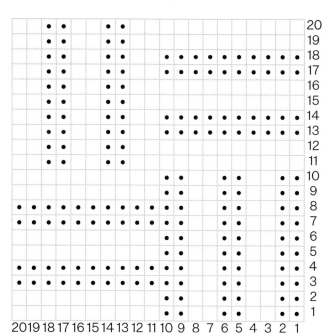

20 19 18 17 16 15 14 13 12 11 10 9 8 7 6 5 4 3 2 1

A deep texture of vertical and horizontal welts. This fabric looks its best if not blocked or stretched; leave the texture alone. Almost perfectly reversible but not quite.

Worked Flat over a Multiple of 20 Stitches

ROW 1 (RS): [(P2, k2) twice, p2, k10] to end.

ROW 2: [P10, (k2, p2) twice, k2] to end.

ROW 3: [(P2, k2) twice, p12] to end.

ROW 4: [K12, (p2, k2) twice] to end.

ROW 5–8: Repeat Rows 1–4 once more.

ROWS 9–10: Repeat Rows 1 and 2 once more.

ROW 11: [K12, (p2, k2) twice] to end.

ROW 12: [(P2, k2) twice, p12] to end.

ROW 13: [P10, (k2, p2) twice, k2] to end.

ROW 14: [(P2, k2) twice, p2, k10] to end.

ROWS 15–18: Repeat Rows 11–14 once more.

ROWS 19 AND 20: Repeat Rows 11 and 12 once more.

Worked in the Round over a Multiple of 20 Stitches

ROUNDS 1 AND 2: [(P2, k2) twice, p2, k10] around.

ROUNDS 3 AND 4: [(P2, k2) twice, p12] around.

ROUND 5–8: Repeat Rounds 1–4 once more.

ROUNDS 9 AND 10: Repeat Rounds 1 and 2 once more.

ROUNDS 11 AND 12: [K12, (p2, k2) twice] around.

ROUNDS 13 AND 14: [P10, (k2, p2) twice, k2] around.

ROUNDS 15–18: Repeat Rounds 11–14 once more.

ROUNDS 19 AND 20: Repeat Rounds 11 and 12 once more.

Lace and Openwork

There are two types of lace patterns: those that alternate patterned and plain rows (also called lace knitting), and those that don't have any plain rows (also known as close-worked or knitted lace).

Lace patterns that have a plain row can be worked on a Garter background or a Stockinette background. A Garter-background lace has the WS rows knit, or alternate rounds purled if working in the round. A Stockinette-background lace has the WS rows purled, or alternate rounds knit if working in the round. Garter-background lace patterns are fully reversible, and more textured in appearance. Stockinette-background patterns are smoother and more refined in appearance, but this means that they look very different on the WS—and are therefore not reversible.

Lace Ribs

There are many patterns like this, all based upon a simple 2-stitch yarnover/decrease pair. The variations are created through changing up the decrease, changing the position of the yarnover relative to the decrease, and changing whether or not there's a plain row and how it's worked if there is one.

These all make excellent background stitches, and both horizontal and vertical insertions. To work them as a vertical insertion, simply eliminate the selvage stitches.

2-Stitch Lace Ribs are close-worked over an even number of stitches. (Putting a rest row between pattern rows would give a strongly biased fabric, because the yarnover/decrease position and slant would always be the same.)

Although these are closely related, they do have differences. The Turkish Stitch appears smoothest on both sides and the yarnovers the least twisted, because the decrease is worked so that the yarnover from the previous row lies on top, hiding the purl bump from the previous row's decrease. The Purse Stitch is the most textured since the decrease lies with the purl from the previous row to the front, making little knots, and the yarnovers are the most twisted. The classic Faggoting Stitch is somewhere in between.

TURKISH STITCH

▲▲ ≡ ||| ⩣

Worked Flat over a Multiple of 2 Stitches
ALL ROWS: K1, [yo, k2tog] to last st, k1.

Worked in the Round over a Multiple of 2 Stitches
ROUND 1: [Yo, k2tog] around.

ROUND 2: [Ssp, yo] around.

CLASSIC FAGGOTING STITCH

▲▲ ≡ ||| ⩣

Worked Flat over an Even Number of Stitches
ALL ROWS: K1, [yo, ssk] to last st, k1.

Worked in the Round over an Even Number of Stitches
ROUND 1: [Yo, ssk] around.

ROUND 2: [P2tog, yo] around.

PURSE STITCH

▲▲ ≡ ||| ⩣

Worked Flat over an Even Number of Stitches
ALL ROWS: K1, [yo, p2tog] to last st, k1.

Worked in the Round over an Even Number of Stitches
ROUND 1: [Yo, p2tog] around.

ROUND 2: [Ssk, yo] around

UNBIASED LACE RIB OVER AN ODD NUMBER OF STITCHES

▲▲ ≡ ||| ⩣

ROW/ROUND 1 (RS): K1, [yo, k2tog] to end.

ROW/ROUND 2: Knit or purl for desired background (see below).

ROW/ROUND 3: [Ssk, yo] to last st, k1.

ROW/ROUND 4: Knit or purl for desired background (see below).

For a Garter background: If working flat, knit the alternate rows; if working in the round, purl the alternate rounds.

For a Stockinette background: If working flat, purl the alternate rows; if working in the round, knit the alternate rounds.

3-STITCH LACE RIB: VERSION 1

```
\ O     3
   O /  1
3 2 1
```

ROW/ROUND 1 (RS): [K2tog, yo, k1] to end.

ROW/ROUND 2: Knit or purl for desired background (see below).

ROW/ROUND 3: [K1, yo, ssk] to end.

ROW/ROUND 4: Knit or purl for desired background (see below).

Close-Worked Version: Worked Flat over a Multiple of 3 Stitches

ALL ROWS: [K2tog, yo, k1] to end.

For a Garter background: If working flat, knit the alternate rows; if working in the round, purl the alternate rounds.

For a Stockinette background: If working flat, purl the alternate rows; if working in the round, knit the alternate rounds.

3-STITCH LACE RIB: VERSION 2

```
|||
```

```
O Λ O   1
3 2 1
```

This can be worked as a vertical insertion over 3 stitches.

ALL ROWS/ROUNDS: Yo, CDD, yo.

To work as a repeated pattern, add stitches between the repeats so you're not working double yarnovers, as follows:

In Rounds over a Multiple of 4 Stitches

ALL ROUNDS: [K1, yo, CDD, yo] to end.

If you're working this flat, you'll need to add a stitch for the end-of-row selvage, as follows:

In Rows over a Multiple of 4 Stitches + 1

ROW 1 (RS): [K1, yo, CDD, yo] to last stitch, k1.

ROW 2: Knit or purl for desired background (see below).

This is a special case of the traditional Razor Shell pattern.

For a Garter background: If working flat, knit the alternate rows; if working in the round, purl the alternate rounds.

For a Stockinette background: If working flat, purl the alternate rows; if working in the round, knit the alternate rounds.

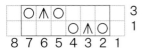

Change the pattern up by working more even rows/rounds between pattern rows/rounds. You can also create a great background pattern by staggering the pattern, as per the chart.

3-STITCH LACE RIB: VERSION 3

When Working in the Round, work only the red-bordered repeat.

In Rounds over a Multiple of 3 Stitches

ROUND 1: [K1, yo, ssk] around.

ROUND 3: [K1, k2tog, yo] around.

In Rows over a Multiple of 3 Stitches + 1

ROW 1 (RS): [K1, yo, ssk] to last st, k1.

ROW 3: [K1, k2tog, yo] to last st, k1.

This version looks best if worked on a Stockinette background: If working flat, purl the alternate rows; if working in the round, knit the alternate rounds.

Working on 4 stitches yields an attractive vertical insertion—2 knit ribs with a waving rib in between. Working on a larger multiple of 3 stitches plus 1 makes this into a great background pattern.

5-STITCH LACE RIB

Stockinette background

ROW/ROUND 1 (RS): [K2tog, yo, k1, yo, ssk] to end.

ROW/ROUND 2: Knit or purl for desired background (see below).

For a Garter background: If working flat, knit the alternate rows; if working in the round, purl the alternate rounds.

For a Stockinette background: If working flat, purl the alternate rows; if working in the round, knit the alternate rounds.

Variations: Create a background pattern by working repeats right next to each other, or work this ribbing-style with purl stitches between repeats.

Smaller Lace Repeats

These all make great background patterns, and many work well as vertical or horizontal insertions.

BIRD'S EYE/CAT'S EYE

Double yarnovers make pleasing and dramatic holes.

Stockinette background

Worked Flat over a Multiple of 4 Stitches

ROW 1 (RS): K2, [k2, yo twice, k2], k2.

ROW 2: P2, [p2tog, (p1, k1) into double yo, p2tog] to last 2 sts, p2.

ROW 3: K2, yo, [k4, yo twice] to last 6 sts, k4, yo, k2.

ROW 4: P3, [p2tog twice, (p1, k1) into double yo] to last 7 sts, p2tog twice, p3.

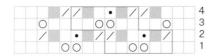

Worked in the Round over a Multiple of 4 Stitches

ROUND 1: [K2, yo twice, k2] around.

ROUND 2: [K2tog, (k1, p1) into double yo, k2tog] around.

ROUND 3: [K4, yo twice] around.

ROUND 4: [K2tog twice, (k1, p1) into double yo] around.

For a more textured fabric, work on a Garter background. To work this flat, work from the In-the-round instructions. To work this in the round, work from the Flat instructions.

Garter background

To create a very effective vertical insertion, repeat Rows/Rounds 1 and 2 only.

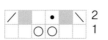

ARROWHEAD
Worked over 7 stitches

Stockinette background

Garter background

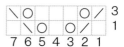

ROW/ROUND 1 (RS): [K1, k2tog, yo, k1, yo, ssk, k1] to end.

ROW/ROUND 2: Knit or purl for desired background (see below).

ROW/ROUND 3: [K2tog, yo, k3, yo, ssk] to end.

ROW/ROUND 4: Knit or purl for desired background (see below).

For a Garter background: If working flat, knit the alternate rows; if working in the round, purl the alternate rounds.

For a Stockinette background: If working flat, purl the alternate rows; if working in the round, knit the alternate rounds.

Variations: Create a background pattern by working repeats right next to each other, or work it ribbing-style, with purl stitches between repeats.

CHEVRON REPEATS

This pattern is a variant of the Arrowhead. Where two repeats meet, one double decrease is worked in place of two consecutive decreases. It's easily adjusted to create larger repeats.

This is a terrific background pattern. The fabric scallops make it an excellent stitch pattern for use in the final rows/rounds before the bind-off.

To work in the round, work the repeat only, skipping the red text.

Stockinette background

To work in the round, work only the outlined repeat.

6-Stitch Repeat

ROW/ROUND 1 (RS): [K1, yo, ssk, k1, k2tog, yo] to last st, k1.

ROW/ROUND 2: Knit or purl for desired background (see below).

ROW/ROUND 3: [K2, yo, CDD, yo, k1] to last st, k1.

ROW/ROUND 4: Knit or purl for desired background (see below).

For a Garter background: If working flat, knit the alternate rows; if working in the round, purl the alternate rounds.

For a Stockinette background: If working flat, purl the alternate rows; if working in the round, knit the alternate rounds.

10-Stitch Repeat

Stockinette background

To work in the round, work only the outlined repeat.

ROW/ROUND 1: [K1, (yo, ssk) twice, k1, (k2tog, yo) twice] to last st, k1.

ROW/ROUND 2: Knit or purl for desired background (see below).

ROW/ROUND 3: [K2, yo, ssk, yo, CDD, yo, k2tog, yo, k1] to last st, k1.

ROW/ROUND 4: Knit or purl for desired background (see below).

For a Garter background: If working flat, knit the alternate rows; if working in the round, purl the alternate rounds.

For a Stockinette background: If working flat, purl the alternate rows; if working in the round, knit the alternate rounds.

14-Stitch Repeat

Stockinette background

To work in the round, work only the outlined repeat.

ROW/ROUND 1: [K1, (yo, ssk) 3 times, k1, (k2tog, yo) 3 times] to last st, k1.

ROW/ROUND 2: Knit or purl for desired background (see below).

ROW/ROUND 3: [K2, (yo, ssk) twice, yo, CDD, (yo, k2tog) twice, yo, k1] to last st, k1.

ROW/ROUND 4: Knit or purl for desired background (see below).

For a Garter background: If working flat, knit the alternate rows; if working in the round, purl the alternate rounds.

For a Stockinette background: If working flat, purl the alternate rows; if working in the round, knit the alternate rounds.

Expand further by adding multiples of 4 stitches, working more repeats of the (yo, ssk) and (k2tog, yo) pair.

Old Favorites and Classic Shetland Patterns

All of these patterns cause the fabric to scallop. They can be used as background patterns or horizontal insertions. If you work them at the bind-off edge of a piece, the edge will be pleasingly wavy.

THE FEATHER AND FAN/OLD SHALE/ CREST OF THE WAVE FAMILY

This is a group of closely related stitch patterns; there are many variations and many different names for them. The basic pattern row is the same; the variations are created by how often the pattern row is worked and what background fabric is used, how it's spaced out. There are also versions that expand the repeat.

The Basic Pattern row (11-stitch repeat): K2tog twice, (yo, k1) 3 times, yo, ssk twice.

The Basic Pattern row (17-stitch repeat): K2tog 3 times, (yo, k1) 5 times, yo, ssk 3 times.

Old Shale/Feather and Fan is typically a 4-row/round repeat: the Basic Pattern Row, followed by a Garter ridge, then 2 rows/rounds of Stockinette.

Old Shale/Feather and Fan (Worked Flat)

ROW 1 (RS): Basic Pattern Row.

ROW 2 (WS): Knit.

ROW 3: Knit.

ROW 4: Purl.

Old Shale/Feather and Fan (Worked in the Round)

ROUND 1: Basic Pattern Row.

ROUND 2: Purl.

ROUNDS 3 AND 4: Knit.

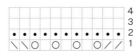

CREST OF THE WAVE

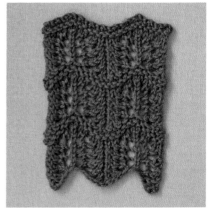

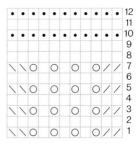

This is typically a 12-row/round repeat: 8 rows/rounds of the Basic Pattern row worked every other row/round on a Stockinette background, and then 2 Garter ridges (2 Garter rows/rounds).

Some variations eliminate the Garter ridges and have only Stockinette between groups of pattern rows.

Others use k2tog as the only decrease, replacing all of the ssks.

RAZOR SHELL

6-stitch repeat

Stockinette background

Garter background

8-stitch repeat

Stockinette background

As with the previous patterns, you can easily change the size of the repeat.

Worked flat, the pattern requires a 1-stitch selvage at the end of the pattern row; eliminate that to work in the round.

The Basic Pattern row (6-stitch repeat): [K1, yo, k1, CDD, k1, yo] to last st, k1.

The Basic Pattern row (8-stitch repeat): [K1, yo, k2, CDD, k2, yo] to last st, k1.

For a Garter background: If working flat, knit the alternate rows; if working in the round, purl the alternate rounds.

For a Stockinette background: If working flat, purl the alternate rows; if working in the round, knit the alternate rounds.

Add a knit stitch either side of the CDD to expand the repeat size by 2 stitches. The scallop is more dramatic with a smaller repeat; the curve softens the plainer stitches that are worked between the yarnover and the decrease.

VINE LACE

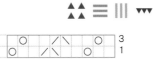

To work in the round, work only the outlined repeat.

This stitch is so simple, but so effective. It makes a great allover pattern or a wide vertical insertion.

Requires a multiple of 10 stitches plus 1 when worked flat; a multiple of 10 stitches when worked in the round. If working in the round, omit the final k1 (in red here).

ROW/ROUND 1 (RS): [K2, yo, k2, ssk, k2tog, k2, yo] to last st, k1.

ROW/ROUND 2: Knit on RS, purl on WS.

ROW/ROUND 3: [K1, yo, k2, ssk, k2tog, k2, yo, k1] to last st, k1.

ROW/ROUND 4: Knit on RS, purl on WS.

It looks best on a Stockinette background: If working flat, purl the alternate rows; if working in the round, work only the repeat and knit the alternate rounds.

TRAVELING VINE

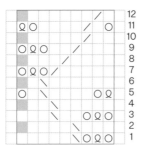

The stitch count increases by 1 stitch on the patterned rows/rounds and decreases back down to the original number after the alternate rows/rounds.

Worked Flat over a Multiple of 8 Stitches + 2

ROW 1 (RS): K1, [yo, k tbl, yo, ssk, k5] to last st, k1.

ROW 2: P1, [p4, ssp, p3] to last st, p1.

ROW 3: K1, [yo, k tbl, yo, k2, ssk, k3] to last st, k1.

ROW 4: P1, [p2, ssp, p5] to last st, p1.

ROW 5: K1, [k tbl, yo, k4, ssk, k1, yo] to last st, k1.

ROW 6: P1, [p1, ssp, p6] to last st, p1.

ROW 7: K1, [k5, k2tog, yo, k tbl, yo] to last st, k1.

ROW 8: P1 [p3, p2tog, p4] to last st, p1.

ROW 9: K1, [k3, k2tog, k2, yo, k tbl, yo] to last st, k1.

ROW 10: P1, [p5, p2tog, p2] to last st, p1.

ROW 11: K1 [yo, k1, k2tog, k4, yo, k tbl] to last st, k1.

ROW 12: P1, [p6, p2tog, p1] to last st, p1.

Worked in the Round over a Multiple of 8 Stitches

ROUND 1: [Yo, k tbl, yo, ssk, k5] around.

ROUND 2: [K3, ssk, k4] around.

ROUND 3: [Yo, k tbl, yo, k2, ssk, k3] around.

ROUND 4: [K5, ssk, k2] around.

ROUND 5: [K1 tbl, yo, k4, ssk, k1, yo] around.

ROUND 6: [K6, ssk, k1] around.

ROUND 7: [K5, k2tog, yo, k tbl, yo] around.

ROUND 8: [K4, k2tog, k3] around.

ROUND 9: [K3, k2tog, k2, yo, k tbl, yo] around.

ROUND 10: [K2, k2tog, k5] around.

ROUND 11: [Yo, k1, k2tog, k4, yo, k tbl] around.

ROUND 12: [K1, k2tog, k6] around.

Lace Motifs

WATERFALL STITCH

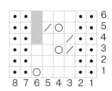

This stitch is an excellent vertical insertion. Change the number of purl stitches worked either side, or work on a Stockinette background for a softer look.

This is typically worked as an insertion rather than a repeat.

Worked Flat over 7 Stitches

ROW 1 (RS): P2, k3, yo, p2.

ROW 2: K2, p4, k2.

ROW 3: P2, k1, k2tog, yo, k1, p2.

ROW 4: K2, p2, p2tog, k2.

ROW 5: P2, k1, yo, k2tog, p2.

ROW 6: K2, p3, k2.

Worked in the Round over 7 Stitches

ROUND 1: P2, k3, yo, p2.

ROUND 2: P2, k4, p2.

ROUND 3: P2, k1, k2tog, yo, k1, p2.

ROUND 4: P2, k2tog, k2, p2.

ROUND 5: P2, k1, yo, k2tog, p2.

ROUND 6: P2, k3, p2.

ZIGZAGS

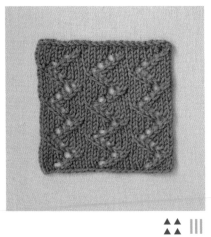

You can create a lot of different patterns with just the (k2tog, yo) and (yo, ssk) pairs.

These charts and photographs show a number of variations.

You can close-work them, eliminating the plain rows between. They also look fantastic on a Garter background, with WS rows knit rather than purled.

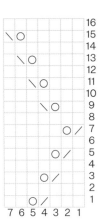

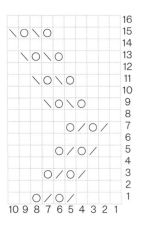

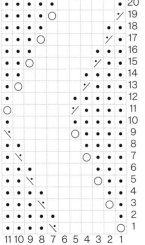

Edgings

Edging-Appropriate Stitch Patterns

If you don't want to work an attached edging, there are lots of other stitch patterns which make excellent finishing patterns. Any pattern that makes a scalloped or wavy edge creates a lovely effect if worked in the final section before the bind-off. And of course, a scalloped edge makes pinning easier, if that's how to you plan to block the shawl (page 38).

Ribbing or ribbing-based patterns work very well, too; a deep band of these types of patterns reduces any roll in the fabric and makes a nice, clean edge.

Attached Edgings

These stitch patterns are specifically designed for working along the edge of a shawl. Their traditional use is as an attached edging or as a bind-off alternative (page 35). When worked as an attached edging, they are placed perpendicularly to the main fabric.

The following edgings can be used that way or worked as a more standard stitch pattern on one edge of your fabric. In this case, the rows will be aligned with the rest of the fabric.

All of the charts are shown flat, as that's how they are worked. For each pattern, a cast-on number is given; the stitch counts shown are only for the edging portion. As outlined in "Techniques" (page 22), the decrease at the end of the

RS rows is worked on the last of the edging stitches and the next available stitch from the shawl.

Many traditional lace patterns add a column of a 2-stitch lace pattern between the main pattern and the attachment element.

When used as attached edgings, they're most often worked on a Garter background, as that helps balance the difference in tensions between the two fabrics.

You can also work them integrated with the rest of the stitches, so that they're part of the body rows. Work the stitches at the start of RS rows and the end of WS rows, omitting the attachment element—the RS end-of-row decrease and WS slip that sits above it. If you choose to work it this way, subtract one from the cast-on number (since you will no longer be working the RS end-of-row decrease) to determine how many stitches you need to work the pattern. The Ancoats design (page 141) uses this technique.

If working them integrated with the rest of the stitches, you may purl rather than knit the WS rows for a Stockinette background, since the row gauge will match that of the main fabric.

I-CORD BIND-OFF

CO 3 sts at start of RS row. You may use a provisional CO if you want to be able to graft both ends of the BO together.

[K2, ssk; do not turn. Sl 3 sts back to left-hand needle.] Continue in this manner until all sts of main fabric have been bound off, and only 3 sts of i-cord remain. Bind off the i-cord sts or join to starting sts.

PLAIN GARTER EDGING

CO any number of sts at start of RS row. The number of sts you CO sets the width of the edging.

ROW 1 (RS): Knit to last CO st, ssk, turn.

ROW 2: Sl 1 wyif, k to end.

BIG LOOPS 1

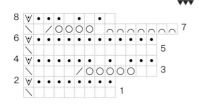

CO 9 sts at start of RS row.

ROW 1 (RS): K8, ssk, turn. 9 sts.

ROW 2: Sl 1 wyif, k8.

ROW 3: K2, yo 5 times, k2tog, k4, ssk, turn. 13 sts.

ROW 4: Sl 1 wyif, k6, p1, k1, p1, k3.

ROW 5: K12, ssk, turn.

ROW 6: Sl 1 wyif, k12.

ROW 7: BO 7 sts, k1, yo 4 times, k2tog, k1, ssk, turn. 9 sts.

ROW 8: Sl 1 wyif, k3, (p1, k1) twice, p1.

BIG LOOPS 2

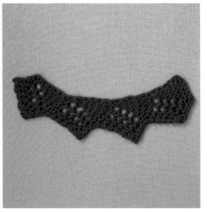

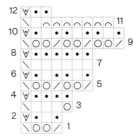

CO 3 sts at start of RS row.

ROW 1 (RS): K2tog, yo twice, ssk, turn. 4 sts.

ROW 2: Sl 1 wyif, k1, p1, k1.

ROW 3: Yo, k3, ssk, turn.

ROW 4: Sl 1 wyif, k4.

ROW 5: (K2tog, yo twice) twice, ssk, turn. 7 sts.

ROW 6: Sl 1 wyif, k1, p1, k2, p1, k1.

ROW 7: K6, ssk, turn.

ROW 8: Sl 1 wyif, k6.

ROW 9: (K2tog, yo twice) 3 times, ssk, turn. 10 sts.

ROW 10: Sl 1 wyif, k1, (p1, k2) twice, p1, k1.

ROW 11: BO 7 sts, k1, ssk, turn.

ROW 12: Sl 1 wyif, k2.

SIMPLE LEAF MOTIF

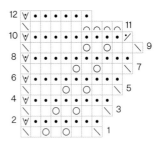

CO 7 sts at start of RS row.

Variation: Work on a Stockinette background by purling WS rows.

ROW 1 (RS): Ssk, k2, (yo, k1) twice, ssk, turn. 8 sts.

ROW 2: Sl 1 purlwise wyif, k7.

ROW 3: Ssk, k2, yo, k1, yo, k2, ssk, turn. 9 sts.

ROW 4: Sl 1 purlwise wyif, k8.

ROW 5: Ssk, k2, yo, k1, yo, k3, ssk, turn. 10 sts.

ROW 6: Sl 1 purlwise wyif, k9.

ROW 7: Ssk, k2, yo, k1, yo, k4, ssk, turn. 11 sts.

ROW 8: Sl 1 purlwise wyif, k10.

ROW 9: Ssk, k2, yo, k1, yo, k5, ssk, turn. 12 sts.

ROW 10: Sl 1 purlwise wyif, k9, k2tog. 11 sts.

ROW 11: BO 4 sts, k5, ssk, turn. 6 sts.

ROW 12: Sl 1 purlwise wyif, k6. 7 sts.

DROPS

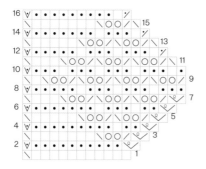

CO 12 sts at start of RS row.

ROW 1 (RS): K11, ssk.

ROW 2: Sl 1, k10, kfb. 13 sts.

ROW 3: Kfb, k2tog, yo twice, ssk, k7, ssk, turn. 14 sts.

ROW 4: Sl 1 wyib, k9, p1, k2, kfb. 15 sts.

ROW 5: Kfb, (k2tog, yo twice, ssk) twice, k5, ssk, turn. 16 sts.

ROW 6: Sl 1 wyib, k7, p1, k3, p1, k2, kfb. 17 sts.

ROW 7: Kfb, (k2tog, yo twice, ssk) 3 times, k3, ssk, turn. 18 sts.

ROW 8: Sl 1 wyib, k5, (p1, k3) 3 times.

ROW 9: (K2tog, yo twice, ssk) 4 times, k1, ssk, turn.

ROW 10: Sl 1 wyib, (k3, p1) 4 times, k1.

ROW 11: Ssk, (k2tog, yo twice, ssk) 3 times, k3, ssk, turn. 17 sts.

ROW 12: Sl 1 wyib, k5, (p1, k3) twice, p1, k2tog. 16 sts.

ROW 13: Ssk, (k2tog, yo twice, ssk) twice, k5, ssk, turn. 15 sts.

ROW 14: Sl 1 wyib, k7, p1, k3, p1, k2tog. 14 sts.

ROW 15: Ssk, k2tog, yo twice, ssk, k7, ssk, turn. 13 sts.

ROW 16: Sl 1 wyib, k9, p1, k2tog.

SHARK'S TOOTH

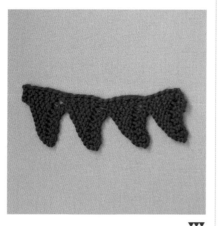

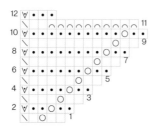

CO 4 sts at start of RS row.

ROW 1 (RS): K2, yo, k1, ssk, turn. 5 sts.

ROW 2: Sl 1 wyif, k2, yo, k2. 6 sts.

ROW 3: K2, yo, k3, ssk, turn. 7 sts.

ROW 4: Sl 1 wyif, k4, yo, k2. 8 sts.

ROW 5: K2, yo, k5, ssk, turn. 9 sts.

ROW 6: Sl 1 wyif, k6, yo, k2. 10 sts.

ROW 7: K2, yo, k7, ssk, turn. 11 sts.

ROW 8: Sl 1 wyif, k8, yo, k2. 12 sts.

ROW 9: K2, yo, k9, ssk, turn. 13 sts.

ROW 10: Sl 1 wyif, k10, yo, k2. 14 sts.

ROW 11: BO 11 sts, k2, ssk, turn.

ROW 12: Sl 1 wyif, k2. 3 sts.

This is endlessly adjustable—more rows, or fewer. Add in pairs of (yo, ssk).

ASPEN LEAF

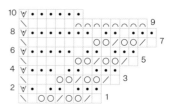

CO 7 sts at start of RS row.

ROW 1 (RS): K1, (k2tog, yo twice) twice, k1, ssk, turn. 9 sts.

ROW 2: Sl 1 wyif, k1, p1, k2, p1, k3.

ROW 3: K1, (k2tog, yo twice) twice, k3, ssk, turn. 11 sts.

ROW 4: Sl 1 wyif, k3, p1, k2, p1, k3.

ROW 5: K1, (k2tog, yo twice) twice, k5, ssk, turn. 13 sts.

ROW 6: Sl 1 wyif, k5, p1, k2, p1, k3.

ROW 7: K1, (k2tog, yo twice) twice, k7, ssk, turn. 15 sts.

ROW 8: Sl 1 wyif, k7, p1, k2, p1, k3.

ROW 9: BO 8 sts, k5, ssk, turn. 6 sts.

ROW 10: Sl 1 wyif, k6. 7 sts.

THE GODMOTHER'S EDGING

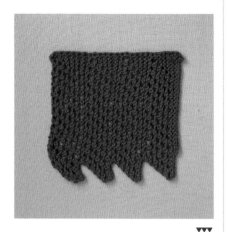

▼▼▼

CO 24 sts at start of RS row.

ROW 1 (RS): K2, (yo, k2tog) 10 times, yo, k1, ssk, turn. 25 sts.

ROW 2: Sl 1 wyif, k24.

ROW 3: K2, (yo, k2tog) 10 times, yo, k2, ssk, turn. 26 sts.

ROW 4: Sl 1 wyif, k25.

ROW 5: K2, (yo, k2tog) 10 times, yo, k3, ssk, turn. 27 sts.

ROW 6: Sl 1 wyif, k26.

ROW 7: K2, (yo, k2tog) 10 times, yo, k4, ssk, turn. 28 sts.

ROW 8: Sl 1 wyif, k27.

ROW 9: K2, (yo, k2tog) 10 times, yo, k5, ssk, turn. 29 sts.

ROW 10: Sl 1 wyif, k28.

ROW 11: BO 5 sts, k22, ssk, turn. 24 sts.

ROW 12: Sl 1 wyif, k23. 24 sts.

VANDYKE EDGING

▼▼▼

CO 11 sts at start of RS row.

ROW 1 (RS): K2, (yo, k2tog) 3 times, yo, k2, ssk, turn. 12 sts.

ROW 2: Sl 1 wyif, k11.

ROW 3: K2, (yo, k2tog) 3 times, yo, k3, ssk, turn. 13 sts.

ROW 4: Sl 1 wyif, k12.

ROW 5: K2, (yo, k2tog) 3 times, yo, k4, ssk, turn. 14 sts.

ROW 6: Sl 1 wyif, k13.

ROW 7: K2, (yo, k2tog) 3 times, yo, k5, ssk, turn. 15 sts.

ROW 8: Sl 1 wyif, k14.

ROW 9: K2, (yo, k2tog) 3 times, yo, k6, ssk, turn. 16 sts.

ROW 10: Sl 1 wyif, k15.

ROW 11: K2, (yo, k2tog) 3 times, yo, k7, ssk, turn. 17 sts.

ROW 12: Sl 1 wyif, k16.

ROW 13: K2, (yo, k2tog) 3 times, yo, k8, ssk, turn. 18 sts.

ROW 14: Sl 1 wyif, k17.

ROW 15: K1, (ssk, yo) 4 times, ssk, k6, ssk, turn. 17 sts.

ROW 16: Sl 1 wyif, k16.

ROW 17: K1, (ssk, yo) 4 times, ssk, k5, ssk, turn. 16 sts.

ROW 18: Sl 1 wyif, k15.

ROW 19: K1, (ssk, yo) 4 times, ssk, k4, ssk, turn. 15 sts.

ROW 20: Sl 1 wyif, k14.

ROW 21: K1, (ssk, yo) 4 times, ssk, k3, ssk, turn. 14 sts.

ROW 22: Sl 1 wyif, k13.

ROW 23: K1, (ssk, yo) 4 times, ssk, k2, ssk, turn. 13 sts.

ROW 24: Sl 1 wyif, k12.

ROW 25: K1, (ssk, yo) 4 times, ssk, k1, ssk, turn. 12 sts.

ROW 26: Sl 1 wyif, k11.

ROW 27: K1, (ssk, yo) 4 times, ssk twice, turn. 11 sts.

ROW 28: Sl 1 wyif, k10.

This is endlessly adjustable. Add or remove multiples of 2 stitches, adding in extra repeats of the zigzag motif. Add a little lace repeat in the plain section at the widest part of the pattern. Add or remove rows to make the points wider or narrower.

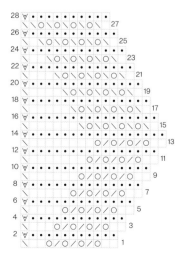

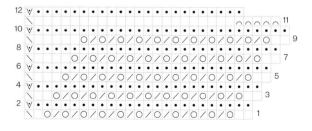

Break-ing the Rules

"I've gone from thinking [that] shawls equal lace to thinking of them as giant knitted doodles, using any kind of knitted fabric."
—Amanda Schwabe, designer

When you begin to create something new, every skein of yarn is like a blank page. You know you want to make something unique, and you're not entirely sure what that looks like. The blank-page stage can be completely overwhelming. For all of us. That is the same for every other artist. Every maker. Every designer.

Welcome to the blank page. Let's fill it up.

These doodles in Kim's sketchbook, trying to work out combinations of triangles, eventually became the Adjacent (page 179) and Radialactive (page 174) shawls.

Creativity Is Play

When you play, you explore. When you explore, you learn. Allowing yourself the time to play with your knitting can be as simple as having materials available to you so that when you have five minutes in your day, you can try something. This is what Kim's creativity kit looks like:

- Small balls of leftover yarn, replenished as needed

- Spare knitting needles

- Office supplies to keep track of what she's done: sticky notes, index cards, tags to tie onto experiments, a pen or pencil to write down what she's done so that she can replicate it later

- Lots of stitch markers

Kim keeps all this in a small bag that she can pick up and take with her on the bus, in the car, on a trip, or anywhere she might have a few minutes. We lead busy, busy lives and often think there is no time for being creative. But there are pockets in every day that you can make use of. Even a few minutes a day can spark the best ideas.

Inspiration, Ideas, and Making Your Own Rules

Inspiration sparks ideas. Ideas can come from anywhere at any time, usually when least expected— when our minds are empty and allowed to ramble. Over and over creatives say things like, "I have to wait to be inspired before I can make anything." And while there are times when ideas jump into your brain fully formed, genuine creativity is a skill, a muscle. You can learn it. You can practice it. You can make it stronger.

Here are some ways to spark your creative mind:

Go through your stash and find some skeins you love that you want to work with. Think about what they might want to be. Kim often has a skein of yarn sitting on her coffee table so that she sees it every day and thinks about what she might do with it.

Make a date with yourself to go to a museum or art gallery for a few hours. A visit to a glass gallery inspires ideas for color combinations and wild organic shapes. An exhibit about how fashion designers form clothing to change the shapes of bodies inspires us to think more carefully about how to design in a way that celebrates our different shapes. An exhibit about feminine archetypes and how they are portrayed in clothing influences the stories behind designs.

Go for a walk. A drive. A bike ride. These are the times when your mind can truly wander. You start with an inner dialogue about your to-do list, or that meeting you have tomorrow, but once those thoughts have run their course, your mind is allowed to open up. Ideas will start coming when your mind is emptiest. Start collecting them.

Get out a piece of paper and start scribbling and doodling without any end goal in mind. When listening, many find that doodling helps them absorb the words. It also leaves a record of shapes, lines, and textures to think about using in future designs.

Practice being fearless. All children are artists, until they're taught not to be, and then they spend a lifetime trying to relearn qualities that were instinctive in the early years. When Kim first started teaching textile classes, she had a weekly class of children under six and another weekly class of women over seventy-five. When it came to being artistic and creative, they were exactly the same in temperament. They created beautiful, innovative work with absolutely no reservations. They were fearless! There was nothing they wouldn't try, nothing they would say no to. Something happens to us in the middle of our lives, between being a small child (prior to being told to color inside the lines) and late in life (when you no longer care about the lines). We stop playing and stop thinking we are creative. To cultivate fearlessness, we need to take on the spirit of both generations and simply play.

Collecting Ideas

Kim has a sketchbook. A bunch of them. They're filled with really good and really bad drawings, tons of words to explain what the sketches are supposed to be, pictures ripped out of magazines or printed from her computer, yarn scraps, colored blobs of pencil crayon, watercolors—and anything else that inspires her at the moment. An entry sticker from a museum or art gallery reminds her of a day spent there and the ideas that sprang from it. Pictures of rocks and driftwood from her last trip to the ocean remind her how important it is to have small pockets of time to just let her mind wander. A napkin with a rough sketch of a completely unwearable sweater, drawn in green crayon from a dinner conversation last weekend. These books are the keepers of her ideas.

Your sketchbook doesn't have to be a book. It can be a shoebox, a Pinterest board, a folder on your computer, a bulletin board. Ideas can come to you fully formed and ready to go. And when they do, record them in some way: a voice memo, some words scribbled down, photographs, and so on. Record every idea. Many ideas are not good ones. They are scraps and shards and bits and pieces. All ideas are important, no matter how small. An idea that doesn't work for one shawl is the magic ingredient for another.

Choosing Yarn to Match Inspiration

Choosing yarn based on a visual inspiration like a photograph, painting, or object is one way to use yarn as the jumping-off point for a shawl.

Find an image or object you like because of its color content. Maybe it's a vacation photo or magazine image. Maybe it's a painting from your childhood or the fabric from a favorite piece of clothing. Using watercolors, markers, or pencil crayons, find colors from the image and record them on pieces of card or paper. This gives you a palette to start with and helps isolate colors, which is less overwhelming.

Everything changes when you're in front of your yarn source (your stash or local yarn store, for example) and begin pulling colors of yarn that match your palette. When working with a source of yarn, you're limited by the colors dyed by yarn companies, so you may not find an exact match. Allow yourself some room to experiment by pulling colors that are similar to, as well as ones that match, your color palette. Start putting colors together. In our studio, we play a game of color roulette whenever we have to choose color combinations:

Determine how many colors you need for your project, and randomly choose skeins to put together. Take photos of each combination, whether you like it or not. When you're finished, go through the photos. Give yourself three seconds to decide whether you like the photo or not—no more than three seconds! Your gut reaction to the colors is what is important here. If given time to think too much about it, you can convince yourself you like or hate anything. Delete anything that is a definite no. When you have only a few combinations left, take the skeins of yarn in those combinations and look at the colors in different lights (indoor, outdoor) to help you choose a final combination.

Alternative Ways to Think About Color

KEEP A COLOR NOTEBOOK.

Start a color notebook. This can be an actual notebook, a shoebox, a Pinterest board, or a drawer in your desk. It's a collection point for color ideas and inspiration. Use it to store swatches of colors

Pages from Kim's color notebook

and color combinations that appeal to you. Fill it with watercolors, pencil crayon rubbings, yarn scraps, magazine images, postcards, and other imagery to inspire your color brain.

You can often find sources for color imagery in other aspects of your life that interest you. Kim loves movies. Nothing thrills her more than watching a movie that has a distinct, memorable color palette. The first time she saw the French film *Amélie*, the color palette astounded her. Color became as much of a character as the actors. Images from movies that capture her eye is one example of how to combine her interests in color form.

PEOPLE AS INSPIRATION

People you love and the colors that remind you of them.

Choose three to five people in your life whom you love, who inspire you, who make you laugh or make you think. Choose three to five colors that remind you of them. Try to think of creative ways of choosing colors. What do they do for a living? What do they like to read? What are their hobbies? How could color represent those things?

If Kim were to choose colors that remind her of Kate, Kate would expect her to choose black and white. Now, she may wear a lot of black, but when Kim sees her working with yarn, it's usually some kind of orange

Pacific Northwest color inspiration in Kim's Travelogue shawl

Shape

Kate has given us an array of recipes to make a variety of shaped shawls, but what if you're looking for something a little unusual? This is where we start experimenting with how increases and decreases can be worked to change the basic shape of a shawl.

Changing the Placement of Increases and Decreases

As a standard, increase and decrease placement in a shawl is set to specific regions, such as the center spine and wingspan edges. The shawl recipes (page 6) clearly show how to make specific shapes based on the placement of increases and decreases. For the sake of simplification, when we refer to increases alone in this section, the same methodology applies to recipes that have decrease points instead of increase points. If increases and decreases cause the shape to do more complex things, we will refer to both.

In a standard top-down triangle, you have four points of increase: two at the spine, which helps create more fabric for the depth of the shawl, and two at the wingspan edge, which gives the shawl width.

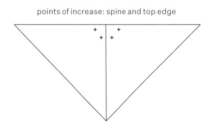

points of increase: spine and top edge

When you move the spine increases to different places within the shawl, the weight and direction of the fabric shift. To maintain the top-down triangle form, you need to keep the wingspan increases, but others can be moved to create different triangles:

This is exactly what Kate did in her Hespero design (page 161). It's a wide top-down triangle with the points of increase moved away from the center spine to create a new triangle in the center.

or yellow or something neon. When we came across the yarn for Hollerith, Kate's face lit up with sheer love and excitement about designing with it. Kim has been shopping with her and seen her attracted to wild and crazy 1960s textiles. So her palette for Kate would be inspired by 1960s prints, 1980s color sensibilities, and just a dash of animal print.

PLACE AS INSPIRATION
Where in the world do you feel most calm and relaxed?
Where in the world do you feel most at home?
Where in the world do you feel most inspired?
Where in the world are you happiest?
Where do you dream of visiting?
Find colors that remind you of that place. What are the colors of the sky? The water? The landscape? The town? When you find a combination that gives you the same feeling as that place, you can use it in a shawl that reminds you of that place.

Kim's color inspiration for the Travelogue shawl (page 134) was a trip to the Pacific Northwest. Every color in the finished shawl is found there: the bright yellow green of fresh spring leaves; the moody blue of the ocean; the gray and rust of the beaches, rusty ships, and tall pines that reach the sky. Every moment of working on that shawl reminded her of good friends, beautiful scenery, and the deep calm she felt while there.

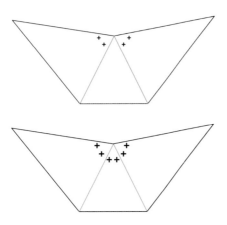

In these examples, we've taken the standard top-down triangle and changed the spines in the first to create another shape in the center. This flattens out the point. In the second example, Kim has added increases within the center shape to push the sides of the center shape out, which pushes the wing triangles out farther.

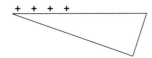

In a standard sideways triangle, you have one point of increase at the wingspan edge that gives the shawl width that is weighted to one side.

Because there's only one point of increase at the wingspan, changing the placement can be either simple or complex. If you move the single point of increase to a different position along the row (marked, so that it remains consistent), you will get a similar shape with a new point of increase to design around. This could be an interesting way to work with simple intarsia or different stitch patterns.

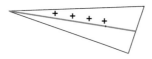

You could also look at creating two or more points of increase, and cycling through them. In this example, Kim has set up a series of faux spines. In every row, the increase moves laterally to the next spine.

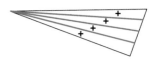

Similarly, when you apply this concept to a standard rectangle, the shape changes from a rectangle to a trapezoid. In this standard rectangle, there is a series of faux spines similar to the last triangle example. Every spine is a point of increase on every increase row. When increases happen at every spine, the shape changes rapidly, as every increase row's stitch count increases by 4.

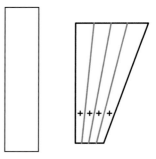

When increases happen at a single spine per increase row, cycling laterally to the next spine in subsequent increase rows, the shape changes slowly, as every increase row's stitch count increases by one.

It doesn't even need to be that complex. Simply adding an increase to one or both sides of a row in a rectangle takes you to a trapezoid shape that is easy to construct.

Changing and Combining the Number of Increases

Changing the number of stitches increased can not only change the shape of your shawl but also change how it sits on the body, as curves help shapes sit on your shoulders more securely.

Here is the example of the top-down triangle with four points of increase:

points of increase: spine and top edge

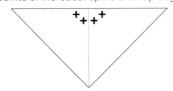

To get this shape, there is one stitch increased at every point of increase. When you increase two stitches per row at the wingspan points of increase and two at the spine points of increase, the wings of the shawl curve up.

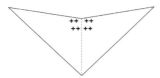

Looking at the sideways triangle with one point of increase, the standard shape looks like this:

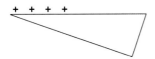

The basic Side-to-Side Triangle recipe (page 16) increases one stitch at the point of increase, to create a straight line. If you change the number of stitches increased to two stitches at the point of increase, one side of the triangle curves beautifully around your neck.

BIAS SHAPING

When you're combining increases and decreases to a shape at the same time, it not only shifts the shape of the shawl, but also shifts the angle of the fabric from straight to biased.

The simplest example of this is a bias rectangle. In a standard rectangle, there are no increases: Cast on the desired number of stitches. Work rows with no increases or decreases until it is the desired size. Bind off.

When you increase on one side edge of a rectangle and decrease on the other, the fabric changes. The fabric is knit on the bias. This changes the way the fabric behaves, how it drapes on the body, and how stitch patterns look.

Because increases add fabric, the increases on one side push the rest of the fabric to the decrease edge. The decrease then removes the same amount of fabric. This allows the angle of the fabric to change without changing the basic shape itself.

But can you create bias shaping within another shape? Yes, you can. In this case, it helps to separate the two concepts:
1) Shawl shaping
2) Bias shaping

You will be working both sets of shaping concurrently. When doing this, Kim often finds it easier to do shawl shaping on RS rows and bias shaping on WS rows.

Take the sideways triangle: The basic recipe shaping tells us to increase one stitch at the same edge every second row.

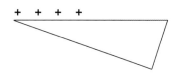

Now add bias shaping. Reminder: Bias shaping happens when you increase on one edge of the shawl and decrease on the other. The bias will always tilt towards the decrease side.

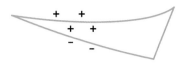

In fact, that is exactly what happens in the main body of Flexture (page 145). Rather than create a simple sideways triangle (page 16), Kim wanted to make the knitting and the effect of shape on the stripes more interesting. Bias panels interspersed with non-bias spines create visual interest. The result is fabric that looks almost pleated.

The vortex shape is what happens when you combine increases and decreases to push the shape. It's not quite on the bias, but it's headed in that direction. The basic recipe for a vortex shape is as follows:

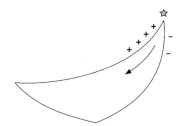

The RS increase-only rows are making the shape wider and tilting the angle of one side of the triangle. The WS rows, with a decrease and an increase, are just changing the angle of the fabric.

If you take that basic concept further, you can change the number of increases versus decreases in a vortex shawl and push that shape even further. Working two increase-only rows for every one decrease/increase row forces the neck edge of the shawl to make a tighter curve. Increase more than one stitch per increase row and that curve gets even tighter.

Changing the Rate of Increase

Changing the rate of increase and/or decrease will dramatically change the shape and size of your shawl. Increases add width to your shawl; decreases take it away. If your increase rows are close together, your shawl size will grow wider and deeper more quickly. If they are farther apart, then the shape will grow wider and deeper more slowly.

Again, working with the shape of the top-down triangle in its standard form:

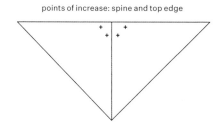

points of increase: spine and top edge

Change the increase rate on one side, and you get an asymmetrical triangle shape.

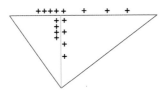

The standard sideways triangle recipe has one point of increase in its standard shape. Here we show it with one increase every second row.

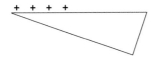

When you decrease the rate of increase to one increase every row, you get a deeper triangle with a shorter wingspan.

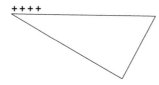

When you decrease the rate of increase to every four rows, you get a shallower triangle with a wider wingspan.

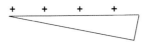

Combining Shapes

Combining shapes can be as simple as putting squares or rectangles together, or as complex as combining two totally different constructions, like a top-down triangle and a half-pi shawl.

Combining squares and rectangles is fairly simple. Start with a center shape and work other shapes around it. You could start with a square and build rows and columns from that.

In the Travelogue shawl (page 134), you start with a mitered square (A), add columns to either side of it to create a rectangle (B and C), then pick up stitches on either side of the rectangle and work away from the center panel.

Log Cabin is another construction that uses squares and rectangles. Start with a center square or rectangle (1) and add blocks of color by turning the square one-quarter turn to one side, picking up stitches and adding a new block (2, 3, 4 . . .).

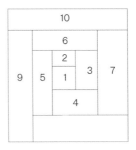

What would happen if you combined a top-down triangle with a half-pi shawl?

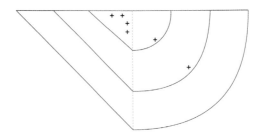

To make this shape work, you must separate the shaping aspects of these two shapes and make sure you're aware of them at all times. The top-down triangle side needs two increases every two rows: one at the wingspan edge and one at the spine. The half pi requires working an increase row every time the number of rows doubles: row 3, row 6, row 12, and so on. Keeping track of rows separately for each side is essential to success.

Carving into Shape

Some shapes give the opportunity to skip the beginning and carve out a bit of the shape to create new shapes. Arc Nemesis (page 169) does just this. It takes the recipe for the pi shawl, starts at the point where five full increase rows have been worked, and then reduces the number of stitches by 25%. Because it's no longer a pi shawl, Kim also added selvage stitches at each edge of the opening.

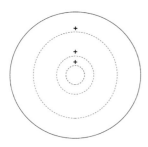

This is what a standard pi shawl looks like, with increase rows marked.

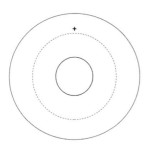

Started five full increase rows into the shape, allowing for a larger, body-hugging curve. This meant calculating the number of stitches needed to start at that point based on the basic pi shawl recipe (page 21).

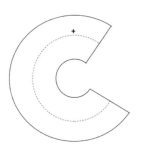

To avoid having a poncho rather than a shawl, and to reduce the amount of fabric in this design, Kim reduced the number of stitches required by 25%. That left her with this shape.

This concept can be applied to many of the shapes in the "Shapes and Recipes" chapter, such as the top-down triangle, the half pi, and the mitered square. The difference is that you are no longer starting with one to three stitches, but instead are starting by casting on 15 or 25 or 35 stitches and placing markers at appropriate points of increase. How large the cutout is depends largely on the weight of yarn you choose and your gauge. Here are some guidelines to help you determine where to start.

This top-down triangle starts several rows into the original recipe. There is no Garter tab, because the part of the shawl that requires it is cut out. You will need two stitches for each selvage and one stitch for the spine, plus enough stitches to make each side of the cutout as long as you want it to be. In this case, the imaginary gauge is 5 stitches per 1 inch (2.5 cm), so 15 stitches will give 3 inches (7.5 cm) of length along each edge of the cutout. Whatever length you choose, make sure it looks deliberate.

Formulas:

2 selvage stitches + side stitches + 1 spine stitch + side stitches + 2 selvedge stitches

side stitches = gauge (5 stitches per inch) × desired side length (3 inches each side) = 15 stitches

2 (selvage) + 15 + 1 (spine) + 15 + 2 (selvage) = 35 sts

CO 35 sts.

Place st markers either side of the center st.

Work 4 increases every RS row, 1 at each end and 2 in the center, until desired size is achieved.

BO.

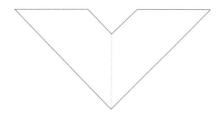

A mitered square is also set up for change. If you look at the recipe for the mitered-square shawl shape (page 13), all rows are mitered, folded at a 90-degree angle at the center, leaving an opportunity to start several rows in to create a different shape.

The standard recipe has you casting on with a single stitch, then increasing only at the center until the shawl is the desired size.

If you change that first stitch to 11 or 21, and mark the center stitch, you create a shape that wraps better around the body.

Start with an odd number of stitches.

Eleven stitches will create a small notch, 21–35 will create a large enough space for your neck to fit into, and more than 35 stitches will create a shawl that should sit on your shoulders well.

CO desired number of sts. Mark the center sts.

RS ROWS: K to center st, yo, sm, k1, sm, yo, k to end. 2 sts increased.

WS ROWS: Knit.

Work to desired size. BO.

To work in Stockinette stitch, purl all WS rows.

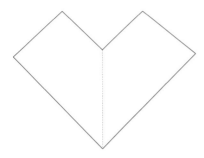

To do the same with a half-pi shawl, determine how deep you want the cutout to be. When you look at the standard half-pi recipe (page 21), you have increase rows at row 3 (15 sts), row 6 (25 sts), row 12 (45 sts), row 24 (85 sts), row 48 (165 sts), and so on. You can start your shawl at any of those increase rows by casting on the number of stitches you would have after working the increase row.

The smallest option—start at row 3 with 15 stitches—will be just enough space to create a curve for the back of your neck to nestle into. Starting at row 6 with 25 stitches takes you a bit deeper to make a cozy place for your whole neck to fit into. Starting at row 12 will make a roomier shawl opening that will sit nicely on your shoulder.

This example starts at row 12. Cast on the stitch count at row 12 of the recipe—45 sts—continuing to work the recipe as written until the shawl is the desired size:

CO 45 sts.

Work 11 rows even for Stockinette st; 13 rows for Garter st.

INCREASE ROW (RS): K3, [yo, k1] to last 3 sts, yo, k3. 85 sts.

Work 23 rows even for Stockinette st; 29 rows for Garter st.

Repeat Increase row. 165 sts.

Work 47 rows even for Stockinette st; 57 rows for Garter st.

Repeat Increase row. 325 sts.

Work up to 95 rows even for Stockinette st; 119 rows for Garter st. BO.

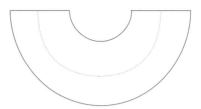

Short Rows and Shaping

Short rows, the act of working over a partial row before turning around and knitting back, are an excellent tool for changing the shape of your shawl, or changing the shape within a color block or stripe in your shawl. They can transform straight lines into angled ones. They can create intriguing shapes within your shawl. They can turn a symmetrical shawl into an asymmetrical one. And they can add length or width to your shawl in targeted areas.

Adding short rows to a stripe or a color block changes the angle of the lines created by those shapes and can also change the shape of your shawl.

Here is a simple rectangle with even stripes:

Add some short rows that focus only on one side of a few stripes, and the shape changes.

If you create the same short rows on each side of the shawl shape, the shape can remain the same, but the color pattern is different. We love these kinds of stripes! They look thrown together and random, but to get the edges of the fabric to line up is very precise work.

You can apply the same concepts you use with stripes to color block shapes. Take, for example, the log cabin construction:

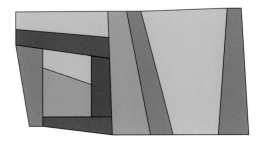

- Center block
- Quarter turn to the left or right (It doesn't matter, but it needs to be consistent.)
- New block/stripe
- Quarter turn

A few randomly placed short rows can be used to change the shape of any of these blocks. Using short rows in this shape can also change the overall shape of the shawl.

In five of the shawls in this book, Kim has used short rows. In Radialactive (page 174), short rows create the basic shape of the shawl. She also used short rows to create an inset piece when she realized she was using less of one of the two yarns than she had intended. Short rows allowed her to retain the integrity of the shape of the piece but squeeze in a little more yarn.

In Travelogue (page 134), Kim has used short rows to shift the angle of some of the color blocks, creating an off-kilter look that she loves.

In Arc Nemesis (page 169), a simple Stockinette and Garter ridge three-quarter pi shawl is transformed when small short-row flame shapes are added to the Garter ridges—but only within one half of the shawl. These shapes add extra rows in an organic way, transforming not only the shape of the shawl, but the depth and symmetry as well.

In Soundscape (page 157), short rows are used to take a symmetrical shape and stripe pattern and push its boundaries. The stripes are interesting because they are not all the same shape and size and aren't even across the entire length. The shape is interesting because it softens a hard, geometric shape, pushing it gently to one side.

And finally, in Flexture (page 145), the fins added to the bottom of the shawl were created with short rows to echo the shape of the main body of the shawl. The stripes narrow close to the point of the triangle and widen as the shawl widens.

Stitch Patterns

What follows is a series of ways you can manipulate established stitch patterns as a leaping-off point for creating something new.

Each method will be applied to the Seed stitch pattern.

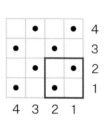

Magnify/Compress

To magnify, take the basic stitch motif and expand it equally both horizontally and vertically. This essentially pixelates the stitch pattern. Compress means to shrink the motif equally both horizontally and vertically.

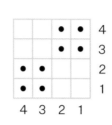

Expand/Contract

To expand, take elements of a stitch pattern and either double or triple them; to contract, reduce their size by half horizontally or vertically. This happens in one direction only: up, down, right, or left.

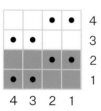

Expand horizontally

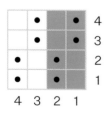

Expand vertically

Isolate

Isolate a section of a stitch pattern to prepare it for use as a new motif. Working a few repeats of the original stitch pattern helps you find interesting motifs.

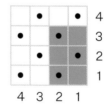

Isolate 1

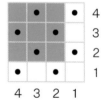

Isolate 3

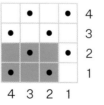

Isolate 2

RS: knit
WS: purl

● RS: purl
WS: knit

Morph

Change one portion of a stitch pattern so that it changes the shapes made within the stitch pattern.

In Morph 1, I've added purl stitches as indicated by the highlight. In Morph 2, I've added knit stitches.

Dissect/Transform/Transplant

Take pieces of a stitch pattern apart and rearrange them in new ways.

Dissect 1 takes the motif isolated in Isolate 1 and repeats it horizontally and vertically. Dissect 2 does the same with the motif isolated in Isolate 2. The motif is highlighted. The blue border shows the full repeat of the pattern.

Morph 1

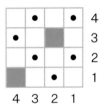

Morph 2

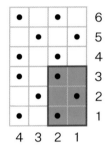

Dissect 1

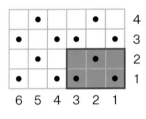

Dissect 2

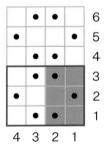

Transform 1

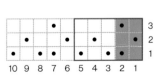

Transform 2

Transform dissected pieces of a stitch pattern by turning them upside down, rotating them, or mirroring them.

In Transform 1, I've mirrored the motif from Dissect 1 horizontally and vertically. In Transform 2, I've rotated the motif counterclockwise once. The original motif is highlighted. The blue border outlines the whole pattern repeat.

Reintroduce the transformed pieces to create something new.

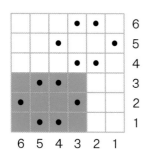 

This example takes the new motif created in Transform 1 and builds a stitch pattern by transplanting it in new ways. The motif is shifted two stitches to the right and stacked on top of the original motif brought over from Transform 1.

Connecting

Use elements from two or more of the other sections and connect them in new ways.

Taking the motif developed in Transform 2, I've further transformed it (flipped vertically and horizontally) and have connected those pieces together.

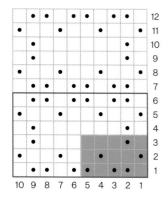 

Incorporating Stitch Patterns into Changing Shapes

When working with a stitch pattern in a shawl shape that has increases, decreases, or a combination of both, you need to be able to manage that changing stitch count within the pattern. There are a few ways to approach this: some simple and some more complex, for those of us who like to challenge ourselves.

Stitch markers are key to this; make sure you have some on hand.

SIMPLE METHOD—FULL REPEATS

If increasing: Place removable markers between the edge of the stitch pattern and all points of increase. For example, if knitting a standard sideways triangle, place a removable marker between the increase side and the edge of the stitch pattern repeat. Keep all stitches between the point of increase and the marker in a plain stitch appropriate for the shawl (the background pattern, usually Stockinette or Garter stitch) until you have enough stitches to incorporate a full pattern repeat. When you do, move the marker over to the new edge of the patterned section.

If decreasing: Place removable markers between the edge of the stitch pattern and all points of decrease. As soon as you have too few stitches to work a pattern repeat, move the stitch markers over/inward by a full repeat, and change the previously patterned stitches (between the decrease and the new marker position) to the plain background pattern stitch.

ONE STITCH AT A TIME

When the stitch pattern and shaping are straightforward, it's not difficult to incorporate new stitches into the pattern one at a time. Many knit/purl patterns, for example, can easily be incorporated in this way. Place a removable marker between the edge of the stitch pattern and all points of increase. As you increase, work the new stitches in pattern, one new pattern stitch per increase (or decrease one pattern stitch, if working with a point of decrease). When a new full pattern repeat has been incorporated, move the stitch marker over to include that new full repeat.

If the pattern stitch is easy to follow, you may find that the markers are not needed. Adjacent (page 179) uses this method.

RS: knit
WS: purl

RS: purl
WS: knit

yo

RS: ssk
WS: ssp

RS: k2tog
WS: p2tog

edge stitches

stitch pattern repeat

new pattern stitch added

marker

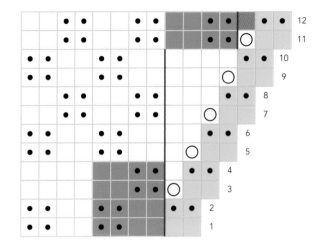

Simple Method

As new stitches are added at the point of increase, work them in a plain stitch pattern appropriate for your fabric until you have enough new stitches to work a full pattern repeat.

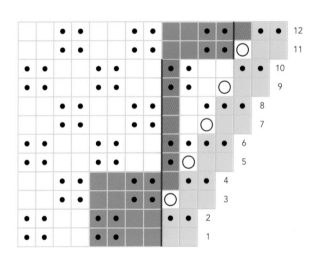

One Stitch at a Time Method

Purple squares indicate new stitches after an increase row. As new stitches are made available, the pattern is easily applied.

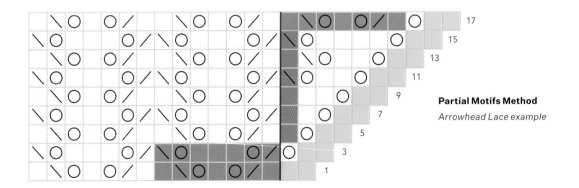

Partial Motifs Method

Arrowhead Lace example

For patterns that have *entangling stitches*—stitches that are worked together in a unit such as a decrease that's worked in conjunction with a yarnover or a cable turn—you can't necessarily add them one at a time, but you can build partial motifs. This strategy reduces the plain areas of fabric and makes the most of really special pattern stitches.

Lace stitch patterns, for example, reply on a yarnover increase and corresponding decrease pair. They're most often placed right next to each other, but not always.

Look at the Arrowhead lace pattern (page 100). There are two yarnover-decrease pairs. If you're adding stitches at the start of the patterned area, you don't need to wait until you have 7 stitches. On pattern row 1, you need 3 stitches to add the (yo, ssk, k1) at the end of the repeat; on pattern row 3, you only need 2 stitches to add the (yo, ssk) element. And if you're adding stitches at the end of the patterned area, on row 1 you need 3 stitches to add the (k1, k2tog, yo) element from the start of the repeat; on row 3 you only need 2 to add the (k2tog, yo) element.

As before, make sure you have markers placed around the main patterned areas—a second color of marker is helpful to separate partially patterned areas. Once you've got enough stitches in your partially patterned area for a full repeat, move the main marker over, just as for the Simple example above.

The key with this method is to ensure that you're adding *stitch-count neutral* patterning. You can't just add the decrease at the start/end of the Arrowhead pattern; you need to make sure you have the yarnover to accompany it.

As with many of these techniques, when in doubt, swatch. It's handy to have a practice swatch in your project bag to try out a technique to see how it will look in the finished shawl. Anytime you have a what-if moment while knitting, try out your idea and see what happens.

Making Your Own Rules

Rules, limits, boundaries—whatever you want to call them—actually allow you to be *more* creative. The smaller the space you have to work in, the more creative you have to be to work within that space. So while this chapter has a lot of information that may be making your head spin, choose one thing in one kind of yarn to start with. Gather the tools around you that you'll need—scrap yarn, needles, stitch markers, stickers, or tags (for you to tag your samples so you can repeat what you did on a larger scale)—and play with shape, color, or stitches. Allow yourself to play and explore, putting restrictions in place when you feel overwhelmed or unfocused.

The only way to gain experience and develop an instinct for how the fabric should look and feel, how stitch patterns can be transformed, and how colors work together, is to start. Right now. Every piece of knitting you do, no matter how small or how complex, teaches your eyes, your mind, and your hands. It teaches you what you like, what fabrics you prefer. It teaches you how to use colors you love but don't feel ready to wear. Living in the space of "What if . . . ?" and "What happens if I change this one tiny thing?" opens your knitting world wide open.

Pat-
terns

Tubulair

The main problem with most cabled scarves is that the fabric isn't generally reversible: They have a distinct RS and WS, making the scarf more difficult to wear than you might expect. This pattern uses ribbed cables that look exactly the same on both sides to make a fully reversible piece, identical on both sides.

For ease and—frankly—fun in knitting, the patterning is random. Once you've read the instructions and have got the hang of the basic cable turn—not a huge challenge—you can work this piece without needing to refer to the instructions. This makes it an ideal travel project, as you don't have to carry the pattern with you.

It's a straightforward rectangle worked from the short side, and it's fairly flexible in size. If you're short on yardage, you only need a piece about 40 inches (101.5 cm) long to create a good double-wrap cowl; additional yardage would allow you to make this into a more standard scarf. See Variations at the end of the pattern for suggestions on how to make it wider, to either accommodate a finer yarn, or to make it into a more dramatic piece.

Finished Measurements

With yarn and at gauge given, piece is 8 inches (20.5 cm) wide by 50 inches (127 cm) long, unstretched.

Yarn

Sweet Fiber Cashmerino Worsted [80% superwash Merino, 10% cashmere, 10% nylon; 200 yds (183 m) per 115 g skein]: 2 skeins Tea Leaves

Yarn Substitution

Look for worsted weight yarns with 3- or 4-ply construction and a touch of luxury. Superwash Merino with a small amount of cashmere, yak, camel, silk, or alpaca will give your yarn the qualities of this beautiful yarn.

Needles

US size 8 (5 mm) needles—straight or short circular

Or size needed to obtain gauge

Notions

Cable needle; stitch markers: 1 standard, 1 removable; 6-sided die and a coin—or a random-number generator/dice app for your phone; tapestry needle

Gauge

25 stitches and 32 rows = 4 inches (10 cm) in Stockinette stitch

Why This Yarn?

Sweet Fiber yarns are lovingly dyed in small batches by Melissa Thompson. Known for multi-layered tonal colorways, her Cashmerino Worsted was an obvious choice for the deep rib and cable scarf/cowl. Superwash Merino brings elasticity and bounce to this cushy yarn. Cashmere adds a touch of soft, downy luxury. And nylon strengthens it up so that you can count on the durability of this everyday-wear piece.

+

PATTERN NOTES

4-over-4 ribbed cable right: Slip next 4 sts to cable needle and hold to back of work; (k2, p2), then (k2, p2) from cable needle.

4-over-4 ribbed cable left: Slip next 4 sts to cable needle and hold to front of work; (k2, p2), then (k2, p2) from cable needle.

The piece is modeled with standard cast-on and bound-off edges, worn with a Jul closure. If you wish to join the edges, you can use the standard cast-on and bind-off methods and seam, or work a provisional cast-on and graft the seam closed (page 25).

CO 60 sts. See Pattern Notes for suggested methods.

SETUP ROW (WS): (K2, p2) 8 times, place standard stitch marker, [k2, p2] to end.

Read before you proceed:

There are 15 two-st knit ribs, designated as follows:

RS: Edge rib, (6 knit ribs), marker, center rib, (6 knit ribs), edge rib.

The marker helps you keep count and divides the first and second groups of sts.

The pattern is a 4-row repeat. In the first RS row, you turn a cable in the first set of 7 knit ribs (before the marker); in the next RS row, you turn a cable in the second set of 7 knit ribs (after the marker and center rib), as follows:

The position and direction of the cable turns are random. Roll the die or use your random number generator to get a number between 1 and 6—this determines which knit rib is the base of the cable. Toss your coin or use your random number generator to determine if the cable turns left or right—heads (or odd numbers) for right, tails (or even numbers) for left.

ROW 1 (RS): [K2, p2] across, working a 4-over-4 ribbed cable somewhere within the first group of knit ribs.

ROW 2: [K2, p2] across.

ROW 3: [K2, p2] across, working a 4-over-4 ribbed cable somewhere within the second group of knit ribs.

ROW 4: Repeat Row 2.

Work the 4-row pattern until you've just about used up the yarn, ending with row 4. Leave yourself about 5–6 times the length of the lower edge in yarn for binding off. BO in pattern, leaving a tail about 32 inches (81.5 cm) long.

Finishing

Wash to block and lay flat to dry—there's no need to stretch it out.

Once dry, join the edges as desired, and weave in ends.

Variations

You can take this basic concept in a number of different directions. Two ideas for making the piece wider:

1. Add More 6-Rib Groups

Casting on 116 stitches gives you four 6-rib groups separated by center ribs, like so:

Edge rib, (6-rib group), center rib, (6-rib group), center rib, (6-rib group), center rib, (6-rib group), edge rib.

Casting on 172 gives you six 6-rib groups separated by center ribs. The sample has an even number of groups, but you needn't stick with that. Adding 28 stitches gives you another 6-rib group and a central rib for dividing it from the neighboring group.

Keep the basic 4-row pattern, turning the cable in groups 1, 3, 5, etc., on row 1, and turning the cable in groups 2, 4, 6, etc., on row 3.

2. Keep the Same Basic Structure, but Expand the Size of the Groups

You'll need a die with more than 6 sides (or different random-number generator), of course. Casting on 76 stitches gives you 2 sets of 8-rib groups. Every additional 8 stitches adds a rib to each group.

If you're using actual dice, then you'll want the number of ribs in a group to be even, e.g., 6, 8, 10, 12, 16, 20.

For a scarf structured like the sample, with two groups of stitches, calculate the stitch count as follows:

4 for edge rib, 4 times the number of sides on your die, 4 for center rib, 4 times the number of sides on your die, 4 for edge rib.

This works out to: 12 + (8 × number of sides on the die).

For example, if you've got a 6-sided die, it's 12 + (8 × 6) = 60 stitches

For example, if you've got a 12-sided die, it's 12 + (8 × 12) = 108 stitches

If you're working a left-leaning cable, work in ribbing pattern up to the selected knit rib. The following 4 stitches, the designated knit rib, are the ones that are slipped to and then worked off the cable needle.

If you're working a right-leaning cable, work in ribbing pattern to 4 *stitches before* the selected knit rib. The following 4 stitches are slipped to the cable needle, and the designated knit rib is worked first.

If you are working 1 Right in the first group, you'll be working a cable at the start of the row. If you are working 6 Left in the second group, you'll be working a cable at the end of the row. In either case, make sure that the yarn is at the back before you start knitting.

If you're working 1 Right in the second group, or 6 Left in the first group, you'll be crossing over the center knit rib. Move and replace the marker as required.

Breaking the rules: There are four cable turns, all involving the edge or center ribs, that will never be generated by the die roll/coin-toss method. They are: turning the first edge rib left, turning the last edge rib right, and turning the center rib either left or right. Once in a while, work one of those turns, too.

The most challenging part of this pattern is keeping track of the RS and the WS. Since the cables are reversible, it's pretty difficult to tell which side you're on. Place a removable stitch marker in the fabric near the start of the RS rows.

Screw-in Closures

These leather closures are screwed into this narrow, rectangular shawl to turn it into an infinity cowl. Wear it loose like this, or wrap around twice for a snug cowl. We like the closures off to one side, as it shows off the cables in the center of the cowl.

Closures by Jul Designs.

Travelogue

The Travelogue shawl records your travels. The idea is simple: Pick up single skeins of yarn on your next trip; choose stitch patterns that remind you of places, architecture, or landscapes that you've seen; and knit as you go. This shawl is based on a trip to Seattle, where Kim spent a week teaching at Seattle Yarn. She chose these yarns because they reminded her of colors in the Puget Sound area: rusty ships, the moody ocean, mountains, gardens overrun with spring greenery, and the slightly gray blue sky. The stitch patterns she's used remind her of textures that surrounded her there. The end result is a shawl that reminds her of friends, beautiful landscapes, and a wonderful week away.

This is a project ripe for experimentation. Change the weight of yarn. Change the stitch patterns. Make it your own! Guidelines are included to let you know what to be aware of when you do decide to make changes.

Finished Measurements

With yarn and at gauge given, piece is 22 inches (56 cm) at deepest point by 68 inches (172.5 cm) wide.

Yarn

Cedar House Yarns Sprig Sport [100% superwash Merino; 328 yds (300 m) per 100 g (3½ oz) skein]: 1 skein each Winesap (MC) and Old Car (CC1)

The Dye Project Ecola Sport [85% Merino, 15% silk; 320 yds (292 m) per 100 g (3½ oz) skein]: 1 skein each Crazy Daisy (CC2) and Tuxedo (CC3)

Round Mountain Fibers Willow [100% superwash Merino; 250 yds (228 m) per 100 g (3½ oz) skein]: 1 skein Pumpkinseed (CC4)

Yarn Substitution

Anything goes! Choose yarn based on how it will remind you of your trip. Kim chose sport- and DK-weight yarns, but you could choose fingering weight or worsted weight and adjust your needle size for the yarns you choose. In her case, she chose a needle one size larger than the recommended size.

Needles

US size 6 (4 mm) needles—32 inch (81 cm) long or longer circular

Or size needed to obtain gauge

Notions

Stitch markers; stitch holder or scrap yarn; blocking pins; blocking wires (optional); tapestry needle

Gauge

22 stitches and 32 rows = 4 inches (10 cm) in Stockinette stitch

---

Why This Yarn?

For this shawl Kim chose two skeins of Sprig Sport from Cedar House Yarns, two skeins of Ecola Sport from The Dye Project, and one skein of Willow, a DK-weight yarn from Round Mountain Fibers. In this case color won out over fiber content, and how the yarn felt won out over everything else. Kim knew the yarns would be a little different in weight and how they behaved as fabric, but for this particular project— essentially a knitted collage—it doesn't matter. Any differences in gauge and texture will add to the individuality of your project.

+

PATTERN NOTES

1/1 LC: Leaving first st on left-hand needle, knit through second st tbl; bring needle around to the front and knit into the front of the first st, and slip both off the needle.

1/1 RC: Skip first st and knit into the front of the second st; leaving both on the needle, knit into the front of the first st, and slip both off the needle.

DS: Create a double stitch with the German short-row method (see "Techniques," page 33). Bring the yarn to the front, slip the next stitch purlwise, and pull the yarn up in front and over to the back of the needle, so that the two legs of the stitch are up on the needle and the yarn is in position to work the following stitch.

Due to the short rows and pick-up rows in this piece, sometimes row 1 of a section or stitch pattern will be a RS row and sometimes it will be a WS row; pay close attention to the directions to ensure you are on the correct side.

Stitch Patterns

Work the following st patterns from charts or written patterns, as you prefer.

Gardens Pattern 1

(multiple of 4 sts + 2)

ROW 1 (RS): K1, yo, ssk, k2tog, [yo twice, ssk, k2tog] to last st, yo, k1.

ROW 2: P1, k1, [p2, (k1, k1 tbl) into double yo] to last 4 sts, p2, k1, p1.

ROW 3: K1, p1, 1/1 RC, [p2, 1/1 RC] to last 2 sts, p1, k1.

ROW 4: P1, k1, [p2, k2] to last 2 sts, p2, k1, p1.

ROW 5: K1, k2tog, yo twice, [ssk, k2tog, yo twice] to last 3 sts, ssk, k1.

ROW 6: P2, [(k1, k1 tbl) into double yo, p2] to last 4 sts, (k1, k1 tbl) into double yo, p2.

ROW 7: K2, p2, [k2, 1/1 RC, p2] to last 2 sts, k2.

ROW 8: P2, [k2, p2] to last 4 sts, k2, p2.

Repeat Rows 1–8 for Gardens Pattern 1.

Gardens Pattern 2

(multiple of 4 sts + 2)

ROW 1 (RS): K1, yo, ssk, k2tog, [yo twice, ssk, k2tog] to last st, yo, k1.

ROW 2: P1, k1, [p2, (k1, k1 tbl) into double yo] to last 4 sts, p2, k1, p1.

ROW 3: K1, p1, k2, [p2, k2] to last 2 sts, p1, k1.

ROW 4: P1, k1, [p2, k2] to last 4 sts, p2, k1, p1.

ROW 5: K1, p1, 1/1 RC, [p2, 1/1 RC] to last 2 sts, p1, k1.

ROW 6: P1, k1, [p2, k2] to last 4 sts, p2, k1, p1.

ROW 7: K1, p1, k2, [p2, k2] to last 2 sts, p1, k1.

ROW 8: P1, k1, [p2, k2] to last 4 sts, p2, k1, p1.

ROW 9: K1, [k2tog, yo twice, ssk] to last st, k1.

ROW 10: P2, [(k1, k1 tbl) into double yo, p2] to end.

ROW 11: [K2, p2] to last 2 sts, k2.

ROW 12: [P2, k2] to last 2 sts, p2.

ROW 13: K2, p2, [1/1 RC, p2] to last 2 sts, k2.

ROW 14: Repeat row 12.

ROWS 15 AND 16: Repeat Rows 11 and 12.

Repeat Rows 1–16 for Gardens Pattern 2.

Forest Pattern

(panel of 25 sts)

ROW 1 (RS): K1, p3, k2, p2, k2, p4, k2, p3, k3, p2, k1.

ROW 2: P1, k2, p3, k3, p2, k4, p2, k2, p2, k3, p1.

ROW 3: K1, p2, 1/1 RC, k1, p2, k2, p4, k1, 1/1 LC, p2, k3, p2, k1.

ROW 4: P1, (k2, p3) twice, k4, p2, k2, p3, k2, p1.

ROW 5: K1, p1, 1/1 RC, k2, p2, k2, p4, k2, 1/1 LC, p1, k3, p2, k1.

ROW 6: P1, k2, p3, k1, p1, k1, p2, k4, p2, k2, p2, (k1, p1) twice.

ROW 7: K1, 1/1 RC, p1, k1, 1/1 LC, p1, k2, p3, 1/1 RC, (k1, p1) twice, k3, p2, k1.

ROW 8: P1, k2, p3, k1, p1, k1, p3, k3, p2, k1, p3, k3, p1.

ROW 9: K1, p3, k2, 1/1 LC, k2, p2, 1/1 RC, k2, p3, k3, p2, k1.

ROW 10: P1, k2, p3, k3, p2, k1, p1, (k2, p2) twice, k3, p1.

ROW 11: K1, p3, k2, p2, k2, p1, 1/1 RC, p1, k2, p3, k3, p2, k1.

ROW 12: P1, k2, p3, k3, p2, k2, p1, k1, p2, k2, p2, k3, p1.

ROW 13: K1, p3, k2, p2, k2, 1/1 RC, p2, k2, p3, k3, p2, k1.

ROW 14: Repeat Row 2.

ROW 15: K1, p3, k2, p2, k2, p4, k2, p3, 1/1 RC, k1, p2, k1.

ROW 16: Repeat Row 2.

ROW 17: K1, p2, 1/1 RC, k1, p2, k2, p4, k2, p2, 1/1 RC, k2, p2, k1.

ROW 18: P1, k2, p4, k2, p2, k4, p2, k2, p3, k2, p1.

ROW 19: K1, p1, 1/1 RC, k2, p2, k1, 1/1 LC, p3, k2, p1, 1/1 RC, k3, p2, k1.

ROW 20: P1, k2, p3, k1, p1, k1, p2, k3, p3, k2, p2, (k1, p1) twice.

ROW 21: (K1, p1) twice, k2, p2, k2, 1/1 LC, p2, k2, 1/1 RC, p1, k3, p2, k1.

ROW 22: P1, k2, p3, k3, p2, k2, p1, k1, p2, k2, p2, (k1, p1) twice.

ROW 23: K1, p3, k2, p2, k2, p1, 1/1 LC, p1, k2, p3, k2, 1/1 LC, p1, k1.

ROW 24: P1, k1, p4, k3, p2, k4, p2, k2, p2, k3, p1.

ROW 25: K1, p3, k2, p1, 1/1 RC, k1, p4, k2, p2, 1/1 RC, k2, 1/1 LC, k1.

ROW 26: P1, k2, p4, k2, p2, k4, p3, k1, p2, k3, p1.

ROW 27: K1, p3, k2, 1/1 RC, k2, p4, k2, p1, 1/1 RC, k3, p2, k1.

ROW 28: P1, k2, p3, k1, p1, k1, p2, k4, p2, k2, p2, k3, p1.

ROW 29: K1, p3, k2, p2, k2, p4, k2, p1, k1, p1, k3, p2, k1.

ROW 30: Repeat Row 28.

Repeat Rows 1–30 for Forest Pattern.

Bridges Pattern

(multiple of 20 sts + 6)

Note: Pattern begins with a WS row.

ROW 1 (WS): K3, [k5, p3, k2, p5, k3, p2] to last 3 sts, k3.

ROW 2: K3, [k1, p3, k5, p2, k3, p5, k1] to last 3 sts, k3.

ROW 3: K3, [p2, k5, p3, k2, p5, k3] to last 3 sts k3.

ROW 4: K3, [p2, k5, p2, k3, p5, k2, p1] to last 3 sts, k3.

ROW 5: K3, [k2, p2, k5, p3, k2, p5, k1] to last 3 sts, k3.

ROW 6: K3, [k5, p2, k3, p5, k2, p3] to last 3 sts, k3.

ROW 7: K3, [p1, k3, p2, k5, p3, k2, p4] to last 3 sts, k3.

ROW 8: K3, [k3, p2, k3, p5, k2, p3, k2] to last 3 sts, k3.

ROW 9: K3, [p3, k3, p2, k5, p3, k2, p2] to last 3 sts, k3.

ROWS 10-18: Repeat Rows 1–9.

ROW 19: K3, [k1, p2, k3, p5, k2, p3, k4] to last 3 sts, k3.

ROW 20: K3, [p5, k3, p2, k5, p3, k2] to last 3 sts, k3.

ROW 21: K3, [p1, k3, p5, k2, p3, k5, p1] to last 3 sts, k3.

ROW 22: K3, [k2, p5, k3, p2, k5, p3] to last 3 sts, k3.

Repeat Rows 1–22 for Bridges Pattern.

Waves Pattern

(multiple of 6 sts)

ROW 1 (RS): K3, [k3, k2tog, yo, k1] to last 3 sts, k3.

ROW 2: K3, [p2, yo, p2tog, p2] to last 3 sts, k3.

ROW 3: K3, [k1, k2tog, yo, k3] to last 3 sts, k3.

ROW 4: K3, [p4, yo, p2tog] to last 3 sts, k3.

ROW 5: K3, [k1, yo, ssk, k3] to last 3 sts, k3.

ROW 6: K3, [p2, ssp, yo, p2] to last 3 sts, k3.

ROW 7: K3, [k3, yo, ssk, k1] to last 3 sts, k3.

ROW 8: K3, [ssp, yo, p4] to last 3 sts, k3.

Part A: Pine Tree (Mitered Square Medallion)

With MC, CO 1 st.

SETUP ROW 1 (RS): Kfbf. 3 sts.

SETUP ROW 2: K1, sl1 wyif, pm, k1.

ROW 1 (RS): K to marker, M1R, sm, k1, M1L, k to end. 5 sts.

ROW 2: K to 1 st before marker, s1 wyif, k to end.

ROW 3: K to marker, M1R, sm, k1, M1L, k to end. 7 sts.

ROW 4: K to 1 st before marker, s1 wyif, k to end.

ROW 5: K to marker, M1R, sm, k1, M1L, k to end. 2 sts increased.

ROW 6: K1, p to 1 st before marker, sl1 wyif, p to last st, k1.

ROW 7: K to marker, M1R, sm, k1, M1L, k to end. 2 sts increased.

ROW 8: K to 1 st before marker, sl1 wyif, k to end.

Repeat Rows 5–8 once more, then repeat Rows 5 and 6 once more. 17 sts.

Alternating Branches:

ROW 1 (RS): K to marker, M1R, sm, k1, M1L, k to end. 2 sts increased.

ROW 2: K to 1 st before marker, sl1 wyif, p to last st, k1.

ROWS 3, 5, 7, 9, AND 11: K to marker, M1R, sm, k1, M1L, k to end.

ROWS 4 AND 8: K1, p to 1 st before marker, sl1 wyif, k to end.

ROW 6: K to 1 st before marker, sl1 wyif, p to last st, k1.

ROW 10: K to 1 st before marker, sl1 wyif, k to end.

+

HOW TO ADJUST FOR SIZE AND STITCH PATTERNS

1 The length of the center panel will determine the wingspan of your final shawl. To make it wider, extend Parts B and C. To make the wingspan shorter, decrease the height of Parts B and C.

2 The height of all additional stripes will determine the depth of the shawl. To make a shallower shawl, decrease the height of the stripes by decreasing the number of pattern rows worked. To make a deeper shawl, increase the height of the stripes by increasing the number of pattern rows worked.

3 To replace the pattern's stitch patterns with those of your choice, simply make sure that the stitch counts for each part allow for full repeats of the chosen stitch pattern. You can cast on or bind off stitches to make sure this happens.

NOTES FOR SUBSTITUTION

As noted in the recipe for a mitered-square shawl (page 13), this type of square needs to be 100% Garter stitch in order to be a true square. In this shawl, Kim compromised the shape in order to get the motif she wanted. As a result, the medallion is not quite square.

Whatever you choose to do with this centerpiece, it will dictate how wide this center panel is. You can control how wide or narrow the panel is by making the mitered motif smaller (narrower panel) or larger (wider panel).

ROW 12: K to 1 st before marker, sl1 wyif, p to last st, k1. 29 sts.

Repeat Rows 3–12 twice more. 49 sts.

Place first 24 sts on a st holder or scrap yarn; do not turn. 25 sts.

Cut MC, leaving a tail of about 4 inches (10 cm).

Part B: Forest

With RS facing, join CC1 and knit across the remaining 25 live sts.

SETUP ROW (WS): P1, k2, p3, k3, p2, k4, p2, k2, p2, k3, p1.

NEXT ROW: Work Forest Pattern to end.

Work as set until you have worked all 30 rows of Forest Pattern 7 times, then work row 1 once more.

Short-row Section:

Work German short rows in Garter stitch, as follows (see "Techniques," page 33):

SHORT ROW 1 (RS): K to last 5 sts, turn.

SHORT ROW 2: DS, k to end.

SHORT ROW 3: Knit to 5 sts before previous DS, turn.

SHORT ROW 4: DS, knit to end.

SHORT ROWS 5–8: Repeat Short Rows 3 and 4 twice more.

Knit 3 rows, knitting into both legs of DSs as you come to them.

BO all sts purlwise.

Part C: Gardens

Turn work so that Part B is at the bottom of work, and Part A is at the top.

With RS facing, and starting at the top right corner of Part A, join CC2 and pick up and knit 26 sts along the top edge.

Purl 1 row.

NEXT ROW (RS): Work Gardens Pattern 1, working repeat 5 times.

Work as set until you have worked all 8 rows of Gardens Pattern 1 three times.

NEXT ROW (RS): Work Gardens Pattern 2, working repeat 5 times.

Work as set until you have worked all 16 rows of Gardens Pattern 2 three times.

Work Gardens Pattern 1 three more times.

Knit 4 rows.

BO all sts purlwise.

Part D: Blocks

Hold piece with RS facing and rotate it clockwise so that Part C is at the right of the work and Part B is at the left. Use a removable marker to mark a spot on the edge of the panel 1½ inches (4 cm) from the bind-off edge of Part C.

Starting at this just-placed marker, join CC3 and pick up and knit 2 sts for every 3 rows along the side edge of Part C, knit across the held sts from Part A, pick up and knit 2 sts for every 3 rows along the side edge of Part B, and CO 10 sts at the end of row. The exact st count is not important, but must be a multiple of 4 sts + 6 to accommodate the pattern. We picked up 212 sts and CO 10 sts for a total of 222 sts for the sample. Remove marker.

NEXT ROW (WS): Knit across, placing markers at the following points (see Schematic):

Marker AA about one-third of the way along the edge of Part B. The number of sts between the beginning of pick-up and Marker AA should be a multiple of 4 sts + 3.

Marker BB about two-thirds of the way along the edge of Part B. The number of sts between Markers AA and BB should be a multiple of 4 sts.

Marker CC at the intersection of Part B and Part A. The number of sts between Markers BB and CC should be a multiple of 4 sts.

Straight Section:

ROW 1 (RS): K3, [k3, p1] to last 3 sts, k3.

ROW 2: K3, [k1, p3] to last 3 sts, k3.

Work row 1 once more.

Short-row Section:

SHORT ROW 1 (WS): Work as set to Marker AA, turn; leave marker in place.

SHORT ROW 2: DS, work as set to end.

SHORT ROW 3: Work as set to Marker BB, purling into both sts of DS as you come to it, turn; leave marker in place.

SHORT ROW 4: DS, work as set to end.

SHORT ROW 5: Work as set to Marker CC, purling into both sts of DS as you come to it, turn; leave marker in place.

SHORT ROW 6: DS, work as set to end.

Purling into both sts of remaining DS as you come to it, repeat Row 2 of Straight Section once, Rows 1 and 2 once, then Row 1 once more.

Repeat Short-row Section once.

Repeat row 2 of Straight Section once, then Rows 1 and 2 once, removing markers on final row.

Cut CC3.

Part E: Garter Ridge

With RS facing, join CC4 and k across sts from Part D.

Knit 3 more rows.

Cut CC4.

Part F: Bridges

With MC, CO 16 sts using long-tail method or cast-on of your choice; with RS facing, continuing with yarn attached to these cast-on sts (cast-on sts are on right-hand needle), k across sts from Part E, then CO 8 sts using backwards loop method (page 24). The exact st count is not important, but must be a multiple of 20 sts + 6 to accommodate the pattern. If st count is not a multiple of 20 sts + 6, adjust the number of sts cast on at the end to get to the correct multiple.

NEXT ROW (WS): Work Bridges Pattern to end.

Work as set until you have worked all 22 rows of Bridges Pattern.

LAST ROW (WS): BO 14 sts, k to end.

Cut MC.

Part G: Garter Ridge

With RS facing and CC2, CO 6, 8, or 10 sts using long-tail method or cast-on of your choice at start of row, then k across sts from Part F, making sure that the final st count is a multiple of 6 sts.

Knit 3 more rows.

Cut CC2.

Part H: Cliffs

With RS facing, join CC1 and work across sts from Part G as follows:

ROW 1 (RS): K3, [k3, p3] to last 3 sts, k3.

ROWS 2 AND 3: Repeat row 1.

ROWS 4–6: K3, [p3, k3] to last 3 sts, k3.

Repeat Rows 1–6 once more, then repeat Rows 1–3 again.

Knit 5 rows.

BO all sts.

Cut yarn.

Turn work 180 degrees so that opposite edge of center panel is facing.

Part I: Garter Ridge

With CC3, CO 5 sts using long-tail method or cast-on of your choice; with RS facing, continuing with yarn attached to these cast-on sts (cast-on sts are on right-hand needle), and starting at top right corner of center panel, pick up and knit 2 sts for every 3 rows along side edges of Parts B, A, and C, ending 1 inch (2.5 cm) from end of center panel. The exact st count is not important, but must be a multiple of 6 sts.

Knit 3 rows.

Cut CC3.

Part J: Ships and Nets

ROW 1 (RS): With RS of Part I facing, join CC4 and k across, placing markers at the following points:

Marker DD at the intersection of Part A and Part B, and Marker EE halfway along the edge of Part B.

ROW 2: Knit.

ROW 3: K3, [yo, k2tog] to last 3 sts, k3.

SHORT ROW 4: K to Marker DD, turn; leave marker in place.

SHORT ROW 5: DS, k to end.

ROW 6: K across, knitting into both legs of DS as you come to it.

ROW 7: K3, [yo, k2tog] to last 3 sts, k3.

ROWS 8 AND 9: Knit.

SHORT ROW 10: K to Marker EE, turn; leave marker in place.

SHORT ROW 11: DS, [yo, k2tog] to last 3 sts, k3.

ROWS 12 AND 13: K across, knitting both legs of remaining DS as you come to it.

Knit 1 row.

BO 10 sts.

Cut CC4.

Part K: Garter Ridge

With RS facing, join MC and k across sts from Part J, CO 10 sts.

Knit 3 more rows.

Cut MC.

Part L: Waves

NEXT ROW (RS): Work Waves Pattern across.

Work as set until you've worked all 4 rows of Waves Pattern.

Knit 4 rows.

BO all sts.

Finishing

Block by soaking with a wool-wash, roll in towel, and/or use spin cycle to wring out most of the moisture; lay flat to dry, using pins or blocking wires to stretch the shawl and open up the stitch patterns.

Once dry, weave in ends.

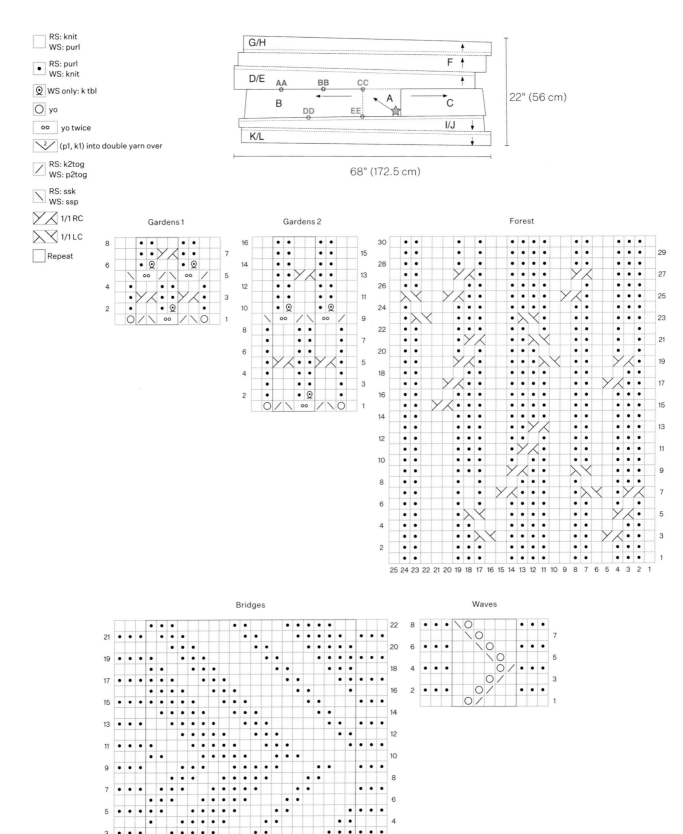

Ancoats

This design uses the side-to-side symmetrical triangle shape (page 16), adding a fairly complex but rewarding lace-stitch pattern. Unlike in many triangular shawls, the bulk of the patterning is placed along the top edge for a distinctive look. The edge of the pattern is scalloped, making blocking much easier. It's easily adjusted to suit the yardage you have or the finished size you want. The naturally dyed yarn is somewhere between a lace weight and a light fingering, making for a delicate and fine piece.

Finished Measurements

With yarn and at gauge given, piece is 13 inches (33 cm) deep by 74 inches (188 cm) wide.

Yarn

Sincere Sheep Cormo Fingering [100% domestic Cormo wool; 500 yds (457 m)]: 1 skein Quercus

Needles

US size 6 (4 mm) needles—straight or circular

Or size needed to obtain gauge

Notions

Markers—two ring-style; blocking pins; tapestry needle; digital scale (optional)

Gauge:

25 stitches and 32 rows = 4 inches (10 cm) in Garter stitch, after blocking

Shawl Cuffs and Belts

Wrap a shawl around your shoulders and secure in place with a shawl cuff or belt. We've placed the cuff at the back of one shoulder, with long ends hanging down. You could also place it in front or wrapped around once, securing shorter ends together.

Shawl cuffs and belts are not only a great way to secure your shawl while you're wearing it, they can also extend the size of smaller shawls. Connect two shawls together by securing one end of each with a shawl belt, and wrap the combined shawl around you.

Shawl belt by Purl & Hank.

Why This Yarn?

Brooke Sinnes of Sincere Sheep naturally dyes breed-specific wool yarns in a palette of colors rarely seen in natural dyes. Her Cormo yarns are legendary, and the fingering weight is what we've chosen for this shawl. The yarn is light, with lots of bounce and elasticity. The yarn has enough twist to work with the lace pattern, but enough elasticity to plump up the Garter stitch and make a cozy, cushy shawl you'll want to wear all the time.

Section 1: First Increases

CO 2 sts.

Work Section 1 Chart. 31 sts when chart is complete.

Section 2—Pattern Transition Increases

Work Section 2 Chart, placing a marker in the spot indicated on Row 1. 45 sts when chart is complete.

Because the st count changes in the charted pattern, in addition to the shawl shaping increases at the start of the RS rows, the marker is crucial to help you keep track.

Section 3: Main Increase Section

Work Main Increase Section Chart.

On Row 1, place a second marker in the spot indicated, just after the patterned section at the start of the row. The other marker remains in place (to the left of the red box in the charts) and designates the end of the plain section and the start of the second patterned section.

Work Rows 1–12 until you've used up a little less than half your available yarn, or until the shawl is half your desired length.

Note: As you work the increases, the number of sts between the markers will grow. On Rows 1, 5, and 9 of the chart, work the increases after the first marker as shown, and then work Garter stitch to the next marker. On the remaining rows, work Garter stitch between the markers.

Section 4: Main Decrease Section

Work Main Decrease Section Chart.

Work Rows 1–12 until 3 sts remain between the markers, ending with Row 12. 45 sts.

Note: As you work the decreases, the number of sts between the markers will reduce. On Rows 3, 7, and 11 of the chart, work the decreases after the first marker as shown, and then work Garter stitch to the next marker. On the remaining rows, work Garter stitch between the markers.

Section 5: Pattern Transition Decreases

Work Rows 1–48 of Section 5 Chart, removing the first marker as you work Row 1, and removing the remaining marker as you work Row 48. 32 sts when chart is complete.

Section 6: Final Decreases

Work Rows 1–74 of Section 6 Chart. 2 sts when chart is complete. BO sts.

Finishing

Block by soaking with a wool-wash, roll in towel, and/or use spin cycle to wring out most of the moisture; lay flat to dry. Stretch and use pins to catch the scallops on both the top and bottom edges.

Once dry, weave in ends.

Key

- ☐ RS: knit / WS: purl
- • RS: purl / WS: knit
- O yo
- ⋎ M1R
- ╱ k2tog
- ╲ ssk
- ⋀ CDD
- ⋏ sssk
- ▨ no stitch
- ⌄ (k1, p1, k1) into double yarnover
- ☐ Work even in garter stitch
- ▯ Marker position

Main Increase Section

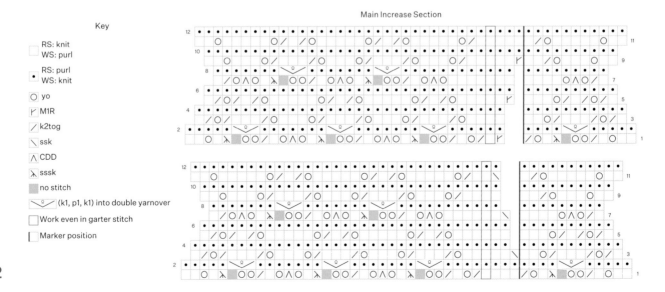

Section 2

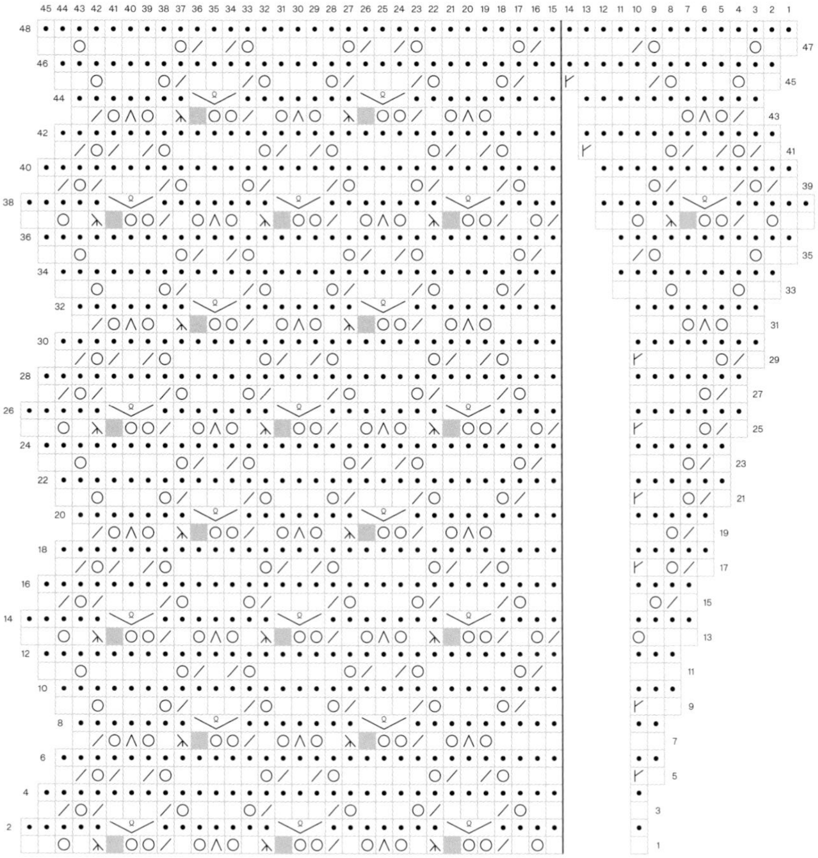

Section 1

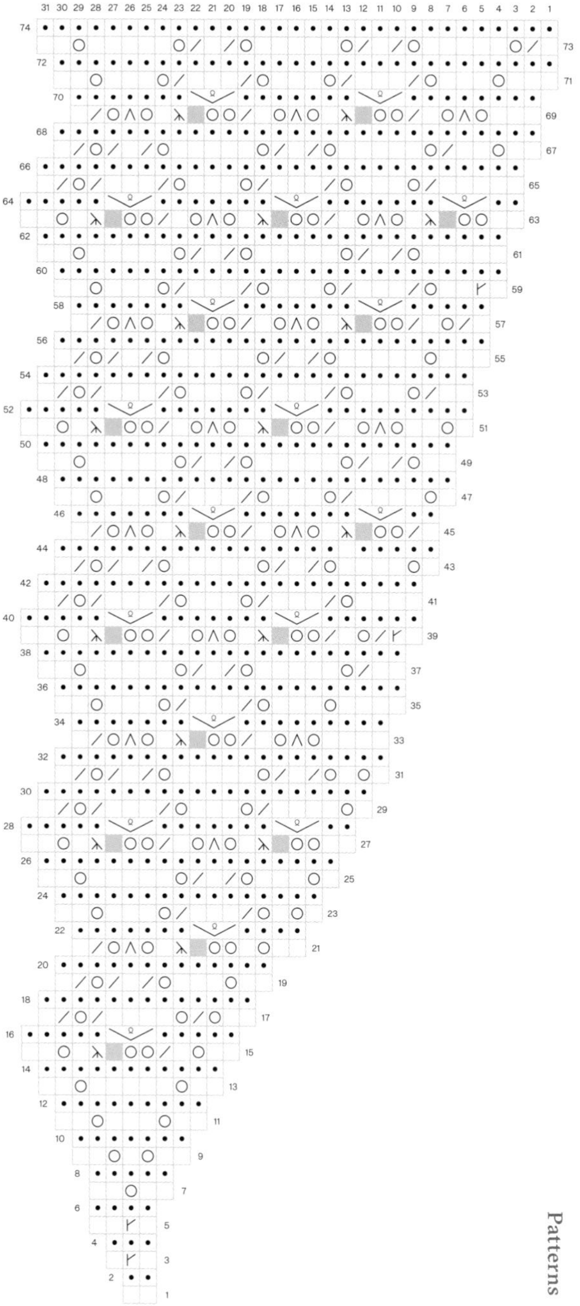

Key

RS: knit
WS: purl

RS: purl
WS: knit

O yo

ʁ m1r

╱ k2tog

∧ CDD

λ sssk

⌄ (K1, p1, k1) into double yarnover

marker position

no stitch

Section 5

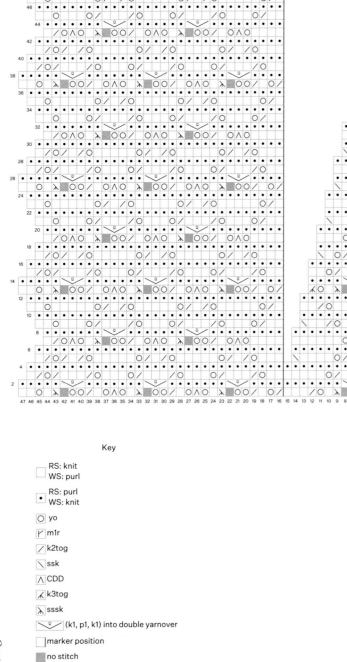

Section 6

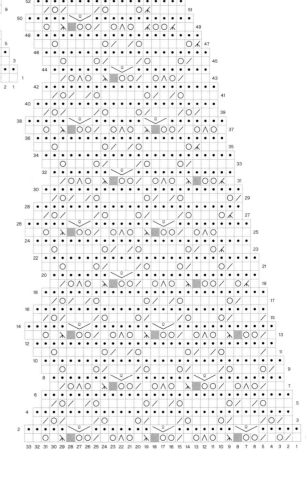

Key

	RS: knit WS: purl
•	RS: purl WS: knit
O	yo
⋎	m1r
/	k2tog
\	ssk
∧	CDD
⊀	k3tog
⋌	sssk
⌣	(k1, p1, k1) into double yarnover
	marker position
▪	no stitch

Flexture

Sideways triangles (page 16) are a joy to wear. They wrap around your neck and shoulders with lots of coverage but not a lot of bulk. Stripes are addictive to knit, pushing you forward to knit the next one. Add some bias shaping in the mix to create fault lines and the illusion of folds, and you have Flexture.

Finished Measurements

With yarn and at gauge given, piece is 26 inches (66 cm) at deepest point by 76 inches (193 cm) wide.

Yarn Substitution:

Drape is the primary quality needed for the body of this shawl. The high level of silk content takes care of that in the Gobsmacked gradient, but fibers like linen, bamboo, and rayon will work as well.

If you can't find a long gradient, consider putting together your own using individual skeins of yarn in colors that blend well into each other, along with accent colors for the stripes (see "Breaking the Rules," page 110). The stripes make excellent break points for changing colors.

Yarn

Gobsmacked Yarn Merino/Silk DK Double [50% superwash Merino, 50% silk; 462 yds (422 m) per 200 g (7 oz) cake]: 1 cake; sample uses a custom color (MC)

Murky Depths Dyeworks Triton MCN DK [80% superwash Merino, 10% cashmere, 10% nylon; 230 yds (210 m) per 100 g (3½ oz) skein]: 1 skein each No. 9 (CC1), Mysore Silk (CC2), Picante (CC3), and Tempest (CC4)

Needles

US size 7 (4.5 mm) needle—32 inches (81 cm) or longer circular

Or size needed to obtain gauge

Notions

Stitch markers; tapestry needle

Gauge

20 stitches and 30 rows = 4 inches (10 cm) in Stockinette stitch

Why This Yarn?

For the sideways triangle, Kim wanted to work with Marit Munson of Gobsmacked Yarn and Debbie Bresler of Murky Depths Dyeworks: two dyers whose work stands beautifully on its own, but also complements each other. The Merino/Silk DK from Gobsmacked Yarn has a beautiful sheen and drapes like a dream. The Triton MCN DK from Murky Depths has a matte finish that contrasts perfectly with the shiny Merino/Silk. Both bases have a four-ply construction, which makes the stitches play well together without causing changes in gauge or the structure of the shawl.

Color was important in choosing these yarns. Kim chose colors from Murky Depths that were both close in value and hue, and very different in value and hue from various points in the Gobsmacked gradient. Gobsmacked gradients are one of a kind, so start with one you love and add accent colors from there.

+

PATTERN NOTES

DS: Create a double stitch with the German short-row method (page 33). Bring the yarn to the front, slip the next stitch purlwise, and pull the yarn up in front and over to the back of the needle, so that the two legs of the stitch are up on the needle and the yarn is in position to work the following stitch.

+

IMPORTANT—PLEASE READ BEFORE BEGINNING.

Each section has the same structure: setup rows are worked, placing markers to divide up pattern sections. Once the markers are in position, you'll work the same RS pattern row throughout each section; the pattern row will change from section to section.

In the different sections, you'll be changing colors and varying the fabric by working either a WS Stockinette row or a WS Garter row.

All WS Stockinette rows are worked as follows: K2, p to last 2 sts, k2.

All WS Garter rows are worked as follows: Knit.

With MC, CO 3 sts.

Bias Section 1

ROW 1 (WS): Knit.

ROW 2: (K1, M1Z) twice, k1. 5 sts.

ROW 3: K2, p1, k2.

ROW 4: (K1, M1Z) twice, k2tog, k1. 6 sts.

ROW 5: K2, p to last 2 sts, k2.

ROW 6: (K1, M1Z) twice, k to last 3 sts, k2tog, k1. 1 st increased.

Repeat Rows 5 and 6 twenty-three more times, then repeat row 5 once more. 30 sts.

Spine 1

SETUP ROW 1 (RS): K1, M1Z, k1, pm, M1Z, k to last 3 sts, k2tog, k1. 31 sts.

SETUP ROW 2: K2, p to last 2 sts, k2.

PATTERN ROW 1 (RS): K1, M1Z, k to marker, sm, M1Z, k to last 3 sts, k2tog, k1. 1 st increased.

Work a WS Stockinette row.

Repeat the last 2 rows once more. 33 sts.

With CC1, work (Pattern row 1 followed by a WS Garter row) twice. 35 sts.

With MC, work Pattern row 1 followed by a WS Garter row. 36 sts.

With CC1, work Pattern row 1 followed by a WS Garter row. 37 sts.

Bias Section 2

SETUP ROW 1 (RS): With MC, k1, M1Z, ssk, k1, M1Z, pm, k to next marker, sm, M1Z, k to last 3 sts, k2tog, k1. 38 sts.

SETUP ROW 2: K2, p to last 2 sts, k2.

PATTERN ROW 2 (RS): K1, M1Z, ssk, k to marker, M1Z, sm, work as set to end. 1 st increased.

Work a WS Stockinette row.

Repeat the last 2 rows 8 more times. 47 sts.

With CC1, work (Pattern row 2 followed by a WS Garter row) twice. 49 sts.

With MC, work Pattern row 2 followed by a WS Stockinette row. 50 sts.

Spine 2

SETUP ROW 1 (RS): K1, M1Z, pm, ssk, k to marker, M1Z, sm, work as set to end. 51 sts.

SETUP ROW 2: K2, p to last 2 sts, k2.

SETUP ROW 3: K1, M1Z, pm, k1, sm, work as set to end. 52 sts.

SETUP ROW 4: K2, p to last 2 sts, k2.

PATTERN ROW 3 (RS): K1, M1Z, k to marker, sm, work as set to end. 1 st increased.

Work a WS Stockinette row.

With CC1, work Pattern row 3 followed by a WS Garter row. 54 sts.

With MC, work Pattern row 3 followed by a WS Stockinette row. 55 sts.

Bias Section 3

PATTERN ROW 4 (RS): K1, M1Z, k1, M1Z, k to 2 sts before marker, k2tog, sm, work as set to end. 1 st increased.

Work a WS Stockinette row.

With CC1, work Pattern row 4 followed by a WS Garter row. 57 sts.

With MC, work (Pattern row 4 followed by a WS Stockinette row) 46 times. 103 sts.

With CC1, work Pattern row 4 followed by a WS Garter row. 104 sts.

With MC, work Pattern row 4 followed by a WS Stockinette row. 105 sts

Spine 3

SETUP ROW 1 (RS): K1, M1Z, pm, k1, pm, M1Z, k to 2 sts before marker, k2tog, sm, work as set to end. 106 sts.

SETUP ROW 2: K2, p to last 2 sts, k2.

PATTERN ROW 5 (RS): K1, M1Z, k to marker, sm, k1, sm, work as set to end. 1 st increased.

Work a WS Stockinette row.

Repeat the last 2 rows twice more. 109 sts.

Bias Section 4

PATTERN ROW 6 (RS): K1, M1Z, ssk, k to marker, M1Z, sm, work as set to end. 1 st increased.

Work a WS Stockinette row.

Repeat the last 2 rows twice more. 112 sts.

With CC1, work Pattern row 6 followed by a WS Garter row. 113 sts

With MC, work (Pattern row 6 followed by a WS Stockinette row) 3 times. 116 sts.

With CC1, work (Pattern row 6 followed by a WS Garter row) 3 times. 119 sts.

With MC, work Pattern row 6 followed by a WS Stockinette row. 120 sts.

With CC1, work Pattern row 6 followed by a WS Garter row. 121 sts.

Spine 4

SETUP ROW 1 (RS): With MC, k1, M1Z, pm, ssk, k to marker, M1Z, sm, work as set to end. 122 sts.

SETUP ROW 2: K2, p to last 2 sts, k2.

PATTERN ROW 7 (RS): K1, M1Z, k to marker, sm, work as set to end. 1 st increased.

Work a WS Stockinette row.

Repeat the last 2 rows 4 more times. 127 sts.

Bias Section 5

SETUP ROW 1 (RS): With CC2, k1, M1Z, k1, M1Z, k2tog, pm, k to marker, sm, work as set to end. 128 sts.

Work a WS Garter row.

PATTERN ROW 8 (RS): With MC, k1, M1Z, k1, M1Z, k to 2 sts before marker, k2tog, sm, work as set to end. 1 st increased.

Work a WS Garter row.

With CC2, work Pattern row 8 followed by a WS Stockinette row. 130 sts.

With MC, work Pattern row 8 followed by a WS Garter row. 131 sts.

With CC2, work (Pattern row 8 followed by a WS Garter row) twice. 133 sts.

Spine 5

SETUP ROW 1 (RS): With MC, k1, M1Z, pm, M1Z, k to 2 sts before marker, k2tog, sm, work as set to end. 134 sts.

SETUP ROW 2: K2, p to last 2 sts, k2.

SETUP ROW 3: K1, M1Z, pm, k1, sm, work as set to end. 135 sts.

Work a WS Stockinette row.

Bias Section 6

PATTERN ROW 9 (RS): K1, M1Z, k to marker, sm, work as set to end. 1 st increased.

Work a WS Stockinette row.

Repeat the last 2 rows twice. 138 sts.

PATTERN ROW 10 (RS): K1, M1Z, ssk, k to marker, M1Z, sm, work as set to end. 1 st increased.

Work a WS Stockinette row.

Repeat the last 2 rows 12 times. 151 sts.

With CC1, work Pattern row 10 followed by a WS Garter row. 152 sts.

With MC, work (Pattern row 10 followed by a WS Stockinette row) 6 times. 158 sts.

With CC1, work (Pattern row 10 followed by a WS Garter row) twice. 160 sts.

With MC, work (Pattern row 10 followed by a WS Stockinette row) 8 times. 168 sts.

With CC3, work (Pattern row 10 followed by a WS Garter row) twice. 170 sts.

With MC, work (Pattern row 10 followed by a WS Stockinette row) twice. 172 sts.

With CC3, work Pattern row 10 followed by a WS Garter row. 173 sts.

With MC, work (Pattern row 10 followed by a WS Stockinette row) 14 times. 187 sts.

With CC1, work Pattern row 10 followed by a WS Garter row. 188 sts.

With MC, work (Pattern row 10 followed by a WS Stockinette row) twice. 190 sts.

With CC1, work Pattern row 10 followed by a WS Garter row. 191 sts.

With MC, work Pattern row 10 followed by a WS Stockinette row. 192 sts.

With CC1, work Pattern row 10 followed by a WS Garter row. 193 sts.

With MC, work (Pattern row 10 followed by a WS Stockinette row) 3 times. 196 sts.

With CC1, work Pattern row 10 followed by a WS Garter row. 197 sts.

With MC, work Pattern row 10 followed by a WS Garter row. 198 sts.

With CC1, work Pattern row 10 followed by a WS Garter row. 199 sts.

With MC, work (Pattern row 10 followed by a WS Stockinette row) 3 times. 202 sts.

Spine 6

SETUP ROW 1 (RS): K1, M1Z, pm, ssk, k to marker, sm, work as set to end. 203 sts.

SETUP ROW 2: K2, p to last 2 sts, k2.

PATTERN ROW 11 (RS): K1, M1Z, k to marker, sm, work as set to end. 1 st increased.

Work a WS Stockinette row.

With CC4, work (Pattern row 11 followed by a WS Garter row) twice. 206 sts.

Bias Section 7

SETUP ROW 1 (RS): With MC, k1, M1Z, k1, M1Z, k2tog, pm, k1, sm, work as set to end. 207 sts.

SETUP ROW 2: K2, p to last 2 sts, k2.

PATTERN ROW 12 (RS): (K1, M1Z) twice, k2tog, sm, work as set to end. 1 st increased.

Work a WS Stockinette row.

Repeat the last 2 rows once more. 209 sts.

With CC3, work Pattern row 12 followed by a WS Garter row. 210 sts.

With MC, work (Pattern row 12 followed by a WS Stockinette row) twice. 212 sts.

With CC3, work (Pattern row 12 followed by a WS Garter row) twice. 214 sts.

With MC, work Pattern row 12 followed by a WS Stockinette row. 215 sts.

With CC3, work Pattern row 12 followed by a WS Garter row. 216 sts.

With MC, work (Pattern row 12 followed by a WS Stockinette row) 3 times. 219 sts.

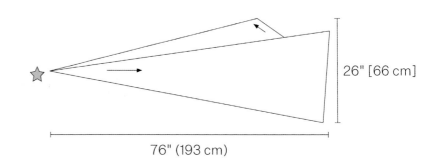

26" [66 cm]

76" (193 cm)

Spine 7

SETUP ROW 1 (RS): With MC, k1, M1Z, pm, k3, pm, M1Z, k to 2 sts before marker, k2tog, sm, work as set to end. 220 sts.

SETUP ROW 2: K2, p to last 2 sts, k2.

PATTERN ROW 13 (RS): K1, M1Z, k1, sm, k3, sm, work as set to end. 1 st increased.

Work a WS Stockinette row.

With CC2, work Pattern row 13 followed by a WS Garter row. 222 sts.

Bias Section 8

PATTERN ROW 14 (RS): (K1, M1Z) twice, k to 2 sts before marker, ssk, sm, k3, sm, work as set to end. 1 st increased.

Work a WS Garter row.

Repeat the last 2 rows once more. 224 sts.

With MC, work (Pattern row 14 followed by a WS Stockinette row) 3 times. 227 sts.

With CC4, work Pattern row 14 followed by a WS Garter row. 228 sts.

With MC, work Pattern row 14 followed by a WS Stockinette row. 229 sts.

With CC4, work (Pattern row 14 followed by a WS Garter row) twice. 231 sts.

With MC, work (Pattern row 14 followed by a WS Stockinette row) 18 times. 249 sts.

With CC1, work Pattern row 14 followed by a WS Garter row. 250 sts.

With MC, work (Pattern row 14 followed by a WS Stockinette row) twice. 252 sts.

With CC1, work (Pattern row 14 followed by a WS Garter row) twice. 254 sts.

With MC, work Pattern row 14 followed by a WS Stockinette row. 255 sts.

Hem

With CC1, knit 10 rows.

BO all sts.

Fins

With RS facing, place a marker on the left edge of your shawl, 2 inches (5 cm) in from the widest end.

With RS facing, join CC1 at marker, and pick up and knit 2 sts for every 3 rows along the left edge of the shawl.

SETUP ROW (WS): K50, pm B, k50, pm A, k to end of row.

Cut CC1.

Fin 1

Fin section:

ROW 1: With CC2, k2, ssk, knit to end. 1 st decreased.

ROW 2: Knit.

SHORT ROW 1: K2, ssk, knit to 1 st before marker B, turn. 1 st decreased.

SHORT ROW 2: DS, k to end.

Work Rows 1 and 2 once more.

SHORT ROW 3: K2, ssk, knit to 1 st before marker A, turn. 1 st decreased.

SHORT ROW 4: DS, k to end.

Work Rows 1 and 2 once more.

Transition:

ROW 1: BO 15 sts, with CC1, k2, ssk, knit to end.

ROW 2: Knit.

Fin 2

With CC4, work Fin Section.

Transition:

With CC2, work Rows 1 and 2.

Fin 3

With CC1, work Fin Section.

BO all sts.

Finishing

Block by soaking with a wool-wash, roll in towel, and/or use spin cycle to wring out most of the moisture; lay flat to dry.

Once dry, weave in ends.

Drape

Drape your shawl casually over one shoulder. It shows off the whole design of the shawl, while adding a unique flair to your outfit. Not practical for all situations, but add a brooch to hold your shawl in place and this would make an excellent dinner or cocktail party look.

Counterfort

This design is a straightforward application of the vortex shape (page 17), worked with a very simple but effective lace motif. The double yarnovers and the very simple, linear patterning make for a bold look—geometric and clean rather than fussy or delicate. The first section of the shawl is worked in a pattern spaced out between Garter ridges. The lacier edging is created by working the patterned row from the first section every RS row, with no Garter ridges in between.

As worked, half the yardage is used for the first pattern, and the other half of the yardage for the edging pattern. This is easily adjusted; just make sure that you end Section 1 with Row 8 to get a tidy transition.

The yarn choice makes this a light piece for warmer weather.

Finished Measurements

With yarn and at gauge given, piece is 14 inches (35.5 cm) deep by 80 inches (203 cm) wide.

Yarn Substitution

Look for sport/DK-weight substitutes in plant fibers to most closely match this shawl. Merino-silk blends or even silk-linen blends would also work well and would make your shawl more luxurious.

Yarn

Kelbourne Woolens Mojave [60% cotton, 40% linen; 185 yds (169 m) per 50 g skein (1¾ oz)]: 2 skeins; samples use #950 Mauve and #585 Raspberry

Needles

US size 7 (4.5 mm) needles—long circular

Or size needed to obtain gauge

Notions

Tapestry needle

Gauge

18 stitches and 40 rows (20 ridges) = 4 inches (10 cm) in Garter stitch, after blocking

Why This Yarn?

Summer shawls require summer yarns, and Kelbourne Woolens Mojave is one of our favorites. Kate Gagnon Osborn and Courtney Kelley develop thoughtfully designed yarns "by knitters, for knitters," and it shows. It's a sport/DK-weight cotton-linen blend with just a touch of texture. It's light and drapes like a dream, making it perfect for that shawl you throw on as you leave the house. We love the color palette so much that we can imagine knitting a few of these shawls to layer up!

Layer It Up

Soft, lacy shawls are ripe for layering up! Here we've taken two shawls in different colors and wrapped them loosely around the neck. A fun replacement for jewelry.

Setup Section

CO 1 st.

SETUP ROW (WS): Kfb. 2 sts.

ROW 1 (RS): Kfb, k1. 3 sts.

ROW 2: K2tog, kfb.

ROW 3: Kfb, k to end. 1 st increased.

ROW 4: K2tog, k to last st, kfb.

ROWS 5–8: Repeat Rows 3 and 4 twice more. 6 sts after row 7.

ROW 9: Kfb, k2tog, yo twice, ssk, k1. 7 sts.

ROW 10: K2tog, [(k1, p1) into double yo, k2] to last st, kfb.

ROWS 11–16: Repeat Rows 3 and 4 three more times. 10 sts.

Section 1

ROW 1 (RS): Kfb, [k2tog, yo twice, ssk] to last st, k1. 1 st increased.

ROW 2: K2tog, [(k1, p1) into double yo, k2] to last st, kfb.

ROW 3: Kfb, k to end. 1 st increased.

ROW 4: K2tog, k to last st, kfb.

ROWS 5–8: Repeat Rows 3 and 4 twice more.

Repeat Rows 1–8 until you've used up the first skein—or approximately half of the yardage, if you're making a substitution—ending after Row 8.

Section 2

ROW 1 (RS): Kfb, [k2tog, yo twice, ssk] to last st, k1. 1 st increased.

ROW 2 (WS): [K2tog, (k1, p1) into double yo, k2] to last st, kfb.

ROW 3: K1, yo twice, ssk, [k2tog, yo twice, ssk] to end. 1 st increased.

ROW 4: K2tog using first leg of yo as the second stitch, p1, k1, [k2, (k1, p1) into double yo] to last 4 sts, k2, p1, kfb.

ROW 5: Kfb, [k2tog, yo twice, ssk] to last 3 sts, k3. 1 st increased.

ROW 6: K2tog, k1, [k2, (k1, p1) into double yo] to last 2 sts, k1, kfb.

ROW 7: K1, yo twice, ssk, [k2tog, yo twice, ssk] to last 2 sts, k2. 1 st increased.

ROW 8: K2tog, [k2, (k1, p1) into double yo] to last 4 sts, k2, p1, kfb.

Repeat Rows 1–8 until you've just about run out of yarn, ending after any WS row. Leave yourself about 5–6 times the length of the lower edge in yarn for binding off.

BO using the Russian Lace method (page 35).

Finishing

Block by soaking with a wool-wash, roll in towel, and/or use spin cycle to wring out most of the moisture; lay flat to dry. There's no need to pin the shawl.

Once dry, weave in ends.

Key

☐	RS: knit WS: purl
•	RS: purl WS: knit
╱	RS: k2tog
╱	WS: k2tog
╲	ssk
O	yo
ⱱ	kfb
☐	Repeat

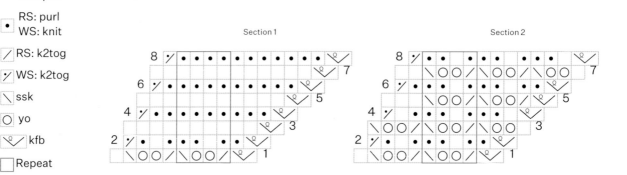

Section 1   Section 2

Hollerith

A classic standard version of the top-down triangle shawl (page 14) in traditional and lovely lace stitch patterns. An unexpected yarn and color choice results in a distinctive piece: a not-at-all delicate shawl that becomes a fantastic statement, like wearing your own personal blanket. The Edging Pattern takes a single element of the Body Pattern and repeats that, for a natural transition. The sample shows the edging started when two thirds of the yardage has been used, but that transition can be made at any point you wish. Just make sure you've completed Row 22 of the Body Pattern before you move to the next section.

Finished Measurements

With yarn and at gauge given, piece is 35 inches (89 cm) deep by 74 inches (188 cm) wide.

Yarn Substitution

Go bulky in a color that makes you happy. This yarn is a pseudo-single, a two-ply yarn where plies are twisted together in the same direction as the individual plies. So look for a single, a slub yarn, or a highly textured two-ply. To get the same effect, the plies should be low twist so the fabric fluffs up like the down jacket version of a shawl.

Yarn

Amano Yana [100% fine highland wool; 175 yds (160 m) per 200 g (7 oz) skein]: 3 skeins #1310 Pineapple

Needles

US size 11 (8 mm) needles—long circular

Or size needed to obtain gauge

Notions

Stitch markers; digital scale to assess yarn usage; blocking pins; blocking wires (optional); tapestry needle

Gauge

10 stitches and 12 rows = 4 inches (10 cm) in Garter stitch

Why This Yarn?

Have you ever stood in the middle of a yarn shop and been completely taken by a skein of yarn? You can't stop thinking about it, and you instantly know what it wants to be.

That's exactly what happened when Kate saw Amano Yana. The color! The bulky size! She immediately had a vision of a huge, cozy, simple lace shawl that she would wear all winter long.

+

PATTERN NOTES

Work patterns from charts or written instructions, as you prefer.

Key

☐ RS: knit
WS: purl

☐• RS: purl
WS: knit

○ yo

╲ ssk

╱ k2tog

⋀ CDD

☐ Lace Pattern Repeat

☐ Work Twice

Stitch Patterns

Body Pattern

ROW 1 (RS): K2, [(yo, k1) twice, place a removable st marker on the base of the last st worked] twice, k1. 11 sts. Move marker up as you go.

ROW 2 AND ALL WS ROWS: Knit.

ROW 3: K2, [yo, k3, yo, k1] twice, k1. 15 sts.

ROW 5: K2, [yo, k5, k1] twice, k1. 19 sts.

ROW 7: K2, [yo, k1, yo, ssk, k1, k2tog, yo, k1] twice, k1. 23 sts.

ROW 9: K2, [yo, k3, yo, CDD, yo, k3, k1] twice, k1. 27 sts.

ROW 11: K2, [yo, k2, (k2, k2tog, yo, k2) to 3 sts before marked st, k3, yo, k1 (marked st)] twice, k1. 4 sts increased.

ROW 13: K2, [yo, k1, yo, ssk, (k1, k2tog, yo, k1, yo, ssk) to 4 sts before marked st, k1, k2tog, yo, k1, yo, k1 (marked st)] twice, k1. 4 sts increased.

ROW 15: K2, [yo, k3, yo, (CDD, yo, k3, yo) to 6 sts before marked st, CDD, yo, k3, yo, k1 (marked st)] twice, k1. 4 sts increased.

ROW 17: K2, [yo, k4, k2tog, (yo, k4, k2tog) to 5 sts before marked st, yo, k5, yo, k1] twice, k1. 4 sts increased.

ROW 19: K2, [yo, k1, yo, ssk, k1, k2tog, yo, (k1, yo, ssk, k1, k2tog, yo) to 7 sts before marked st, k1, yo, ssk, k1, k2tog, yo, k1, yo, k1 (marked st)] twice, k1. 4 sts increased.

ROW 21: K2, [yo, k3, yo, CDD, yo, k1, (k2, yo, CDD, yo, k1) to 8 sts before marked st, k2, yo, CDD, yo, k3, yo, k1 (marked st)] twice, k1. 4 sts increased.

ROW 22: Knit.

Repeat Rows 11–22 for Body Pattern.

Edging Pattern

ROW 1 (RS): K2, [yo, k2, (k1, k2tog, yo, k1, yo, ssk) to 3 sts before marked st times, k3, yo, k1 (marked st)] twice, k1. 4 sts increased.

ROW 2 AND ALL WS ROWS: Knit.

ROW 3: K2, [yo, k1, yo, ssk, (k1, k2tog, yo, k1, yo, ssk) to 4 sts before marked st, k1, k2tog, yo, k1, yo, k1 (marked st)] twice, k1. 4 sts increased.

ROW 5: (K2, [yo, k2, yo, ssk, (k1, k2tog, yo, k1, yo, ssk) to 5 sts before marked st, k1, k2tog, yo, k2, yo, k1 (marked st)] twice, k1. 4 sts increased.

ROW 7: K2, [yo, k3, yo, ssk, (k1, k2tog, yo, k1, yo, ssk) to 6 sts before marked st, k1, k2tog, yo, k3, yo, k1 (marked st)] twice, k1. 4 sts increased.

ROW 9: K2, [yo, (k1, k2tog, yo, k1, yo, ssk) to 1 st before marked st, k1, yo, k1 (marked st)] twice, k1. 4 sts increased.

ROW 11: K2, yo, k1, [(k1, k2tog, yo, k1, yo, ssk) to 1 st before marked st, k1, yo, k1 (marked st)] twice, k1. 4 sts increased.

ROW 12: Knit.

Repeat Rows 1–12 for Edging Pattern.

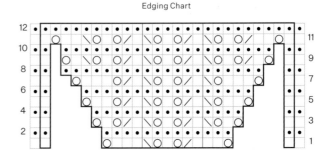

Body Chart

Edging Chart

Directions

Work a 2-st/4-ridge Garter tab (page 26), for 7 sts.

Body of Shawl

Work from Body Pattern, working central repeat twice. Every RS row increases 4 sts.

Once you have completed Row 22, Repeat Rows 11–22 until you have used up 2 of the 3 skeins—or approximately two thirds of the yardage, if you're making a substitution—ending after Row 22.

Edging

Work from Edging Pattern, working central repeat twice.

Repeat Rows 1–12 until you've just about run out of yarn, ending with any odd-numbered chart row. Leave yourself about 5–6 times the length of the lower edge in yarn for binding off.

BO using the Russian Lace method (page 35).

Finishing

Block by soaking with a wool-wash, roll in towel, and/or use spin cycle to wring out most of the moisture, then stretch and pin out. If you have them, use wires along the top edge, and use pins to pull out each of the scallops on the lower edge.

Once dry, weave in ends.

Snug Wrap and Pin

On cold days it feels so good to bundle up with a shawl around your neck and shoulders. Simply wrap the shawl up around your neck and pin to keep it in place. We've let the point of this top-down triangle float down one arm for warmth and an asymmetrical look.

The Snuggle

Shawls wrapped two or three times around your neck keep cold air from sneaking into your coat. This shawl is wrapped twice around the neck and pulled snugly against the neck. Cozy! *Safety pin–style shawl pin by Lisa Ridout.*

Soundscape

Hexagons are fun to knit and hold amazing design possibilities, but can be difficult to wear as a shawl. In order for them to be wide enough to wear comfortably, they also have to be very deep, which is not as manageable. With Soundscape, that issue is solved with short rows. Short rows are worked to increase the width of the shawl faster than the depth would normally be worked. Contrasting stripes emphasize the short-row structure in a playful way. The result is a cozy shawl to wrap up in on cold days.

Finished Measurements

With yarn and at gauge given, piece is 40 inches (101.5 cm) deep at deepest point by 65 inches (165 cm) wide.

Yarn Substitution

Vintage No. 6 is a fingering-weight yarn with a recommended gauge of 24–32 stitches per 4 inches (10 cm); however, because the yarn is worsted spun, lots of air is trapped in the fibers, allowing it to be knit at a larger gauge with no issues. Look for fingering-weight, worsted-spun yarns that have a similar recommended gauge, with the understanding that yarns from individual flocks and breeds will have characteristics that make your shawl unique.

Commercial Substitute

The Fibre Co. Arranmore Light. Although a DK-weight yarn, Arranmore Light is worsted spun, comes in a wide variety of colors, and knits up in a similar fabric to the Middle Brook Vintage No. 6.

Yarn

Middle Brook Fiberworks Vintage No. 6 [40% Shetland wool, 40% fine wool, 10% ramie, 10% silk; 396 yds (362 m) per 100 g (3½ oz) skein]: sample uses 2 skeins Natural Brown (MC) and 1 skein Natural Oatmeal (CC)

Note: Both the Natural Oatmeal and the Natural Brown shades of this yarn were overdyed at Indigodragonfly Studios in the same Smokey Plum color.

Needles

US size 7 (4.5 mm) needles—24 inches (61 cm) or longer

Or size needed to obtain gauge

Notions

Stitch markers; tapestry needle

Gauge

20 stitches and 29 rows = 4 inches (10 cm) in Stockinette stitch

Why This Yarn?

Anne Choi of Middle Brook Fiberworks is shepherdess to a small flock of Shetland sheep. She designs yarns that combine wool from her flock with other fine wools from local farmers, and sometimes silk and/or plant fibers. We wanted to use yarn that represented the skeins we fall in love with at fiber festivals, in a top-down shawl pattern that could easily be adapted for other non-commercial yarns. Vintage No. 6 has bounce and a crisp hand. It bloomed beautifully when washed, filling in the space between stitches. The resulting shawl fabric is light and warm.

+

PATTERN NOTES

DS: Create a double stitch with the German short-row method (page 33). Bring the yarn to the front, slip the next stitch purlwise, and pull the yarn up in front and over to the back of the needle, so that the two legs of the stitch are up on the needle and the yarn is in position to work the following stitch.

With MC, CO 38 sts.

SETUP ROW (WS): K2, (pm, k11) 3 times, pm, k3.

Note: The markers establish four spines around which increases will be worked. When looking at the shawl with RS facing, the st immediately after each marker is a spine st.

Continue with MC.

Increase Section A

ROW 1 (RS): K to marker, sm, (k1, M1Z, k to next marker, M1Z, sm) 3 times, k to end. 6 sts increased.

ROW 2: K2, (p to 1 st before marker, sl1 wyif, sm) 4 times, p to last 2 sts, k2.

ROW 3: K1, M1Z, k to marker, sm, (k1, M1Z, k to next marker, M1Z, sm) 3 times, k to last st, M1Z, k1. 8 sts increased.

ROW 4: Repeat Row 2.

Note: These 4 rows will be repeated throughout in both Increase Section A and Increase Section B. In the A version, all 4 rows are worked with 1 color. In the B version, you change color for Rows 3 and 4.

All WS rows are worked the same way: On a full row, the first and last 2 sts are knit, the spine sts are slipped, and the rest of the row is purled. On short rows, purl back from where you are, slipping the spine sts as established and knitting the last 2 sts.

Continue with MC.

Short-row Section A

ROW 1 (RS): K to marker, sm, k1, M1Z, k to 2 sts before second marker, turn.

ROW 2 (WS): DS, p to 1 st before marker, sl1 wyif, sm, p to last 2 sts, k2.

Increase Section B

With MC, work Rows 1 and 2 of Increase Section A, with CC work Rows 3 and 4 of Increase Section A.

Switch to MC.

Short-row Section B

ROW 1 (RS): K1, M1Z, k to marker, sm, k1, M1Z, k to second marker, M1Z, sm, k1,

M1Z, k to 2 sts before third marker, turn.

ROW 2 (WS): DS, (p to 1 st before marker, sl1 wyif, sm) twice, p to last 2 sts, k2.

Work Short-row Section A once.

Work Increase Section B once.

Switch to MC.

Short-row Section C

ROW 1 (RS): K to marker, sm, (k1, M1Z, k to next marker, M1Z, sm) twice, k1, M1Z, k to 2 sts before fourth marker, turn.

ROW 2 (WS): DS, (p to 1 st before marker, sl1 wyif, sm) 3 times, p to last 2 sts, k2.

Continue with MC.

Work Short-row Section B once.

Work Short-row Section A once.

Work Increase Section B once.

Switch to MC.

Work Short-row Section A once.

Work Increase Section A once.

Switch to CC.

Work Increase Section A once.

Switch to MC.

Work Short-row Section B once.

Work Short-row Section A once.

Work Increase Section A once.

Switch to CC.

Work Increase Section A once.

Switch to MC.

Work Short-row Section C once.

Work Short-row Section B once.

Work Short-row Section A once.

Work Increase Section A once.

Switch to CC.

Switch to MC.

Work Increase Section A once.

Switch to CC.

Work Increase Section A once.

Switch to MC.

Work Short-row Section A once.

Work Increase Section A once.

Work Short-row Section A once.

Switch to CC.

Work Increase Section A twice.

Switch to MC.

Work Short-row Section B once.

Work Short-row Section A once.

Work Increase Section A once.

Work Short-row Section B once.

Work Short-row Section A once.

Switch to CC.

Work Increase Section A twice.

Switch to MC.

Work Short-row Section C once.

Work Short-row Section B once.

Work Short-row Section A once.

Work Increase Section A once.

Work Short-row Section C once.

Work Short-row Section B once.

Work Short-row Section A once.

Switch to CC.

Work Increase Section A twice.

Switch to MC.

Work Short-row Section A once.

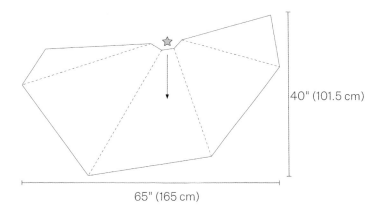

Increase Section C (decrease along right edge)

ROW 1 (RS): K to marker, sm, (k1, M1Z, k to next marker, M1Z, sm) 3 times, k to end. 6 sts increased.

ROW 2: K2, (p to 1 st before marker, sl1 wyif) 4 times, p to last 2 sts, k2.

ROW 3: K1, ssk, k to marker, sm, (k1, M1Z, k to next marker, M1Z, sm) 3 times, k to last st, M1Z, k1. 6 sts increased.

ROW 4: Repeat row 2.

Work Short-row Section A once.

Switch to CC.

Work Increase Section C 3 more times.

Switch to MC.

Short-row Section D (decrease along right edge)

ROW 1 (RS): K1, ssk, k to marker, sm, k1, M1Z, k to second marker, M1Z, sm, k1, M1Z, k to 2 sts before third marker, turn.

ROW 2 (WS): DS, (p to 1 st before marker, sl1 wyif, sm) twice, p to last 2 sts, k2.

Work Short-row Section A once.

Work Increase Section C 3 times.

Notes: If you wish to increase the size of your shawl, you can work more repeats of Increase Section C here before working Garter Hem.

You will need to make sure you have enough yarn to work the Garter Hem Section (see page 55).

Garter Hem Section (decrease along right edge)

ROW 1 (RS): K to marker, sm, (k1, M1Z, k to next marker, M1Z, sm) 3 times, k to end. 6 sts increased.

ROW 2: (K to 1 st before marker, sl1 wyif) 4 times, k to end.

ROW 3: K1, ssk, k to marker, sm, (k1, M1Z, k to next marker, M1Z, sm) 3 times, k to last st, M1Z, k1. 6 sts increased.

ROW 4: Repeat row 2.

Repeat Rows 1–4 once more.

BO all sts.

Finishing

Untreated wools need careful care to avoid felting. Block by soaking shawl in cool water, being careful not to agitate. Squeeze water out gently and roll in a towel to remove excess water. Lay flat to dry.

Once dry, weave in ends.

Front Wrap

Sometimes the design of your shawl is just too good to keep on your back. We've reversed this shawl, spreading it across the front of the model, with the ends behind her. Alternatively, overlap and pin in back for a cape look.

Hespero Brioche Triangle

An interesting alternative to a scarf, based on the wide top-down triangle (page 15), this is a long and relatively narrow piece that wraps extravagantly. It's all about warmth with the double-layer brioche fabric. The shaping is slightly adjusted—rather than working increases around a central spine, they move outward to form a wedge. The wedge is then shaped to a shallow triangle with short rows. This piece was designed to be the very opposite of what many consider to be a shawl: It's casual and sturdy and not at all feminine.

Finished Measurements
With yarn and at gauge given, piece is 13 inches (33 cm) at deepest point by 90 inches (228.5 cm) wide.

Yarn
Erika Knight Wild Wool [85% wool, 15% nettle (viscose); 186 yds (170 m) per 100 g skein (3½ oz)]: 2 skeins #705 Brisk

Needles
US size 8 (5 mm) needles—long circular

Or size needed to obtain gauge

Notions
Two markers of any style; one safety pin or removable marker; blocking pins (optional); tapestry needle

Gauge
14 stitches and 22 rows = 4 inches (10 cm) in Brioche Rib Stitch

Why This Yarn?
Erika Knight's Wild Wool is a wonderfully rustic-looking yarn that's actually quite soft! Nettle fibers combed into the wool give it texture, both physically and visually. The green chosen for this shawl is as at home on a hike through the woods as a walk through city streets. The lightly plied texture works beautifully in concert with the texture of the brioche stitches, resulting in a fantastic, contemporary, everyday favorite.

+

TIPS AND TRICKS

This pattern is actually fairly forgiving. If you're off on stitch counts, it will still work out. There should always be an odd number of stitches in the center section. When working the Main Section, after a WS row, there will be one more stitch in the first segment (between start of row and first marker) than in the second segment (between second marker and end of row).

+

PATTERN NOTES

Sl1yo (slip the next stitch purlwise, while creating a yarnover): Bring the yarn to the front, slip the next stitch purlwise; leave the yarn in front, ready to work the following stitch. When you knit the following stitch, the yarn will drape over the needle to create the yarnover.

Brk1: Knit the stitch and its accompanying yarnover together.

Note: You'll be building up the brioche pattern in each section. In the center, you're adding only one stitch at each end. As with all brioche, once the pattern is established, it's fairly easy to see what needs to be done.

CO 1: Use the backwards loop method (page 24) to CO 1 stitch at the end of the row. That new stitch will be worked at the start of the next row.

M1PR, M1PL: In Row 2 of the Setup Section and Main Section Row 3, use the strand of the yarnover wrap to create the new stitches; lift and work into the strand of the yarnover wrap, rather than into the usual strand that runs between the stitches. For working M1PL, lift the start of the yarnover wrap; for working M1PR, lift the end of the yarnover wrap. If you find these increases tricky, you can use the backwards loop increase instead (M1Z). The M1R and M1L must be worked as written, however.

Pfkb: Purl through the front and knit through the back of the stitch. 1 st increased.

DS: Create a double stitch with the German short-row method (page 33). Bring the yarn to the front, slip the next stitch purlwise, and pull the yarn up in front and over to the back of the needle, so that the two legs of the stitch are up on the needle and the yarn is in position to work the following stitch.

Using long-tail method (page 24), CO 5 sts.

Note: The semicolons in the rows indicate the marker position. Markers are always slipped when you come to them.

Setup

ROW 1 (WS): P1, k1, sl1yo, k1, p1, CO 1 at end of row. 6 sts.

ROW 2 (RS): Kfb, pm; k1, p1, M1PL, brk1, M1PR, p1, k1, pm; CO 1 at end of row. 10 sts.

ROW 3: Pfkb; p1, k2, sl1yo, k2, p1; k1, p1, CO 1 at end of row. 12 sts.

ROW 4: Kfb, k1, sl1yo; k1, p1, M1L, sl1yo, [brk1, sl1yo] to 2 sts before marker, M1R, p1, k1; sl1yo, k1, CO 1 at end of row. 16 sts.

ROW 5: Pfkb, sl1yo, brk1; p1, k1, [sl1yo, brk1] to 3 sts before marker, sl1yo, k1, p1; brk1, sl1yo, k1, p1, CO 1 at end of row. 18 sts.

It's helpful to put a safety pin or removable marker in the fabric at the start of the RS row to help you keep track of where you are.

Main Section

ROW 1 (RS): Kfb, k1, sl1yo, [brk1, sl1yo] to marker; k1, p1, M1PL, brk1, [sl1yo, brk1] to 2 sts before marker, M1PR, p1, k1; sl1yo, [brk1, sl1yo] to last st, k1, CO 1 at end of row. 4 sts increased.

ROW 2 (WS): Pfkb, [sl1yo, brk1] to marker; p1, k2, [sl1yo, brk1] to 4 sts before marker, sl1yo, k2, p1; [brk1, sl1yo] to last 2 sts, k1, p1, CO 1 at end of row. 2 sts increased.

ROW 3: Kfb, k1, sl1yo, [brk1, sl1yo] to marker; k1, p1, M1L, sl1yo, [brk1, sl1yo] to 2 sts before marker, M1R, p1, k1; sl1yo, [brk1, sl1yo] to last st, k1, CO 1 at end of row. 4 sts increased.

ROW 4: Pfkb, [sl1yo, brk1] to marker; p1, k1, [sl1yo, brk1] to 3 sts before marker, sl1yo, k1, p1; [brk1, sl1yo] to last 2 sts, k1, p1, CO 1 at end of row. 2 sts increased.

Repeat Rows 1–4 until you've used about two thirds of your yarn, or piece is the wingspan you want, ending with Row 4.

Lower Triangle—Setup

Note: You're working a pair of short rows in the first wing, before the first marker.

SHORT ROW 1 (RS): Kfb, k1, sl1yo, [brk1, sl1yo] to 2 sts before marker, brk1, turn.

SHORT ROW 2 (WS): DS, [brk1, sl1yo] to last 2 sts, k1, p1, CO 1 st at end of row. 1 st increased.

NEXT ROW (RS): Kfb, k1, sl1yo, [brk1, sl1yo] to 2 sts before marker, k1 working into both legs of DS, p1; k1, p1, M1PL, brk1, [sl1yo, brk1] to 2 sts before marker, M1PR, p1, k1; sl1yo, [brk1, sl1yo] to last st, k1, CO 1 at end of row. 4 sts increased.

Note: You're now working a pair of short rows in the second wing, after the second marker.

SHORT ROW 3 (WS): Pfkb, [sl1yo, brk1] to marker, turn. 1 st increased.

Overwrap

Flip up the collar of your jacket and loosely wrap the shawl around your shoulders. This chic and sophisticated look has an air of *je ne sais quoi*.

SHORT ROW 4 (RS): DS, [brk1, sl1yo] to last st, k1, CO 1 at end of row. 1 st increased.

NEXT ROW (WS): Pfkb, [sl1yo, brk1] to 2 sts before marker, sl1yo, p1 working into both legs of DS; p1, k2, [sl1yo, brk1] to 4 sts before marker, sl1yo, k2, p1; [brk1, sl1yo] to last 2 sts, k1, p1, CO 1 at end of row. 2 sts increased.

Lower Triangle

SHORT ROW 1 (RS): Kfb, k1, sl1yo, [brk1, sl1yo] to marker; k1, p1, M1L, sl1yo, [brk1, sl1yo] to 2 sts before marker, M1R, p1, k1, turn. 3 sts increased.

SHORT ROW 2 (WS): DS, k1, [sl1yo, brk1] to 3 sts before marker, sl1yo, k1, turn.

At this point, the pattern in the center between the markers is set, and you'll discontinue the increases. From here, you'll work short rows, turning every row after working the brk1 st before the previous turn.

SHORT ROW 3 (RS): DS, work in pattern as set to 2 sts before previous DS, brk1, turn.

SHORT ROW 4 (WS): DS, work in pattern as set to 2 sts before previous DS, brk1, turn.

Repeat Short rows 3 and 4 until 3 sts remain between the DSs, ending with a WS row.

NEXT ROW (RS): Work in pattern as set to marker, working into both legs of all DSs as you come to them; sl1yo, [brk1, sl1yo] to last st, k1, CO 1 at end of row.

FOLLOWING ROW (WS): Pfkb, [sl1yo, brk1] to marker; work in pattern as set to marker, working into both legs of all DSs as you come to them; [brk1, sl1yo] to last 2 sts, k1, p1, CO 1 at end of row. 2 sts increased.

Lower Triangle—Final Rows

SHORT ROW 1 (RS): Kfb, k1, sl1yo, (brk1, sl1yo) to 2 sts before marker, brk1, turn.

SHORT ROW 2 (WS): DS, [brk1, sl1yo] to last 2 sts, k1, p1, CO 1 st at end of row. 1 st increased.

NEXT ROW (RS): Kfb, k1, sl1yo, [brk1, sl1yo] to 2 sts before marker, k1 working into both legs of DS, p1; work in pattern as set to marker; sl1yo, [brk1, sl1yo] to last st, k1, CO 1 at end of row. 4 sts increased.

SHORT ROW 3 (WS): Pfkb, [sl1yo, brk1] to marker, turn. 1 st increased.

SHORT ROW 4 (RS): DS, [brk1, sl1yo] to last st, k1, CO 1 at end of row. 1 st increased.

NEXT ROW (WS): Pfkb, [sl1yo, brk1] to 2 sts before marker, sl1yo, k1 working into both legs of DS; work in pattern as set to marker; [brk1, sl1yo] to last 2 sts, k1, p1, CO 1 at end of row. 2 sts increased.

BO using an adjusted Russian Lace method (page 35), working all purl sts as purls and working brk1 as required on any knit/wrap combo sts, as follows:

Work 1 st, *work 1 st, return 2 sts to left-hand needle without twisting and k2tog-tbl; repeat from * until all sts have been worked. Cut yarn and pull through final st to secure.

Finishing

Block by soaking in a wool-wash, roll in towel, and/or use spin cycle to wring out most of the moisture; lay flat to dry. There's no need to stretch, but you may wish to pin out the wings and the central triangle to make straight edges. The sample as shown was not pinned.

Once dry, weave in ends.

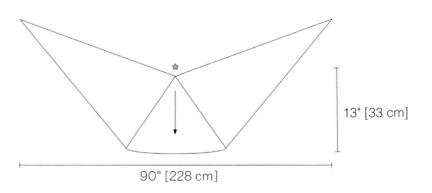

13" [33 cm]

90" [228 cm]

Stoclet Crescent

A two-sided lace stitch pattern combined with a lovely fringe-like finish creates a sophisticated shawl, the patterning reminiscent of Art Deco motifs. This is a straightforward version of the shallow crescent shape (page 18). The lace is structured and very open, almost more hole than fabric, and really should be worked with a solid color. The needles are smaller than you might expect for a lace project, but this ensures the structure of the motifs.

We've used a Stockinette tab here for a smooth side edge, which is continued throughout the shawl. The side edge doesn't have as much stretch as a Garter edge, but this provides a tidy benefit of holding the top edge firm, creating a nice collar-like effect when worn, and keeping the extra-stretchy lace from sagging out of shape.

This is a challenging but very satisfying project. Make sure your needles have good sharp points, and keep lots of stitch markers on hand.

The name is not a terrible typo for Stockinette, but a reference to Stoclet Palace in Brussels, a remarkable private house considered to be a masterpiece of early twentieth-century architecture. It's not strictly Art Deco, but rather in the Viennese Secession style, and has all the gorgeous lines and orderly curves of what we associate with the style.

Finished Measurements
With yarn and at gauge given, piece is 24 inches (60 cm) at deepest point by 75 inches (190.5 cm) wide.

Yarn Substitution
Smooth, luxurious, drapey: those are the qualities you want in a yarn for this shawl. Look for 3- or 4-ply yarns made from blends that contain silk for best results.

Yarn
Crave Yarn Caravan [70% superwash fine Merino, 10% cashmere, 10% camel, 10% mulberry silk; 354 yards (323 m) per 100 g (3½ oz) skein]: 2 skeins Palm Reader

Needles
US size 3 (3.25mm) needles—long circular

Or size needed to obtain gauge

Notions
Crochet hook in a size similar to the size used for knitting; stitch markers—lots of them; at least one removable stitch marker; digital scale to assess yarn usage; blocking pins; tapestry needle

Gauge
16 stitches and 22 rows = 4 inches (10 cm) in Body Pattern

Why This Yarn?
For the delicate, finely drawn lace pattern of the Stoclet shawl, a smooth yarn steeped in luxury was called for. Enter Caravan. This blend of fine Merino, cashmere, camel, and mulberry silk is smooth, soft, and drapey—everything you want a lace shawl to be. Dyer Amor has created a rich, saturated palette of colors, all perfect for this pattern.

Body Pattern

Work from chart or written instructions as you prefer.

ROW 1 (WS): P3, [yo twice, p2tog, p2, yo, p2tog, ssp, yo, p2, ssp] to last 3 sts, yo twice, p3. 2 sts increased.

ROW 2: K2, LLI, k1, yo, k1, [p1, yo, ssk, k6, k2tog, yo, k1] to last 4 sts, p1, yo, k1, RLI, k2. 4 sts increased.

ROW 3: P4, yo, p2, [p2, yo, p2tog, p4, ssp, yo, p2] to last 6 sts, p2, yo, p4. 2 sts increased.

ROW 4: K4, yo, k1, yo, k2, [k2, yo, k1, yo, sssk, k3tog, yo, k1, yo, k2] to last 7 sts, k2, yo, k1, yo, k4. 4 sts increased.

ROW 5: P3, yo twice, p2tog, p2, yo, p2tog, [ssp, yo, p2, ssp, yo twice, p2tog, p2, yo, p2tog] to last 9 sts, ssp, yo, p2, ssp, yo twice, p3. 2 sts increased.

ROW 6: K2, LLI, k1, yo, k1, p1, yo, ssk, k3, [k3, k2tog, yo, k1, p1, yo, ssk, k3] to last 10 sts, k3, k2tog, yo, k1, p1, yo, k1, RLI, k2. 4 sts increased.

ROW 7: (P4, yo) twice, p2tog, p2, [p2, ssp, yo, p4, yo, p2tog, p2] to last 12 sts p2, ssp, (yo, p4) twice. 2 sts increased.

ROW 8: (K4, yo, k1, yo) twice, sssk, [k3tog, yo, k1, yo, k4, yo, k1, yo, sssk] to last 13 sts, k3tog, (yo, k1, yo, k4) twice. 4 sts increased.

Fringe Lace Edging Setup (if Body ended with Row 1)

Note: Do not work last row of Body shown here; this row is given for the purpose of aligning your work with the Setup Row.

LAST ROW OF BODY (WS): P3, [yo twice, p2tog, p2, yo, p2tog, ssp, yo, p2, ssp] to last 3 sts, yo twice, p3. 2 sts increased.

SETUP ROW: K3, LLI, yo, k1 into double yo (dropping second wrap and placing a removable marker around the base of this st), [(p1, k1) twice, p1, RLI, (p1, k1) twice, p1, k1 into double yo (dropping second wrap)], to last 3 sts, yo, RLI, k3. 3 sts increased.

Key

RS: knit
WS: purl

RS: purl
WS: knit

RS: p tbl
WS: k tbl

O yo

Ⅎ LLI

Ⅎ RLI

RS: k2tog
WS: p2tog

RS: ssk
WS: ssp

⅄ sssk

⅄ k3tog

☐ repeat

■ hook a removable marker around the base of this stitch - see pattern

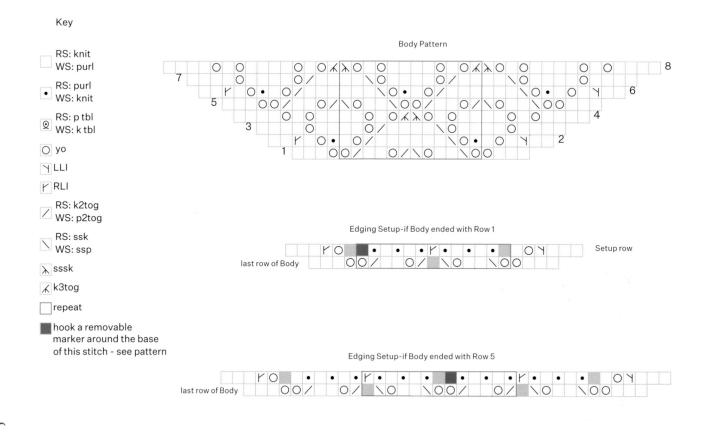

Body Pattern

Edging Setup-if Body ended with Row 1

Setup row

last row of Body

Edging Setup-if Body ended with Row 5

last row of Body

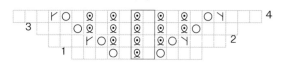

Edging

Note: Do not work last row of Body shown here; this row is given for the purpose of aligning your work with the Setup Row.

Wrap and Pin

Wrap around shoulders, overlap at one shoulder, and secure with a shawl pin or brooch. When doing this with triangles, or any shawl that has a distinctive point, try a variety of placements. Direct the point over one shoulder, down your arm, or off-center on your back.

Twig shawl stick by Jul Designs.

Fringe Lace Edging Setup (if Body ended with Row 5)

Note: Do not work last row of Body shown here; this row is given for the purpose of aligning your work with the Setup Row.

LAST ROW OF BODY (WS): P3, yo twice, p2tog, p2, yo, p2tog, [ssp, yo, p2, ssp, yo twice, p2tog, p2, yo, p2tog] to last 9 sts, ssp, yo, p2, ssp, yo twice, p3. 2 sts increased.

SETUP ROW: K3, LLI, yo, k1 into double yo (dropping second wrap and placing a removable marker around the base of this st), (p1, k1) twice, p1, RLI, [(p1, k1) twice, p1, k1 into double yo (dropping second wrap), (p1, k1) twice, p1, RLI], to last 10 sts (counting double yo as 2 sts), (p1, k1) twice, p1, k1 into double yo (dropping second wrap), yo, RLI, k3. 3 sts increased.

Fringe Lace Edging Pattern

ROW 1 (WS): P3, yo, p1, [k1 tbl, p1] to last 3 sts, yo, p3. 2 sts increased.

ROW 2: K3, LLI, yo, p1 tbl, [k1, p1 tbl] to last 3 sts, yo, RLI, k3. 4 sts increased.

ROW 3: P3, yo, [k1 tbl, p1] to last 4 sts, k1 tbl, yo, p3. 2 sts increased.

ROW 4: K3, LLI, yo, [k1, p1 tbl] to last 4 sts, k1, yo, RLI, k3. 4 sts increased.

Repeat Rows 1–4 for Fringe Lace Edging Pattern.

Directions

Using the backwards loop method, CO 3 sts.

Starting with a knit row, work 16 rows of Stockinette stitch.

SETUP ROW (RS): K3, pick up and knit 12 sts along the edge of the Stockinette strip (working under one leg of the edge st), and pick up and knit 3 more in the CO edge. 18 sts.

Tip: Use markers to divide up the repeats, placing them on Row 2. (It's impossible to place a marker in the middle of a double yarnover.) It's very easy to lose track of where you are in the pattern without markers.

Starting with a WS row, work the Body Pattern until you've used up about three quarters of your yarn (if working with the recommended yarn, when about 50 g of the second skein remains), ending with Row 1 or 5 of the Body Pattern.

Fringe Lace Edging

Work the appropriate Fringe Lace Edging Setup—which one you use is determined by which row of the Body Pattern was last worked on the Body. The Fringe Lace Edging Setup gives you the last Body Pattern row for alignment; work only the RS Setup Row; the last row of Body is shown for the purposes of aligning your sts. To guide you with the final step, you will place a removable st marker around the base of the st indicated in the pattern; the marker just stays around that st as you work.

NEXT ROW (WS): Work Fringe Lace Edging Pattern, working the 2-st repeat as indicated.

Work the 4-row Fringe Lace Edging Pattern until you've almost used up your yarn, ending with a WS row. Leave about 3 rows worth of yarn for the crochet edging.

Do not cut yarn.

Crochet Edging

At this point you will need to identify which sts are to be dropped. You'll be dropping every other knit st on the RS. The removable marker placed when you worked the Fringe Lace Edging Setup identifies one of the sts to be dropped; this st, and every other knit st to either side of it, will be dropped. From this position, count back in multiples of 4 sts [(p tbl, k1, p tbl, k1) when counting backward], towards the start of the row, stopping when you have 6–9 sts left to the start of the row. The last st of the final 4-st multiple will be the first knit st that is to be dropped when working the Crochet Edging; place a removable marker around the base of this st.

If you have 6 sts before the marked st: [Slip 3 sts to your crochet hook (without twisting them), pull up a loop with your crochet hook, and pull it through the 3 sts. Ch 5.] twice.

*[Drop the next knit st (removing marker if necessary), and let it unravel—it will stop once it hits the yo worked in the last rows of the Body Pattern. Slip 3 sts to your crochet hook (without twisting them), pull up a loop with your crochet hook, and pull it through the 3 sts. Ch 5.] to the last 3–5 sts. Slip those remaining sts to your crochet hook (without twisting them), pull up a loop with your crochet hook, and pull it through the sts. Cut yarn, and pull tail through final st to secure.**

If you have 7 sts before the marked st: Slip 4 sts to your crochet hook (without twisting them), pull up a loop with your crochet hook, and pull it through the 4 sts. Ch 5. Slip 3 sts to your crochet hook (without twisting them), pull up a loop with your crochet hook, and pull it through the 3 sts. Ch 5. Repeat from * to ** above.

If you have 8 sts before the marked st: [Slip 4 sts to your crochet hook (without twisting them), pull up a loop with your crochet hook, and pull it through the 4 sts. Ch 5.] twice. Repeat from * to ** above.

If you have 9 sts before the marked st: Slip 5 sts to your crochet hook (without twisting them), pull up a loop with your crochet hook and pull it through the 5 sts. Ch 5. Slip 4 sts to your crochet hook (without twisting them), pull up a loop with your crochet hook and pull it through the 4 sts. Ch 5. Repeat from * to ** above.

Finishing

Block by soaking with a wool-wash—to help the silk in the yarn bloom—then stretch and pin out. The top edge won't stretch out fully straight; let it curve. Place pins in each crochet chain loop in the lower edge, making sure that the dropped sts have fully unraveled.

Once dry, weave in ends.

Arc Nemesis

What happens when you add short rows to one side of a circular shawl, but not the other? That was the question Kim wanted this shawl to answer. Rows of textured flame shapes decorate one half of this shawl, while the other half sports a simple Garter ridge pattern. The resulting shape is unique and wraps around you elegantly. Wear and make waves wherever you go!

Finished Measurements

With yarn and at gauge given, piece is 23 inches (58.5 cm) at deepest point by 75 inches (190.5 cm) wide.

Yarn Substitution

If substituting yarn, the coloring is first priority. Look for a long variegated yarn with color lengths of at least 5 inches (12.5 cm).

Yarn

Indigodragonfly CaribouBaa [100% superwash Merino; 435 yds (398 m) per 100 g (3½ oz) skein]: 3 skeins Kelvin and Hobbes

Needles

US size 4 (3.5 mm) needles—32 inches (80 cm) long or longer circular

Or size needed to obtain gauge

Notions

Removable stitch markers; blocking pins; tapestry needle

Why This Yarn?

Indigodragonfly CaribouBaa is light, soft, holds its shape, and wears beautifully even with regular wearing. Kim dyed this yarn specifically for this shawl, with 7-to-10-inch (18-to-25.5.-cm) lengths of color (page 78). The shifts in color follow the flame sections and bring them to life.

Design Placement

Many of the shawls we make have special design elements that we want to show off. In this case, the rippled edge is showcased by draping it across the front of the body. When wearing your shawls, shape elements like points and ends don't always need to be draped directly in front or down your back. Try turning your shawl so that shape elements drape across your shoulder, down your arm, or off to one side. Changing the angle even a quarter turn can completely change the look from "baby-bib chic" to casual sophistication.

Stitch Patterns

Stockinette Pattern

(any number of sts)

ROW 1 (RS): Knit.

ROW 2: K1, p to last 2 sts, k2.

Work the following Flame Patterns from charts or written patterns as you prefer.

Flame Pattern 1

(st count varies)

ROW 1 (RS): Knit. 16 sts.

ROW 2: DS, k13. 14 sts.

ROW 3: DS, k11. 12 sts.

ROW 4: DS, k8. 9 sts.

ROW 5: DS, k6. 7 sts.

ROW 6: DS, k3. 4 sts.

ROW 7: DS, k2. 3 sts.

ROW 8: DS, k6. 7 sts.

ROW 9: DS, k8. 9 sts.

ROW 10: DS, k11. 12 sts.

ROW 11: DS, k13. 14 sts.

ROW 12: DS, k15. 16 sts.

ROW 13: DS, k16. 17 sts.

Flame Pattern 2

(st count varies)

ROW 1 (RS): Knit. 21 sts.

ROW 2 (WS): DS, k17. 18 sts.

ROW 3: DS, k15. 16 sts.

ROW 4: DS, k11. 12 sts.

ROW 5: DS, k9. 10 sts.

ROW 6: DS, k5. 6 sts.

ROW 7: DS, k3. 4 sts.

ROW 8: DS, k4. 5 sts.

ROW 9: DS, k5. 6 sts.

ROW 10: DS, k9. 10 sts.

ROW 11: DS, k11. 12 sts.

ROW 12: DS, k15. 16 sts.

ROW 13: DS, k17. 18 sts.

ROW 14: DS, k20. 21 sts.

ROW 15: DS, k21. 22 sts.

Flame Pattern 3

(st count varies)

ROW 1 (RS): Knit. 26 sts.

ROW 2 (WS): DS, k22. 23 sts.

ROW 3: DS, k20. 21 sts.

ROW 4: DS, k16. 17 sts.

ROW 5: DS, k14. 15 sts.

ROW 6: DS, p1, k9. 11 sts.

ROW 7: DS, k8. 9 sts.

ROW 8: DS, k5. 6 sts.

ROW 9: DS, k3. 4 sts.

ROW 10: DS, k4. 5 sts.

ROW 11: DS, k5. 6 sts.

ROW 12: DS, k8. 9 sts.

ROW 13: DS, k10. 11 sts.

ROW 14: DS, k15. 16 sts.

ROW 15: DS, k17. 18 sts.

ROW 16: DS, k20. 21 sts.

ROW 17: DS, k22. 23 sts.

ROW 18: DS, k25. 26 sts.

ROW 19: DS, k26. 27 sts.

Flame Pattern 4

(st count varies)

ROW 1 (RS): Knit. 31 sts.

ROW 2 (WS): DS, k27. 28 sts.

ROW 3: DS, k25. 26 sts.

ROW 4: DS, p1, k20. 22 sts.

ROW 5: DS, k19. 20 sts.

ROW 6: DS, k15. 16 sts.

ROW 7: DS, k13. 14 sts.

ROW 8: DS, k9. 10 sts.

ROW 9: DS, k7. 8 sts.

ROW 10: DS, k8. 9 sts.

ROW 11: DS, k9. 10 sts.

ROW 12: DS, k13. 14 sts.

ROW 13: DS, k15. 16 sts.

ROW 14: DS, k19. 20 sts.

ROW 15: DS, k21. 22 sts.

ROW 16: DS, k24. 25 sts.

ROW 17: DS, k26. 27 sts.

ROW 18: DS, k30. 31 sts.

ROW 19: DS, k31. 32 sts.

Directions

CO 164 sts using the long-tail method (see "Techniques," page 24) or cast-on of your choice.

ROWS 1–8: Knit.

Work 7 rows in Stockinette Pattern (see Pattern Notes), ending with a RS row.

Flame shape row (ws): Using the backwards loop method (see "Techniques," page 24), CO 5 sts, work Flame Pattern 2, BO 5 sts, k15, pm, work Flame Pattern 1, k to end.

Work 7 rows in Stockinette Pattern, starting and ending with a RS row.

Flame shape row (ws): K10, pm, work Flame Pattern 3, k to end.

Garter Ridge Section

Work 3 rows in Stockinette Pattern, starting and ending with a RS row.

Knit 1 WS row.

Repeat last 4 rows once more.

INCREASE ROW (RS): K2, [yo, k1] to last 2 sts, k2. 324 sts.

Knit 1 WS row.

Work 5 rows in Stockinette Pattern, starting and ending with a RS row.

FLAME SHAPE ROW (WS): CO 10 sts, work Flame Pattern 2, BO 10 sts, k5, work Flame Pattern 1, k25, work Flame Pattern 3, k to end.

Work 3 rows in Stockinette Pattern, starting and ending with a RS row.

FLAME SHAPE ROW (WS): K85, pm, work Flame Pattern 1, k to end.

Knit 1 RS row.

+

PATTERN NOTES

Use the backwards loop cast-on (page 24) for all stitches cast on after the initial long-tail cast-on.

+

IMPORTANT—PLEASE READ!

All flame shape rows start on WS rows.

Each flame shape section is one row with one or more short-row flame shapes worked in it. Flame shapes are created with German short rows (page 33), requiring work on both the RS and WS of the shawl within each row.

Stitch markers are placed as you work the chart, as guideposts.

Key

☐ RS: knit
  WS: purl

⬒ RS: purl
  WS: knit

⊃ short row right

⊂ short row left

☐ place marker (omit placing marker if working Flame Pattern on the edge of the shawl)

☐ remove marker

◼ omit this stitch if working a Flame Pattern on the edge of the shawl

23" (58.5 cm)

75" (190 cm)

Flame Pattern 1

Note: Numbers in the middle of each row represent the number of stitches to be knit; they allow you to knit without having to count squares in the chart.

Flame Pattern 2

Flame Pattern 3

Flame Pattern 4

FLAME SHAPE ROW (WS): K30, work Flame Pattern 4, k to end.

Work 9 rows in Stockinette Pattern, starting and ending with a RS row.

FLAME SHAPE ROW (WS): CO 5 sts, work Flame Pattern 3, BO 5 sts, k60, work Flame Pattern 1, k to end.

Work 5 rows in Stockinette Pattern, starting and ending with a RS row.

FLAME SHAPE ROW (WS): K50, work Flame Pattern 1, k35, work Flame Pattern 2, k to end.

Work 3 rows in Stockinette Pattern, starting and ending with a RS row.

FLAME SHAPE ROW (WS): CO 7 sts, work Flame Pattern 1, BO 7 sts, k70, work Flame Pattern 3, k to end.

Garter Ridge Section

Knit 2 rows.

Work 7 rows in Stockinette Pattern, starting and ending with a RS row.

FLAME SHAPE ROW (WS): CO 15 sts, work Flame Pattern 4, BO 15 sts, k25, work Flame Pattern 1, k to end.

Work 3 rows in Stockinette Pattern, starting and ending with a RS row.

FLAME SHAPE ROW (WS): K40, work Flame Shape 3, k to end.

Work 3 rows in Stockinette Pattern, starting and ending with a RS row.

FLAME SHAPE ROW (WS): K140, work Flame Shape 1, k to end.

Garter Ridge Section

Work 5 rows in Stockinette Pattern, starting and ending with a RS row.

Knit 1 WS row.

Work 3 rows in Stockinette Pattern, starting and ending with a RS row.

FLAME SHAPE ROW (WS): K10, work Flame Pattern 1, k25, work Flame Pattern 2, k to end.

Work 3 rows in Stockinette Pattern, starting and ending with a RS row.

FLAME SHAPE ROW (WS): CO 5 sts, work Flame Pattern 2, BO 5 sts, k75, work Flame Pattern 3, k to end.

INCREASE ROW (RS): K2, [yo, k1] to last 2 sts, k2. 644 sts.

FLAME SHAPE ROW (WS): CO 15 sts, work Flame Pattern 3, BO 15 sts, k45, work Flame Pattern 4, k75, work Flame Pattern 2, k55, work Flame Pattern 3, k to end.

Work 3 rows in Stockinette Pattern, starting and ending with a RS row.

FLAME SHAPE ROW (WS): CO 10 sts, work Flame Pattern 3, BO 10 sts, k10, work Flame Pattern 2, k140, work Flame Pattern 3, k70, work Flame Pattern 2, k35, work Flame Pattern 1, k to end.

Work 5 rows in Stockinette Pattern, starting and ending with a RS row.

FLAME SHAPE ROW (WS): K10, work Flame Pattern 1, k20, work Flame Pattern 1, k45, work Flame Pattern 4, k5, work Flame Pattern 1, k60, (work Flame Pattern 2, k30) twice, work Flame Pattern 2, k to end.

Work 5 rows in Stockinette Pattern, starting and ending with a RS row.

Garter Ridge Section

Knit 2 rows.

FLAME SHAPE ROW (WS): CO 5 sts, work Flame Pattern 1, BO 5 sts, k20, work Flame Pattern 3, k30, work Flame Pattern 2, k40, work Flame Pattern 1, k80, work Flame Pattern 2, k to end.

Work 3 rows in Stockinette Pattern, starting and ending with a RS row.

FLAME SHAPE ROW (WS): CO 10 sts, work Flame Pattern 4, BO 10 sts, k30, work Flame Pattern 1, k60, work Flame Pattern 3, k20, work Flame Pattern 1, k40, work Flame Pattern 2, k to end.

Garter Ridge Section

Knit 3 rows.

FLAME SHAPE ROW (WS): CO 5 sts, work Flame Pattern 1, BO 5 sts, k40, work Flame Pattern 2, k10, work Flame Pattern 1, k to end.

Knit 1 row.

Edging

SHORT ROW 1 (WS): CO 10 sts, work Flame Pattern 3, BO 35 sts, k16, turn.

SHORT ROW 2: DS, k15, sl1 wyif, CO 5 sts, work Flame Pattern 2.

SHORT ROW 3: BO 30 sts, k6, turn.

SHORT ROW 4: DS, k5, sl1 wyif, CO 10 sts, work Flame Pattern 3.

SHORT ROW 5: BO 40 sts, k6, turn.

SHORT ROW 6: DS, k5, sl1 wyif, CO 7 sts, work Flame Pattern 2.

SHORT ROW 7: BO 30 sts, k3, turn.

SHORT ROW 8: DS, k2, sl1 wyif, CO 3 sts, work Flame Pattern 1.

SHORT ROW 9: BO 25 sts, k16, turn.

SHORT ROW 10: DS, k15, sl1 wyif, CO 5 sts, work Flame Pattern 2.

SHORT ROW 11: BO 50 sts, k4, turn.

SHORT ROW 12: DS, k3, sl1 wyif, CO 10 sts, work Flame Pattern 3.

SHORT ROW 13: BO 70 sts, k6, turn.

SHORT ROW 14: DS, k5, sl1 wyif, CO 3 sts, work Flame Pattern 2.

SHORT ROW 15: BO 25 sts, k11, turn.

SHORT ROW 16: DS, k10, sl1 wyif, CO 7 sts, work Flame Pattern 3.

SHORT ROW 17: BO 45 sts, k3, turn.

SHORT ROW 18: DS, k2, sl1 wyif, CO 3 sts, work Flame Pattern 2.

BO remaining sts.

Finishing

Block by soaking with a wool-wash, roll in towel, and/or use spin cycle to wring out most of the moisture; lay flat to dry. Pin out edges of flame shapes for more definition. The ends of the shapes will curl slightly. This is normal.

Once dry, weave in ends.

Radialactive

A creative take on the wedge recipe (page 19), Radialactive uses two yarn bases in two different weights dyed in the same ombré colorway to create a stripe pattern that fades away in the middle. The ombré is started from different ends of each skein, creating color contrast at the beginning and end of the shape, with texture contrast through the center of the shawl.

Finished Measurements

With yarn and at gauge given, piece is 32 inches (81.5 cm) at deepest point by 82 inches (208.5 cm) wide.

Yarn Substitution

Of course Kim loves how the pattern and yarn play together in this shawl, so a direct substitute of another long ombré is the obvious choice.

However, there are other concepts that would make wonderful use of this structure:

Two yarn bases in different weights (fingering and lace) in the same semi-solid or tonal colorway would be a monochromatic way to play with transparency.

A solid yarn for MC and a gradient for CC would allow you to play with color shifts alongside a solid ground.

Use the same yarns, but start both MC and CC from the same end of the ombré. This would make the alternating texture and transparency the focal point.

Yarn

The Blue Brick Killarney Sock Wooly Mammoth [80% superwash Merino, 20% nylon; 800 yds (731 m) per 200 g (7 oz) skein]: 1 skein Feather (MC)

The Blue Brick Point Pelee Lace [80% superwash Merino, 10% cashmere, 10% nylon; 720 yds (658 m) per 140 g (4.9 oz) skein]: 1 skein Feather (CC)

Needles

US size 4 (3.5 mm) needles—32 inches (81 cm) long or longer circular

Or size needed to obtain gauge

Notions

Blocking pins; tapestry needle

Gauge

22 stitches and 30 rows = 4 inches (10 cm) in Stockinette stitch

22 stitches and 27 rows = 4 inches (10 cm) in Garter Ridge Stitch Pattern

---

Why This Yarn?

Shireen Nadir of the Blue Brick is famous for her ombré yarns that shift from color to color in long, languid lengths. The color technique was paramount to the success of Radialactive, and the shape and pattern of the shawl were integral to making the most out of the ombré. They were important to each other!

Simple Wrap and Drape

Wrap around your shoulders and let ends hang in front. This works even better if your shawl has a curved edge along the neckline, as the curve aligns with your body and allows the shawl to sit casually on your shoulders.

Wedge 1

With MC and starting from one end of the ombré, CO 150 sts.

SETUP ROW 1 (RS): K to last 3 sts, w&t (page 32).

SETUP ROW 2: K to end.

Join CC, starting from the opposite end of the ombré:

Short-row set 1

SHORT ROW 1 (RS): With CC, k to 3 sts before the first wrapped st you come to, w&t.

SHORT ROW 2: P to end.

SHORT ROW 3: With MC, k to 3 sts before the first wrapped st you come to, w&t.

SHORT ROW 4: K to end.

Repeat Short-row set 1 twenty-two more times, then work Short Rows 1 and 2 again. 6 sts remain before the first wrap.

SETUP ROW 1 (RS): With CC, k to first wrapped st, w&t to create a double wrap.

SETUP ROW 2: P to end.

Short-row set 2

SHORT ROW 5: (RS): With MC, k to first double-wrapped st, k this st together with its wraps, k to next wrapped st, w&t to create a double wrap.

SHORT ROW 6: K to end.

SHORT ROW 7: With CC, k to first double-wrapped st, knit this st together with its wraps, k to next wrapped st, w&t to create a double wrap.

SHORT ROW 8: P to end.

Repeat Short-row set 2 until 1 wrapped st remains, ending after Short row 6.

Wedge 2

SETUP ROW 1 (RS): With MC, BO 15 sts, k to last 3 sts, w&t. 135 sts.

SETUP ROW 2: K to end.

Work Short-row set 1 six times, work Short Rows 1 and 2 once more.

Work Short-row set 1 until 6 sts remain before first wrap, ending after Short row 2.

SETUP ROW 1 (RS): With MC, k to first wrapped st, w&t to create a double wrap.

SETUP ROW 2: K to end.

Work Short Rows 7 and 8 once, work Short-row set 2 fourteen times, work Short Rows 7 and 8 once more.

Work Short-row set 2 until 1 wrapped st remains, ending after Short row 6.

Wedge 3

SETUP ROW 1 (RS): With MC, BO 15 sts, k to last 3 sts, w&t. 120 sts.

SETUP ROW 2: K to end.

Work Short-row set 1 six times, then work Short Rows 1 and 2 once more.

Work Short-row set 1 five times, work Short Rows 1 and 2 once more.

Work Short-row set 1 until 6 unwrapped sts remain, ending after Short row 2.

Wedge 3 Garter Stitch Insert

ROW 1 (RS): With MC, k75, w&t.

ROW 2: K to end.

ROW 3: K to 3 sts before first wrapped st you come to, w&t.

ROW 4: K to end.

Repeat Rows 3 and 4 twenty-two more times. 6 uwrapped sts remain.

ROW 5: K to first wrapped st, w&t to create a double wrap.

ROW 6: K to end.

ROW 7: K to first double-wrapped st, knit this st together with its wraps, knit to next wrapped st, w&t to create a double wrap.

ROW 8: K to end.

Repeat Rows 7 and 8 twenty-two more times.

Second Half of Wedge 3 (mirrors first half, not including Garter Stitch Insert):

SETUP ROW 1 (RS): With CC, k6, w&t.

SETUP ROW 2: P to end.

Short-row set 3

SHORT ROW 9 (RS): With MC, k to first wrapped st, knit this st together with its wrap, k3, w&t.

SHORT ROW 10: K to end.

SHORT ROW 11: With CC, k to first wrapped st, knit this st together with its wrap, k3, w&t.

SHORT ROW 12: P to end.

Work Short-row set 3 five more times, then work Short rows 11 and 12 once more.

Work Short-row set 3 until you have reached top of Garter Stitch Insert, with 4 wraps around final Garter Stitch Insert st.

SETUP ROW 1 (RS): With CC, k to first wrapped st, knit wrapped st together with its wraps, k3, w&t to create a double wrap.

SETUP ROW 2: P to end.

Work Short-row set 2 until 1 wrapped st remains, ending with Short row 6.

Wedge 4

With MC, knit 2 rows, working remaining wrapped sts together with their wraps. Using backwards loop method (page 24), CO 15 sts. 135 sts.

SETUP ROW 1 (RS): With CC, k to last 3 sts, w&t.

SETUP ROW 2: K to end.

Work Short rows 3 and 4 once, work Short-row set 1 five times, then work Short rows 1 and 2 once more.

Work Short-row set 1 five times, then work Short rows 1 and 2 once more.

Work Short-row set 1 three times, work Short rows 1 and 2 once, then work Short-row set 1 until 6 unwrapped sts remain.

SETUP ROW 1 (RS): With MC, k to first wrapped st, w&t to create a double wrap.

SETUP ROW 2: K to end.

SETUP ROW 3: With CC, k to first double-wrapped st, knit this st together with its wraps, knit to next wrapped st, w&t to create a double wrap.

SETUP ROW 4: P to end.

Work Short-row set 2 five times, then work Short rows 7 and 8 once more.

Work Short-row set 2 three times, then work Short rows 7 and 8 once more.

Work Short-row set 2 five times, work Short rows 7 and 8 once more.

Work Short-row set 2 until 1 wrapped st remains.

Wedge 5

With MC, knit 2 rows, working remaining wrapped sts together with their wraps. Using backwards loop method, CO 15 sts.

With MC, knit 2 rows.

SETUP ROW 1 (RS): With CC, k to last 3 sts, w&t.

SETUP ROW 2: K to end.

Work Short rows 3 and 4 once, work Short-row set 1 five times, then work Short rows 1 and 2 once more.

Work Short-row set 1 five times, then work Short rows 1 and 2 once more.

Work Short-row set 1 three times, then work Short rows 1 and 2 once more.

Work Short-row set 1 twice, then work Short rows 1 and 2 once more.

Work Short-row set 1 once, then work Short rows 1 and 2 once more.

Work Short-row set 1 until 6 unwrapped sts remain.

SETUP ROW 1 (RS): With CC, k to first wrapped st, w&t to create a double wrap.

SETUP ROW 2: P to end.

Work Short-row set 2 four times, then work Short rows 7 and 8 once more.

Work Short-row set 2 once, then work Short rows 7 and 8 once more.

Work Short-row set 2 twice, then work Short rows 7 and 8 once more.

Work Short-row set 2 three times, then work Short rows 7 and 8 once more.

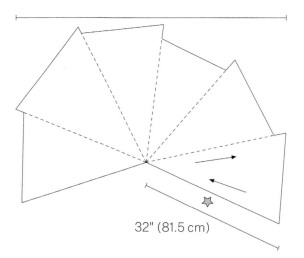

32" (81.5 cm)

Work Short-row set 2 five times, then work Short rows 7 and 8 once more.

Work Short-row set 2 until 1 wrapped st remains.

With MC, knit 2 rows, working remaining wrapped sts together with their wraps.

Wedge 6

SETUP ROW 1 (RS): With MC, BO 15 sts, k to end. 135 sts.

SETUP ROW 2: K to end.

SETUP ROW 3: With CC, k to last 3 sts, w&t.

SETUP ROW 4: P to end.

Work Short Rows 3 and 4 once, work Short-row set 1 five times, then work Short rows 3 and 4 once more.

Work Short-row set 1 five times, then work Short rows 3 and 4 once more.

Work Short-row set 1 three times, then work Short rows 3 and 4 once more.

Work Short-row set 1 until 6 unwrapped sts remain.

SETUP ROW 1 (RS): With MC, k to first wrapped st, w&t to create a double wrap.

SETUP ROW 2: K to end.

Work Short rows 7 and 8 once, work Short-row set 2 five times, then work Short rows 5 and 6 once more.

Work Short-row set 2 three times, then work Short rows 5 and 6 once more.

Work Short-row set 2 five times, then work Short rows 5 and 6 once more.

Work Short-row set 2 until 1 wrapped st remains.

Using MC, knit 6 rows, working remaining wrapped sts together with their wraps.

BO all sts.

Finishing

Block by soaking with a wool-wash, roll in towel, and/or use spin cycle to wring out most of the moisture; lay flat to dry. Stretching is not required, however pinning out corners will help them keep their defined shape.

Once dry, weave in ends.

Adjacent

Adjacent is designed to use the predictability of self-striping yarn in a structured, organized way utilizing atypical shapes for this yarn. Individual triangles are worked and attached as you go without cutting yarn. The sample yarn has a striping pattern of ten colors. Nine stitch patterns were chosen to cycle through the color sequence, ensuring each color is worked in a different stitch pattern each time it comes around again.

The wingspan/width can be lengthened by working more triangles in the first tier. The depth can be made shallower by completing fewer tiers of triangles, or deeper by adding tiers.

Finished Measurements

With yarn and at gauge given, piece is 12 inches (30.5 cm) deep by 60 inches (152.5 cm) wide.

Yarn Substitution

Look for self-striping sock yarn designed to have 5-to-7-row stripes in a standard sock. Charts are written with this amount of yarn in mind. If you choose a yarn with different stripe lengths, you will have to adjust the charts accordingly, adding or subtracting rows.

This pattern is also perfect for using up small amounts of yarn or for mini skeins. If working this option, consider changing colors every time you change to a new shape.

Yarn

Gauge Dye Works Classic: Merino Twist [80% superwash Merino, 20% nylon; 655 yds (599 m)]: 1 hank in Azurite F

Needles

US size 4 (3.5 mm) needles—straight or circular

Or size needed to obtain gauge

Notions

Removable stitch markers; blocking pins; tapestry needle

Gauge

24 stitches and 36 rows = 4 inches (10 cm) in Stockinette stitch

Why This Yarn?

Catherine Gamroth of Gauge Dye Works is a genius. She engineers fixed-stripe yarns for both socks and shawls, and gradient yarns that use complex color arrangements to cycle through a color sequence. The colorway chosen for this design, Azurite F, is reminiscent of the azurite stone. The crystal structure of azurite inspired this shawl.

+ ALTERNATIVES

In addition to working the pattern as written, you can:

1) Choose a few stitch patterns and work the whole shawl in only those patterns.

2) Roll dice to determine which stitch pattern to work next.

3) Choose a single stitch pattern to use throughout the shawl.

4) Make up your own stitch pattern! A blank chart that you can copy has been provided for this purpose.

Construction Essentials

Overview and Basic Module Instructions—read before you begin

This rectangular shawl is constructed in tiers of triangles, linked together at connection points. Connection points attach to adjacent triangles in an orderly way, as indicated in diagrams throughout the pattern.

In this hank of Gauge Dye Works yarn, there are ten colors in the stripe sequence. Kim has provided you with nine knit/purl stitch patterns. Make sure that you change stitch pattern when you repeat a color, so that no two triangles are alike.

Yarn Management

Self-striping yarn is dyed in a precise manner; however not every length of color is identical. You will find that different stripe colors will transition into the next triangle. Expect to see a transition area between colors. Some triangles will start or end with a little bit of other colors—this should be expected. When you look at the final shawl from a distance, only individual colored squares are seen. No cutting is required when using self-striping yarn.

Each triangle is intended to use as much of each color stripe as possible. You may find you need to add or subtract rows to do this with the yarn you've chosen. Once you've established how many rows are in a triangle, this should remain consistent for the rest of your shawl.

If using mini skeins or yarn scraps, you will need to cut your yarn and attach new yarn each time you want to start a new color. The most secure way to do this is to cut before the bind-off, and work the bind-off and subsequent cast-on in the new color. This will establish a strong base for your connection points.

RS versus WS

All the stitch patterns in this pattern are reversible and look identical on both sides of the triangle. For this reason, we recommend using removable markers to mark the RS of your shawl. We like to use two. One marker is placed on the RS of the first triangle and should not be moved. It will help you sanity-check RS

vs. WS at any point in your shawl. The second marker is placed on the RS of the last triangle worked.

Changing Size

The width and depth of this shawl can be changed easily. To widen the wingspan, work more triangles in Tier 1 to establish width. Work fewer triangles for a narrower wingspan. To increase depth, work more tiers. To make a shallower shawl, work fewer tiers.

Connection Points

Connection points indicate where to attach the triangles together as you go.

At a connection point, pick up and knit a stitch from an adjacent triangle at the point indicated (always at the end of a row). On the following row, work a ssk at the start of the row to decrease one stitch and maintain the proper stitch count. Connection points are indicated in the diagrams throughout the pattern.

Directions

Setup Tier

Leaving a tail of around 4 inches (10 cm), make a slipknot to CO 1 st.

Work an A Triangle, ending with a RS row.

BO sts until 1 st remains on right-hand needle.

Starting with the 1 remaining st, work a B Triangle, working connection points as indicated in Setup Tier diagram (page 183) and ending with a WS row.

BO sts until 1 st remains on right-hand needle.

Work triangle charts in numerical order, alternating shape A and B until a chain of twenty triangles has been completed, or desired shawl width has been achieved. End Tier 1 with a B Triangle, bound off on a RS row.

Odd Tier Turnaround

This sequence turns your work at the end of an Odd Tier and readies it for starting an even-numbered tier of triangles.

With yarn still attached to the last triangle of the previous tier, work a B Triangle, ending with a RS row.

BO sts until 1 st remains on right-hand needle.

Work a B Triangle on that st, ending with a WS row.

BO sts until 1 st remains on right-hand needle; pick up and knit 1 st from the center of the hypotenuse of the last A Triangle from Tier 1 (as indicated by blue Xs in Odd Tier Turnaround diagram [page 183]), psso.

Even Tier (Tier 2, and all following even-numbered tiers):

Work an A Triangle, ending with a RS row. Pick up and knit 1 st from the second intersection you come to (intersection between A and B Triangles in the previous tier, as indicated in Tier 2 diagram, below, by a green circle), turn work.

BO sts until 1 st remains on right-hand needle.

Work a B Triangle, ending with a RS row.

BO sts until 1 st remains on right-hand needle; pick up and knit 1 st from the center of the hypotenuse of the closest A Triangle in Tier 1, psso.

Continue as set, alternating Triangles B and A, until this Tier is even with the end of the previous tier. End with an A Triangle, bound off on a RS row. 1 st remains on right-hand needle.

Even Tier Turnaround

This sequence turns your work and readies it for starting an odd-numbered tier of triangles.

Work an A Triangle, ending with a WS row.

BO sts until 1 st remains on right-hand needle.

Work an A Triangle, ending with a RS row.

BO sts until 1 st remains on right-hand needle; pick up and knit 1 st from the center of the hypotenuse of the B Triangle from previous tier (see Even Tier Turnaround Diagram, green circle, below), psso.

Odd Tier (Tier 3 and all following odd-numbered tiers):

Wrap with Ends in Front

Wide and narrow shawls can be worn scarf-style like this: Wrap around your neck once, and let the ends hang down in front. A great way to dress up a simple outfit.

After the Even Tier Turnaround is complete:

Work a B Triangle, ending with a WS row; pick up and knit 1 st from the second intersection you come to (intersection between A and B Triangles in the previous tier, as indicated in Even Tier Turnaround diagram by a green X); turn work.

BO sts until 1 st remains on right-hand needle.

Work an A Triangle, ending with a RS row.

BO sts until 1 st remains on right-hand needle; pick up and knit 1 st from the center of the hypotenuse of the closest B Triangle in previous tier (blue Xs in Even Tier turnaround diagram), psso.

Continue as set, alternating B and A Triangles until this tier is even with the end of the previous tier, ending with a B Triangle.

Continue as set, alternating Odd Tier/ Odd Tier Turnaround with Even Tier/ Even Tier Turnaround until shawl is desired size.

Finishing

Block by soaking with a wool-wash, roll in towel, and/or use spin cycle to wring out most of the moisture; lay flat to dry. Stretch by pinning out triangles at edges of shawl.

Once dry, weave in ends.

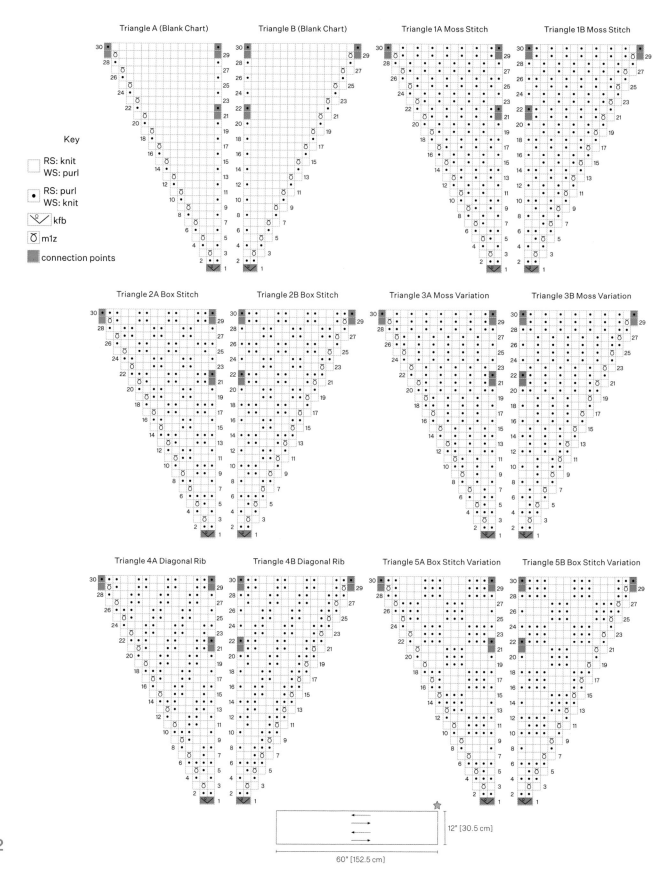

Triangle A (Blank Chart)

Triangle B (Blank Chart)

Triangle 1A Moss Stitch

Triangle 1B Moss Stitch

Key

RS: knit
WS: purl

RS: purl
WS: knit

kfb

m1z

connection points

Triangle 2A Box Stitch

Triangle 2B Box Stitch

Triangle 3A Moss Variation

Triangle 3B Moss Variation

Triangle 4A Diagonal Rib

Triangle 4B Diagonal Rib

Triangle 5A Box Stitch Variation

Triangle 5B Box Stitch Variation

12" [30.5 cm]

60" [152.5 cm]

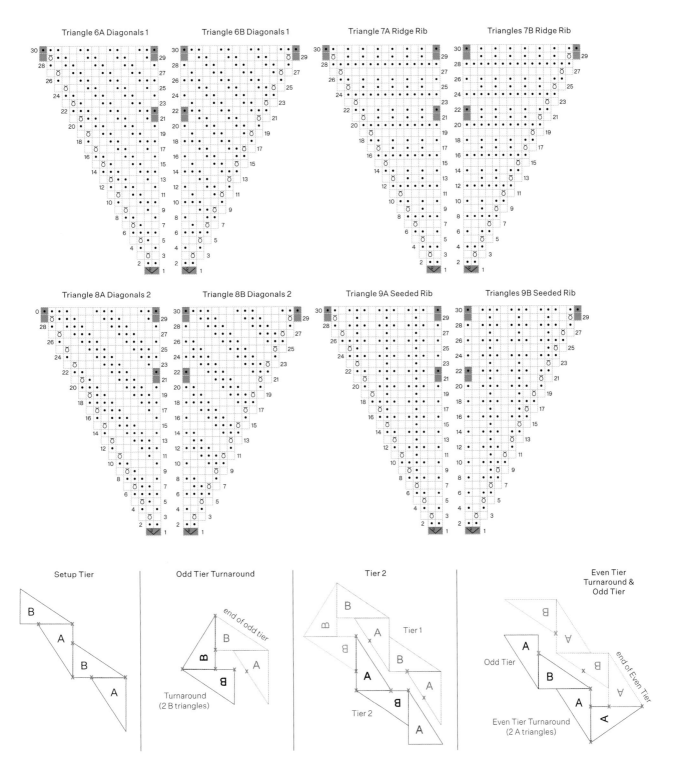

Triangle 6A Diagonals 1   Triangle 6B Diagonals 1   Triangle 7A Ridge Rib   Triangles 7B Ridge Rib

Triangle 8A Diagonals 2   Triangle 8B Diagonals 2   Triangle 9A Seeded Rib   Triangles 9B Seeded Rib

Setup Tier   Odd Tier Turnaround   Tier 2   Even Tier Turnaround & Odd Tier

SETUP TIER: *Diagram shows how to build the first tier of triangles. Each red X indicates a connection point. Pick up and knit 1 st from an adjacent triangle at the end of a row, and work ssk to decrease that st and secure the connection at the start of the next row.*

ODD TIER TURNAROUND: *Connection points used to connect Odd Tiers to Even Tiers. Blue Xs connect to each other from one corner of the B*

Triangle to the center of the hypotenuse of an A Triangle in the previous tier.

TIER 2 AND EVEN TIER TURNAROUND: *Green Xs connect to each other from the corner of an A Triangle in the current tier to the second available intersection between B and A Triangles in the previous tier. All other connection points remain as established.*

Askew

Askew is an improvisational shawl for the adventurous knitter. Basic instructions are given to establish the wingspan of your shawl, create the shapes, and securely connect the shapes together. After two tiers of practice squares, where you learn how the basic construction works, you're off on your own to make a shawl that suits your creative spirit.

Finished Measurements

With yarn and at gauge given, piece is 18 inches (45.5 cm) at deepest point by 64 inches (162.5 cm) wide.

Yarn Substitution

If substituting yarn, look for self-striping sock yarns designed to have 5–6 row stripes in a standard sock. This pattern is also perfect for using up small amounts of yarn or for mini skeins. If working this option, consider changing colors every time you change to a new shape.

Yarn

Must Stash Perfect Must Match Set [75% superwash Merino, 25% nylon; 440 yds (402 m) per 100 g (3½ oz) skein]: 2 skeins Bohemian

Needles

US size 4 (3.5 mm) needle—straight or circular

Or size needed to obtain gauge

If using a different yarn, consider using a needle size that is 1–2 sizes larger than the recommended size. The gauge should be loose enough to drape nicely, but dense enough to maintain the square shapes.

Notions

Blocking pins; tapestry needle

Gauge

23 stitches and 31 rows = 4 inches (10 cm) in Stockinette stitch

Why This Yarn?

For Askew, Kim was looking for self-striping sock yarns with 5-to-6-row stripes in a standard sock and a lot of colors. Must Stash Perfect Must Match Set filled the bill perfectly! Twenty different subtle changing colors in predictable stripes made it a joy to knit with, and meant that colors rarely landed next to each other.

Crisscross

This crescent-shaped shawl is worn with the ends crisscrossed over one shoulder. One half of the shawl is draped across the front of the body with one end over one shoulder. The rest is draped across the back with the second end overlapping the first and allowed to hang down. The top end keeps the shawl in place, and wrapping it over from the back means you can easily adjust it throughout your day. Simple and elegant.

Construction Essentials

Overview and Basic Module Instructions—read before you begin

This shawl is constructed using tiers of small squares linked together at connection points. Connection points—made up of bind-offs and cast-ons—attach to nearby squares at a corner, an intersection, or the middle of a side. Each successive tier is several squares shorter than the preceding one, to create a crescent-esque shape.

Yarn Management

Self-striping yarn is dyed in a precise manner, however not every length of color is identical. You will find that different stripe colors will transition into the next square. Expect to see a transition area of 1–2 rows (including bind-off row) between colors. Leaving a small amount of color before working a bind-off ensures that transitions happen somewhere between the last row of a square and the first row of the next one. When you look at the final shawl from a distance, only individual colored squares are seen. No cutting is required when using self-striping yarn.

If using mini skeins or yarn scraps, you will need to cut your yarn and attach new yarn each time you want to start a new color. The most secure way to do this is to cut before the bind-off and work the bind-off and subsequent cast-on in the new color. This will establish a strong base for your connection points.

RS versus WS

The RS of all Basic Squares shows the Stockinette square in the middle of a Garter stitch square. All RSs of all Basic Squares should always be on the RS of the shawl. Because the directions for the Basic Square start with a RS row, in some cases you may need to work a WS row *before* starting the Basic Square instructions.

Changing Size

The width and depth of this shawl can be changed easily.

Tier 1 determines the final width of the shawl. To make the shawl narrower, work fewer repeats of Part A in Tier 1. To make it larger, work more repeats of Part A.

The number of tiers worked determines the depth of the shawl. In the sample shown, seven tiers were worked. To make a shallower shawl, work fewer tiers; to make a deeper shawl, work more tiers.

Stitch Patterns

Basic Square

ROWS 1–5: Knit.

ROW 6 (WS): K3, p6, k3.

ROWS 7–12: Repeat Rows 5 and 6 twice more.

Knit every row until you have a small amount of the current color left, ending with a RS or WS row as indicated in the instructions. (In the sample, a baseline of 1–6 inches [2.5–15 cm] was used. If much more than 6 inches [15 cm] of the current color was available, it was often enough to work another 2 rows.)

Bind-Off A

BO 6 sts (1 st remains on right-hand needle), k5, CO 6 sts using the backwards loop method (page 24). 12 sts.

Bind-Off B

BO 12 sts (1 st remains on right-hand needle), CO 11 sts using the backwards loop method. 12 sts.

Corner Connection Method

Pick up and knit 1 st from the free corner (no other squares attached to the corner) of a nearby square, BO 1 st. This secures the connection point. (Red Xs in Image 1 show examples of corner connection points)

Intersection Connection Method

Pick up and knit 1 st from the intersection (where a minimum of two corners meet) of a nearby square, BO 1 st. This secures the connection point. (Blue Xs in Image 2 show examples of intersection connection points.)

Directions

Tier 1

Leaving a tail of around 4 inches (10 cm), CO 12 sts.

Part A

*Work Basic Square, ending with a WS row.

Work Bind-Off A.

NEXT ROW (WS): Knit.

Repeat from * 4 more times.

Work Basic Square, ending with a RS row.

Work Bind-Off A.

**Work Basic Square, ending with a WS row.

Work Bind-Off A.

NEXT ROW (WS): Knit.

Repeat from ** once more.

Work Basic Square, ending with a RS row.

Work Bind-Off A.

Repeat Part A twice more.

***Work Basic Square, ending with a WS row.

Work Bind-Off A.

NEXT ROW (WS): Knit.

Repeat from *** 3 more times.

Work Basic Square, ending with a RS row.

Work Bind-Off A.

This point marks approximately two-thirds of the final width of your shawl. If adding width, work more repeats of Part A here.

Part B

*Work Basic Square, ending with a RS row.

Work Bind-Off A.

Repeat from * twice more.

Work Basic Square, ending with a WS row.

Work Bind-Off A.

NEXT ROW (WS): Knit.

**Work Basic Square, ending with a RS row.

Work Bind-Off A.

Repeat from ** 4 more times.

Repeat Part B once more.

Work Basic Square, ending with a WS row.

This completes the neck edge of your shawl.

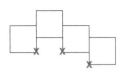

Image 1

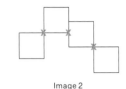

Image 2

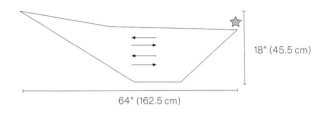

18" (45.5 cm)

64" (162.5 cm)

Tier 2

In Tier 2, you will work squares while connecting them to Tier 1. Please review RS vs WS in the Overview Section before proceeding.

With RS facing, and Tier 1 to your right, work Bind-Off B. You have 12 sts on your needle.

Connect the last stitch of Bind-Off B (this is a newly created st) to the corner of a nearby Tier 1 Square, using the Corner Connection Method.

NEXT ROW (WS): Knit.

*Work Basic Square, ending with a WS row. Remember that all RSs of all Squares should be on the RS of the shawl.

Work Bind-Off A, connecting to the corner of a nearby Tier 1 Square using the Corner Connection Method.

Repeat from * twice more.

Work Basic Square, ending with a WS row.

Work Bind-Off B, connecting to the intersection between 2 nearby Tier 1 Squares using the Intersection Connection Method.

NEXT ROW (WS): Knit.

Work Basic Square, ending with a WS row.

Work Bind-Off A, connecting to the corner of a nearby Tier 1 square using the Corner Connection Method.

NEXT ROW (WS): Knit.

Work Basic Square, ending with a WS row.

Work Bind-Off A, connecting to the intersection between two nearby Tier 1 squares using the Intersection Connection Method.

NEXT ROW (WS): Knit.

**Work Basic Square, ending with a WS row.

Work Bind-Off B, connecting to the corner of a nearby Tier 1 square using the Corner Connection Method.

NEXT ROW (WS): Knit.

Repeat from ** twice more.

At this point in your shawl, you have worked all possible combinations of Basic Square/Bind-Off/Connection Point. In even-numbered tiers, you are always connecting at the end of a RS row.

Continue as set, either working Basic Squares and Connection Points as written for Tier 2, or starting to work them randomly in the following manner:

Work a Basic Square, ending with a WS row.

Work a Bind-Off on a RS row.

Work a Connection Point at the end of the Bind-Off.

Work a WS row.

End Tier 2 approximately three squares from the end of Tier 1.

Tier 3 and all following odd-numbered tiers

In odd-numbered tiers, you are always connecting at the end of a WS row.

Work squares randomly in the following manner:

Work a Basic Square, ending with a RS row.

Work a Bind-Off on a WS row.

Work a Connection Point at the end of the Bind-Off.

End Tier 3 approximately five squares from the end of Tier 1.

Tier 4 and all following even-numbered tiers

Work Squares randomly in the following manner:

Work a Basic Square, ending with a WS row.

Work a Bind-Off on a RS row.

Work a Connection Point at the end of the Bind-Off.

Work a WS row.

End Tier 4 approximately five squares from the end of Tier 3.

Continue until desired size is reached, or until you have enough yarn left for one more square.

Work Basic Square, ending with a WS Row.

BO all sts.

Finishing

Block by soaking with a wool-wash, roll in towel, and/or use spin cycle to wring out most of the moisture; lay flat to dry. Stretch by pinning out squares at edges of shawl.

Once dry, weave in ends.

Glossary

BO: bind off

CC: contrasting color

CDD (CENTERED DOUBLE DECREASE): slip 2 stitches as if to work a k2tog, knit 1, then lift the 2 slipped stitches up and over the just-knit stitch, as if binding off. 2 stitches decreased.

CH : chain

CM: centimeter

CO: cast on

DS (DOUBLE STITCH FOR GERMAN SHORT ROWS [SEE "TECHNIQUES," PAGE 32]): Bring the working yarn to the front and slip the just-worked stitch purlwise to the right-hand needle. Tug on the working yarn, bringing it up and over the needle, around the back, so that the just-worked stitch is pulled up tight, and two strands are sitting on the needle. If you're to knit the next stitch, leave the yarn at the back, keeping the tension, and work back in pattern. If you're to purl the next stitch, bring the yarn around the needle to the front, as if for a yarnover, keeping the tension.

G: grams

K: knit

K TBL: knit through the back loop

K1B: knit into the stitch below the stitch on the left-hand needle

K2TOG: knit 2 stitches together. 1 stitch decreased.

K3TOG: knit 3 stitches together. 2 stitches decreased.

KFB: knit into the front and back of the same stitch. 1 stitch increased.

KFBF: knit into the front, back, and front of the same stitch. 2 stitches increased.

KFBFB: knit into the front, back, front, and back of the same stitch. 3 stitches increased.

KFBFBF: knit into the front, back, front, back, and front of the stitch. 4 stitches increased.

KYOK: work (knit 1, yarnover, knit 1) into the same stitch. 2 stitches increased.

LLI (LEFT LIFTED INCREASE): Insert the left-hand needle from the front into the left leg of the stitch two rows below the last stitch on the right-hand needle. Knit into this loop. 1 stitch increased.

M: marker

M: meter(s)

M1 (MAKE ONE): make one stitch using the method of your choice. 1 stitch increased.

M1L (LEFT-LEANING MAKE ONE): Insert left-hand needle, from front to back, under the horizontal strand of yarn which runs between the stitch just knit and the following stitch; then knit into the back of this loop. 1 stitch increased.

M1PL (LEFT-LEANING PURL MAKE ONE): Insert left-hand needle, from front to back, under the horizontal strand of yarn which runs between the stitch just knit and the following stitch; then purl into the back of this loop. 1 stitch increased.

M1PR (RIGHT-LEANING PURL MAKE ONE): Insert left-hand needle, from back to front, under the horizontal strand of yarn which runs between the stitch just knit and the following stitch; then purl into the front of this loop. 1 stitch increased.

M1R (RIGHT-LEANING MAKE ONE): Insert left-hand needle, from back to front, under the horizontal strand of yarn which runs between the stitch just knit and the following stitch; then knit into the front of this loop. 1 stitch increased.

M1Z (MAKE ONE STITCH USING THE BACKWARDS LOOP METHOD [PAGE 24]): Make a backwards (e-wrap) loop and place it on the right-hand needle. 1 stitch increased.

MC: main color

MM: millimeter(s)

OZ: ounces

P: purl

P1B: purl into the stitch below the stitch on the left-hand needle.

P2TOG: purl 2 stitches together. 1 stitch decreased.

P3TOG: purl 3 stitches together. 2 stitches decreased.

PFB: purl into the front and back of the same stitch. 1 stitch increased.

PFKB: purl into the front of the stitch, leaving it on the needle, then knit into the back of the same stitch. 1 stitch increased.

PM: place marker

PSSO: pass slipped stitch(es) over

RLI (RIGHT LIFTED INCREASE): Insert the right-hand needle into the right leg of the stitch below the next stitch on the left-hand needle; pick up this loop and place it on the left-hand needle with the right leg at the front, then knit into it. 1 stitch increased.

RS: right side

SK2P: Slip the next stitch knitwise, k2tog, then lift the slipped stitch up and over the just-knit stitch, as if binding off.

SKP: slip the next stitch knitwise, knit the following stitch, then lift the slipped stitch up and over the just-knit stitch, as if binding off.. 1 stitch decreased.

SL: slip (purlwise, unless otherwise indicated)

SM: slip marker

SSK: slip the next 2 stitches, individually, knitwise to the right-hand needle. Return them to the left-hand needle without twisting them and knit them together through the back loops. 1 stitch decreased.

SSSK: slip the next 3 stitches, individually, knitwise to the right-hand needle; insert the tip of the left-hand needle, from left to right, into the fronts of those 3 stitches and knit them together. 2 stitches decreased.

SSP: slip the next 2 stitches, individually, knitwise to the right-hand needle. Return them to the left-hand needle without twisting them and purl them together through the back loops. 1 stitch decreased.

SSSP: slip the next 3 stitches, individually, knitwise to the right-hand needle. Return them to the left-hand needle without twisting them and purl them together through the back loops. 2 stitches decreased.

ST(S): stitch(es)

TBL: through back loop(s)

TOG: together

WS: wrong side

W&T (WRAP & TURN [PAGE 32]): Slip the next stitch purlwise, move the working yarn between the tips of the needles to the other side (if it's in knit position, bring it to the front; if it's in purl position, take it to the back), and then return the slipped stitch to the left-hand needle. Turn, ready to work the following row. Bring the yarn to where you need it for the following row, ready to continue in pattern.

WYIB: with yarn in back

WYIF: with yarn in front

YD(S): yard(s)

YO (YARNOVER): create a stitch by wrapping the working yarn over the needle (page 27). 1 stitch increased.

Further Reading

Bernard, Wendy. *Japanese Stitches Unraveled*. Abrams, 2018.

Campochiaro, Cecelia. *Sequence Knitting*. Chroma Opaci, 2015.

Edwards, Betty. *Color*. TarcherPerigee, 2004.

Hemmons Hiatt, June. *The Principles of Knitting*. Touchstone, 2012.

Kleon, Austin. *Keep Going: 10 Ways to Stay Creative in Good Times and Bad*. Workman Publishing Company, 2019.

Kleon, Austin. *Steal Like an Artist: 10 Things Nobody Told You About Being Creative*. Workman Publishing Company, 2012.

Loske, Alexandra. *Color: A Visual History from Newton to Modern Color Matching Guides*. Smithsonian Books, 2019.

Moreno, Jillian. *Yarnitecture*. Storey Publishing, 2016.

Parkes, Clara. *The Knitter's Book of Yarn*. Potter Craft, 2007.

Parkes, Clara. *The Knitter's Book of Wool*. Potter Craft, 2011.

Walker, Barbara. *A Treasury of Knitting Patterns*. Schoolhouse Press, 1998.

Walker, Barbara. *A Second Treasury of Knitting Patterns*. Schoolhouse Press, 1998.

Walker, Barbara. *A Fourth Treasury of Knitting Patterns*. Schoolhouse Press, 2000.

Walker, Barbara. Charted Knitting Designs: A Third Treasury of Knitting Patterns. Schoolhouse Press, 1998.

BLOGS/NEWSLETTERS:

Austin Kleon: austinkleon.com

Austin Kleon is a writer who draws. His weekly newsletter is short and sweet, providing links to ten things that have captured his attention. Sometimes books, sometimes music and movies, and sometimes it's an article about something you had no idea you were interested in!

Maria Popova: Brainpickings.org

Brain Pickings draws from literature, art, science, and philosophy as Maria Popova explores what it means to live a decent, substantive, and rewarding life. Her blog and weekly newsletters provide food for creativity and humanity.

Acknowledgments

We'd like to thank the yarn companies who generously supported our project: Amano Yarns, Berroco Yarns, The Blue Brick, Cedar House Yarns, Crave Yarns, The Dye Project, Erika Knight, Gauge Dyeworks, Gobsmacked Yarns, Indigodragonfly, Kelbourne Woolens, Middle Brook Fiberworks, Murky Depths Dyeworks, Must Stash Yarns, and Sincere Sheep.

Shawl jewelry was generously provided by Jul Designs, Lisa Ridout Jewellery, Purl and Hank, and The Woodlot.

We're very grateful to the community of knitters who supported us as we developed the project. Our sample and test knitters: Meg Anderson Kinfoil, Danielle Baines, Victoria Bingham, Sue Frost, Fiona Hunter, and Keri Williams; our readers and Excel consultants: Meg Anderson Kinfoil, Fiona Ellis, Amy Herzog, Cheryl McLeod, and Jillian Moreno. A special mention to Rachel Brown and Joanna Fromstein for additional tech editing services.

Many thanks to Shawna Mullen, Sue McCain, Glenn Scott, Gale Zucker, Julie Paquette, Minah Campos, Alexis Gray, and Susanna Rodriguez.

Kate wishes to thank Norman, Mum, and Tony, who were particularly supportive and understanding while she worked on this project.

Kim wishes to thank Ron for unfailing love, support, and delicious dinners; Victoria for her patience, humor, and occasional detours into cute videos; and Oz, Willow, and Molly for reminders to eat, sleep, and play.

Index

Editor: Shawna Mullen
Designer: Laura Palese
Production Manager: Kathleen Gaffney

Library of Congress Control Number: 2020931061

ISBN: 978-1-4197-4397-9
eISBN: 978-1-64700-017-2

Text and illustrations copyright © 2020 Kate Atherley and Kim McBrien Evans
Photographs copyright © 2020 Abrams, except:
Photographs pages 24 (right), 25–26, 33–40 copyright © 2020 Gale Zucker
Photographs pages 24 (left), 43, 47, 49, 67, 68, 70–79, 112, 114 copyright © 2020 Kim
McBrien Evans
All other photography by Glenn Scott

Cover © 2020 Abrams

Published in 2020 by Abrams, an imprint of ABRAMS. All rights reserved.
No portion of this book may be reproduced, stored in a retrieval system,
or transmitted in any form or by any means, mechanical, electronic, photocopying,
recording, or otherwise, without written permission from the publisher.

Printed and bound in China

10 9 8 7 6 5 4 3 2 1

Abrams books are available at special discounts when purchased
in quantity for premiums and promotions as well as fundraising or educational
use. Special editions can also be created to specification. For details, contact
specialsales@abramsbooks.com or the address below.

Abrams® is a registered trademark of Harry N. Abrams, Inc.

ABRAMS The Art of Books
195 Broadway, New York, NY 10007
abramsbooks.com